Illustrated Living History Series

EARLY EXPLORERS

OF NORTH AMERICA

C. Keith Wilbur

Chelsea House Publishers

Philadelphia

First published in hardback edition in 1997 by Chelsea House Publishers.

Some of the descriptions on pages 137-38 are derived from, or
originally appeared in, *Explorers and Settlers* by Robert G. Ferris
(National Park Service, 1968).

1 3 5 7 9 8 6 4 2

Library of Congress Cataloging-in-Publication Data

Wilbur, C. Keith, 1923-
Early Explorers of North America / C. Keith Wilbur
p.   cm. --(Illustrated living history)
Originally published: Chester, Conn. : Globe Pequot Press, c1989.
Includes bibliographical references and index.
Summary: Surveys the history of New World explorations from the Viking age to the eighteenth century,
including the latest views on pre-Colombian explorations.
ISBN 0-7910-4531-5 (hc)
1. North America--Discovery and exploration--Juvenile literature.
2. Explorers--North America--History--Juvenile literature.
[1. America--Discovery and exploration. 2. Explorers.] I. Title.
II.Series: Wilbur, C. Keith, 1923- Illustrated living history series.
E101.W56 1996
970.01--dc20   96-43019
                                                        CIP
                                                        AC

CONTENTS

PREFACE

There is a compelling force within us to rise above the humdrum and the ordinary, to take the shunpike, follow an old Indian trail, peer into a microscope, or rediscover some of history's forgotten mysteries. The Old World had its share of such people~ a restless, imaginative lot who had to see for themselves just what lay beyond the great expanse of the Atlantic Ocean. It may seem hard to believe that these explorers were making the crossing some four thousand years ago~ European Stone Agers who left their calling cards of stone caves and monuments! From that time, countless swash-buckling adventurers probed westward, many seeking an easy passage to the rich Orient, only to find the great American continent had blocked the way. Thereafter, exploration and exploitation moved into high gear, with saints and sinners (the latter being in the majority) seeking their fortunes in North America.

There was danger in that wilderness far beyond the contrary winds and currents and the shoals and submerged rocks that could pound a hull into kindling. The native Indians, although still living in their own Stone Age of stone implements, could mount a swift, fierce, and decisive ambush or attack against the latest European armor, musket, or the dreaded Spanish horse. Although at first welcoming the explorers as gods with wondrous trade goods, the Indians realized that they must drive them from the North American shores if the tribal way of life was to survive. However, their constant intertribal wars made it difficult to make a coordinated resistance against the flood of newcomers.

Here, then, was a clash of two opposite cultures~ one living in harmony with nature, the other intent on plundering nature's bounty. The most imaginative fiction writer would fall short of the true-life adventures that took place in the New World! On many of the following pages, the explorers tell of their exploits in their own words. But what are the possibilities that an earlier peoples, without benefit of an alphabet to record their stay, were here much before the Vikings? Many historical detectives consider the silent and curious stone structures as evidence of such a coming. Although the question is far from settled, keen eyes and open minds will hope-fully uncover more of that dim and distant past.

Meanwhile, you are invited to discover the discoverers from your easy chair, free from wading through swamps and swatting hungry mosquitoes!

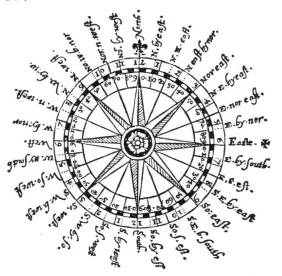

COMPASS ROSE FROM A 1596 SAILOR'S MANUAL. THE SUNDIAL MARKINGS IN THE OUTER CIRCLE TOLD THE TIME AT SEA.

1   BEFORE THE VIKINGS

Imagine the headlines "OLD WORLD MEETS NEW! GREAT CANOE, PUSHED BY WIND, BRINGS WHITE PRIEST ACROSS THE SEA!" If the North American Indians had had a means to write and presses to print the story, that sort of news would have been a sell out. But there were no reporters on hand, no flash bulbs popping to record one of the most momentous events in history. Only word of mouth could pass along important happenings to later generations. Legends became a sort of oral lending library with each telling to be passed along as an embellished original. Wise men held their listeners spellbound around the campfire, weaving the threads of mysticism and magic into the fabric of truth. The message is there, if only we latecomers have the wit to hear it.

The Micmacs of Nova Scotia have their own version of the first contact with foreign travelers. Called "The Dream of the White Robe and the Floating Island," it was recorded by the Reverend Silas T. Rand in 1869.

"When there were no people in this country but Indians, and before any others were known, a young woman had a singular dream. She dreamed that a small island came floating in towards the land, with tall trees on it, and living beings — among whom was a man dressed in rabbit skin garments. The next day she related her dream, and sought for an interpretation. It was the custom in those days, when any one had a remarkable dream, to consult the wise men, and especially the magicians and soothsayers. These pondered over the girl's dream, but could make nothing of it. The next day an event occurred that explained it all. Getting up in the morning, what should they see but a singular little island, as they supposed, which had drifted near to the land and became stationary there. There were trees on it, and branches to the trees, on which a number of bears, as they supposed, were crawling about. They all seized their bows, arrows and spears, and rushed down to the shore, intending to shoot the bears; what was their surprise to find that these supposed bears were men, and that some of them were lowering down into the water a very singularly constructed canoe, into which several of them jumped and paddled ashore. Among them was a man dressed in white — a priest with his white stole on — who came towards them making signs of friendship, raising his hand towards heaven, and addressing them in an earnest manner, but in a language which they could not understand.

"The girl was now questioned respecting her dream. Was it such an island as this that she had seen? Was this the man? She affirmed that they were indeed the same. Some of them, especially the necromancers, were displeased; they did not like it that the coming of these foreigners should have been intimated to this young girl, and not to them. Had an enemy of the Indian tribes with whom they were at war been about to make a descent upon them, they could have foreseen and foretold it by the power of their magic; but of the coming of this teacher and of a new religion they could know nothing."

The new teacher was gradually received into favor.

The square-rigged ship, with rigging alive with sailors furling the sail, seemed like a fanciful floating island with trees. The strange canoe, an oar-propelled longboat, had brought the robed priest with his version of God. The odd alphabetical markings in his prayer book, lacking the word pictures familiar to the prehistoric Indian culture, was much beyond their understanding. Although the kindly missionary converted a number of tribespeople, the powerful medicine men saw him and his message as a threat to their traditional beliefs.

WORD PICTURES FROM THE CHIPPEWA.

A similar legend was shared by all of the North American Indians. A great white god, tall, bearded, and pale of skin and dressed in a flowing white robe came from the sea and returned to the sea. Such eyewitness accounts could only have originated along coastal waters. One might consider Verrazano sailing under the French flag in 1524 and cruising from the Carolinas to New England. Or there was the invasion of Florida by the Spanish. Both countries would likely have had priests aboard, ready and willing to save the "savages."

On the other hand, there is mounting evidence that these expeditions were rather recent arrivals and that there were Old World voyages made well before the birth of Christ! If this seems just this side of preposterous, consider the old gospel that Columbus was first to set foot on America. When Yale University's c.1440 Vinland Map came to light, the Norsemen's voyages became fact. Then archeologists uncovered the remains of a Viking settlement at L'Anse aux Meadows in Newfoundland. It was time to rewrite history. Now it appears that even they were latecomers to our shores. Daring prehistoric mariners ~ those who had no complete alphabet to record their adventures ~ may have left stone calling cards and artifacts as far back as 2000 B.C.! While our evidence is still largely circumstantial and any hard proof dimmed by time, it's an exciting prospect to ponder.

Although the following may seem a wearisome minicourse of Ancient History 101, it's best that we review the prehistoric similarities and ties that were common to both sides of the Atlantic. The early Ages of Man represented the technological advances with the raw materials at hand ~ stone, bronze, and then iron.

THE STONE AGE

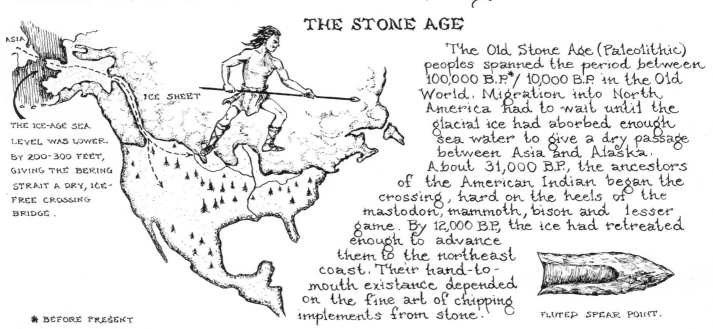

ASIA

ICE SHEET

THE ICE-AGE SEA LEVEL WAS LOWER BY 200-300 FEET, GIVING THE BERING STRAIT A DRY, ICE-FREE CROSSING BRIDGE.

✳ BEFORE PRESENT

FLUTED SPEAR POINT.

The Old Stone Age (Paleolithic) peoples spanned the period between 100,000 B.P.✳/ 10,000 B.P. in the Old World. Migration into North America had to wait until the glacial ice had aborbed enough sea water to give a dry passage between Asia and Alaska.

About 31,000 B.P., the ancestors of the American Indian began the crossing, hard on the heels of the mastodon, mammoth, bison and lesser game. By 12,000 B.P., the ice had retreated enough to advance them to the northeast coast. Their hand-to-mouth existance depended on the fine art of chipping implements from stone.

Some unsung craftsman tried pecking stone to shape and then polishing it smooth with an abrasive stone. It was a modest nicety, but with it the New Stone Age (Neolithic) had arrived. Our northeastern Indians remained in this age until European colonists brought along their more highly developed metalwork techniques.

But about 4300 B.C., there were other Stone Agers who had big ideas. From the region of the Mediterranean and Spain, the Megalithic (great stone) people developed a passion for huge stone structures. Standing stone monuments began to dominate the landscape, chambers of stone slabs were used for ceremonies and burials, and great stone markers were placed in a circle as outdoor astro-nomical observatories. The megalithic fever spread up along the west coast of Europe and into the British Isles. Apparently it even carried to North America, for their counterparts are very much in evidence on this side of the Atlantic.

PECKED, POLISHED NEOLITHIC INDIAN STONE TOOLS

ULU - A WOMAN'S KNIFE

HAFTED CELT - FELLED TREES BY AXING OUT CHARCOAL BASE AFTER BURNING

STANDING STONES (MENHIRS)

Since the days of the Megalithic stone builders, stone has represented strength, power, permanence, and the timelessness of fertility and reproduc-tion. It was therefore fitting that the great stone builders erected upright stone slabs as memorials to the brave and important personages or notable events of their time. The tradition was carried into the Bronze Age, and there are many examples on Spanish lands that are Phoenician in origin and date back to the fifth century B.C. In North America, like stones are clustered in New England and New York and are scattered westward as far as the Ohio River.

Characteristically, the smaller standing stones that rise three to six feet above the ground have slightly tapered ends, while those that rise into the sky for an impressive seven to sixteen feet end in the shape of a blunt cone. Monolithic memorials are very much a part of today, and every cemetery that bristles with inscribed standing stones and our parks that feature carved stone statues of past heroes serve as reminders of their prehistoric origins.

EUOPOEAN STANDING STONE

SOUTH ROYALTON, VERMONT STANDING STONE

STANDING STONE CIRCLES (CROMLECHES)

ATLANTIC OCEAN

ORKNEY ISLANDS

HEBRIDES

SCOTLAND

MAESHOWE, IN THE ORKNEY ISLANDS, HAS THIS ASTRONOMICAL CIRCLE. 2300 B.C.

When standing stones were arranged in a large circle they became markers for astronomical observatories.

3

The prehistorics were sun worshippers~ and understandably so. The earlier days of hunting in small bands had given way to agricultural communities that planted and harvested according to the seasons. With these ancient outdoor calendars, their priests could accurately predict when the sun rose and set behind specific standing stones. In this way, the Megalithic people marked their religious sun observances with the shortest (December 21st) and longest (June 21st) days of the year, and the equinoxes, when the days and nights were of equal length (March 21st and September 21st).

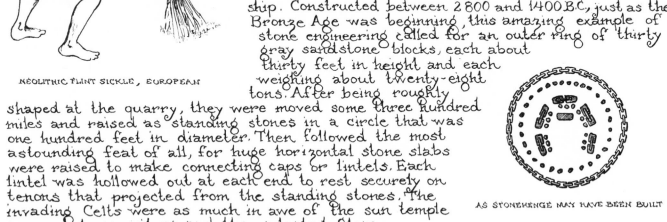

NEOLITHIC FLINT SICKLE, EUROPEAN

It's a rare schoolchild who hasn't heard of Stonehenge. On England's Salisbury Plain still stand the remains of this ultimate in slab stone craftsmanship. Constructed between 2800 and 1400 B.C., just as the Bronze Age was beginning, this amazing example of stone engineering called for an outer ring of thirty gray sandstone blocks, each about thirty feet in height and each weighing about twenty-eight tons. After being roughly shaped at the quarry, they were moved some three hundred miles and raised as standing stones in a circle that was one hundred feet in diameter. Then followed the most astounding feat of all, for huge horizontal stone slabs were raised to make connecting caps or lintels. Each lintel was hollowed out at each end to rest securely on tenons that projected from the standing stones. The invading Celts were as much in awe of the sun temple as are today's visitors, and they adapted Stonehenge to their own worship of the sun, moon, and stars.

AS STONEHENGE MAY HAVE BEEN BUILT

THE REMAINS OF STONEHENGE, WILTSHIRE, ENGLAND

More modest cromlechlike placements are to be found in New England and southern New York. Perhaps the best known is located at New Salem, New Hampshire. Amidst the confusion of stones on that hilltop is still enough raw material to make the ghosts of the Megalithic builders feel quite at home. It was known as Meeting House Hill in the early settlement days, and one colonial letter mentions three great stone chambers that were large enough to "hold a church service in." Since, the "Mystery Hill" complex has fallen on hard times. One owner in the early 1800s found no lack of foundation stones to build his home there. When he passed on to his reward in 1850, all hell broke loose. Sewer and road builders discovered the bonanza of large stone slabs and carted off over 50 percent of the stonework. Then, in the 1930s, history buff William Goodwin bought the site. Substituting enthusiasm for careful research, he tidied up the place by rebuilding some of the stone chambers and walls. Archeologists shuddered and generally turned their backs on any of its possibilities.

Now owned by Robert Stone and his New England Antiquities Research Association, a scientific approach has led to new discoveries. In 1974, an archeo-astronomical survey located a circle of standing stones, long hidden in the brush and brambles that ringed the hilltop. Aligned to sunrises and sunsets, they gave the same seasonal information as that of Stonehenge and other cromleches. Calculations of just when the sun would have risen and set in a proper sequence behind the stone markers gave dates of between 1700 and 2300 B.C. Charcoal samples near bedrock have given a radiocarbon dating as old as 2000 B.C. Although scoffers rightly claim that an ancient forest fire could have given the same results,

4

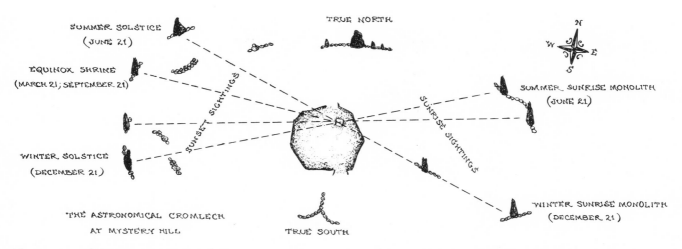

SUMMER SOLSTICE
(JUNE 21)

TRUE NORTH

EQUINOX SHRINE
(MARCH 21; SEPTEMBER 21)

SUNSET SIGHTINGS

SUNRISE SIGHTINGS

SUMMER SUNRISE MONOLITH
(JUNE 21)

WINTER SOLSTICE
(DECEMBER 21)

THE ASTRONOMICAL CROMLECH
AT MYSTERY HILL

TRUE SOUTH

WINTER SUNRISE MONOLITH
(DECEMBER 21)

the search for solid evidence is ongoing. Perhaps the mystery of Mystery Hill will one day be solved. If so, "Neolithic Hill" has a nice ring to it!

TABLE ROCKS (PERCHED ROCKS OR DOLMENS)

Small and large standing stones were sometimes used as supports for a large slab or boulder capstone. The Megalithic people housed their dead in these structures ~ a temporary resting place before the soul departed from its earthly bounds. It was the custom to mound soil over the chamber, sometimes to a height of twenty feet, with a stone passageway connecting the room to the outside world. These European Megalithic structures date between 5000 B.C. and 1200 B.C.

North America has her own ancient versions of the dolmens ~ but with a difference. They apparently were not covered with earth and therefore lack a passageway. Of interest is the spacing of the standing stone legs. Both here and abroad, they are distanced in multiples of the megalithic yard where they meet the capstones. This 2.72-foot Stone Age yardstick was commonly used in Megalithic times.

The function of these stone tables is a bit puzzling. Some point to the Celtic admiration for all things Megalithic. Although these Bronze Age invaders were skilled stone builders in their own right, they may have adapted the earlier technology to their own use. Perhaps, because the Celts practiced cremation to immediately free the spirit from the body, the ashes needed no in-ground burial as with the Megalithic dead. This is pure speculation, of course. Some geologists still feel that the table boulders were propped up by stones left by the glacial melt ~ a whim of nature. For the present, the controversy has raised more intriguing questions than hard facts.

DOLMEN AT NORTH WALES, GREAT BRITAIN

DOLMEN AT CORNWALL, ENGLAND

DOLMEN, LYNN, MASSACHUSETTS

DOLMEN AT BARTLETT, NEW HAMPSHIRE

SLAB STONE CHAMBERS

America's slab-roofed "caves" would seem to be close cousins to the Neolithic dolmens. Here, the massive capstones were formed from whatever rock was handy ~ slate, granite, quartz, or gneiss. Their considerable weight is supported by heavy standing stones or dry-laid (without mortar) walls of roughly squared stones fitted together. All have been built above ground without soil cover and have tamped earth

DOLMEN AT NEW SALEM, NEW YORK. THE 90-TON CAPSTONE IS THE LARGEST KNOWN EXAMPLE IN AMERICA.

SLAB ROOFED WITH STANDING STONES

DRY-LAID SMALL STONE WALLS

floors. They are found east of the Hudson River, high on mountaintops and over- looking a fair-sized waterway. Unlike the dolmens of Europe, no skeletal remains have been found. Still, the archeological investigations have been minimal, and they do have promise of being ancient temples, burial sites or not.

Although the "who" and "why" of the standing stones, dolmens, and slab-roofed chambers remains an open question on this side of the Atlantic, the "how" of it has some reasonable answers. Probably the Megalithic masons shaped their massive blocks at the quarry site. They may have first heated the rock and then split off a fragment by quickly cooling it with water. A safer method involved the drilling of holes with pointed flint, then splitting down the grain of the rock with wooden wedges. Surface irregularities were then bruised smooth with boulders. Stone axes completed the smoothing process. Rollers and a great deal of muscle brought the slab to the building site.

LEVERS RAISED ENDS FOR LOG ROLLERS.

THE SLAB WAS MOVED BY LEVERS AND BY HIDE ROPE.

THE SLAB WAS HAULED UP A SLOPING EMBANKMENT AND LEVERED INTO THE BASE HOLE.

THE SLAB BECAME UPRIGHT BY LEVERING AND ROPES. SMALL STONES WERE RAMMED BETWEEN THE SLAB AND EMBANKMENT TO SECURE IT.

LINTELS WERE EITHER RAISED IN PLACE BY DIGGING A LARGER EMBANK- MENT OR BY LEVERING UPWARD AND BLOCKING.

There is no archeological evidence that the North American Algonquin Indians had any knowledge of Megalithic building. Incredible as it seems, European Stone Agers may have somehow crossed the ocean to become North America's first explorers. There is a striking resemblance between the housing and implements of the Late Archaic Indians (3000 B.C. to A.D. 300) and those of the Old World Neolithic peoples.

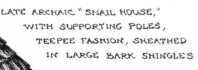

LATE ARCHAIC "SNAIL HOUSE," WITH SUPPORTING POLES, TEEPEE FASHION, SHEATHED IN LARGE BARK SHINGLES

(WILBUR, THE NEW ENGLAND INDIANS)

NEOLITHIC HOUSE WITH SUPPORTING POLES RESTING ON A ROUGH STONE CIRCULAR WALL. NOTE THE STONE SLABS AT THE ENTRANCE, THE ROOFING IS OF THATCH RATHER THAN WITH THE BARK THAT WAS PLENTIFUL IN AMERICA.

(QUENNELL, LIFE IN NEW STONE, BRONZE, IRON AGE)

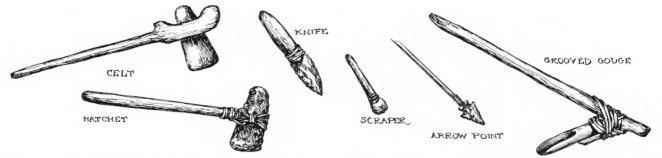

CELT

KNIFE

HATCHET

SCRAPER

ARROW POINT

GROOVED GOUGE

TOOLS SIMILAR TO BOTH EUROPEAN AND INDIAN NEOLITHIC PEOPLE. COULD SOME OF OUR NORTH AMERICAN ARTIFACTS HAVE BEEN INFLUENCED OR MADE BY THE MEGALITHIC BUILDERS?

As for the remarkable dream in the Micmac Indian legend, you may recall that the Indian girl envisioned the priestly newcomer as wearing white "rabbit skin garments." Now this may be reading more into the tale than is warranted, but all Stone Age people dressed in animal skins. The art of spinning and weaving was unknown until the Bronze Age, and any later explorers would dress in the woven cloth of the day.

THE BRONZE AGE

Speaking of clothing, the Greek word "Phoenikes" refers to the Phoenicians, a Mediterranean people who dyed their clothing a rich purple-red. The color came from a secret process of extracting the dye from sea snails. Their tubby-one-hundred-foot cargo ships, manned by fearless seatraders, could be spotted on the horizon by their vivid purple sails. The decks were crammed with any and all goods in demand ~ finely crafted desirables of gold and ivory, Phoenician glass, and, most important of all, handsome objects cast in bronze.

POSSIBLE MEGALITHIC AND PHOENICIAN TRADE ROUTES AND EXPLORATION c. 400 B.C.

ORKNEY ISLANDS

SCANDINAVIA

= MEGALITHIC STRUCTURES

= ? MEGALITHIC ROUTES TO AMERICA.

= PHOENICIAN EMPIRE

PHOENICIAN TRADE ROUTES

STONEHENGE

DANUBE RIVER

IBERIA

CADIZ

CARTHAGE

LIBYA (AFRICA)

PHOENICIA

? TO AMERICA

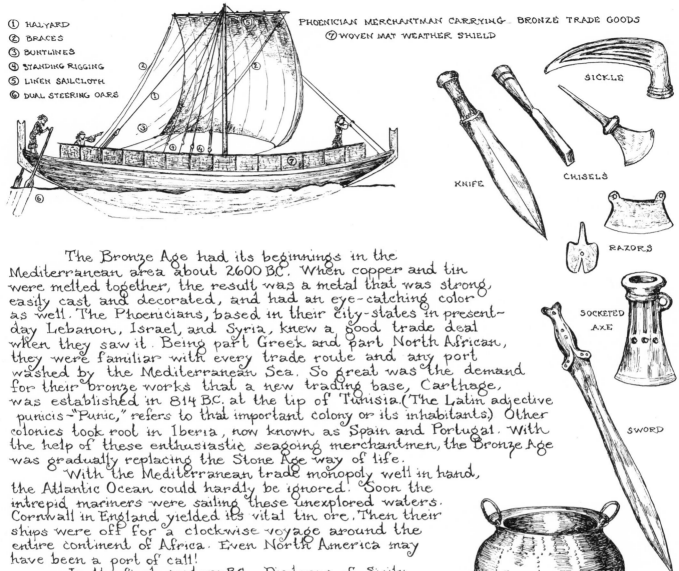

① HALYARD
② BRACES
③ BUNTLINES
④ STANDING RIGGING
⑤ LINEN SAILCLOTH
⑥ DUAL STEERING OARS

PHOENICIAN MERCHANTMAN CARRYING BRONZE TRADE GOODS
⑦ WOVEN MAT WEATHER SHIELD

KNIFE

CHISELS

SICKLE

RAZORS

SOCKETED AXE

SWORD

The Bronze Age had its beginnings in the Mediterranean area about 2600 B.C. When copper and tin were melted together, the result was a metal that was strong, easily cast and decorated, and had an eye-catching color as well. The Phoenicians, based in their city-states in present-day Lebanon, Israel, and Syria, knew a good trade deal when they saw it. Being part Greek and part North African, they were familiar with every trade route and any port washed by the Mediterranean Sea. So great was the demand for their bronze works that a new trading base, Carthage, was established in 814 B.C. at the tip of Tunisia. (The Latin adjective punicis - "Punic," refers to that important colony or its inhabitants) Other colonies took root in Iberia, now known as Spain and Portugal. With the help of these enthusiastic seagoing merchantmen, the Bronze Age was gradually replacing the Stone Age way of life.

With the Mediterranean trade monopoly well in hand, the Atlantic Ocean could hardly be ignored. Soon the intrepid mariners were sailing these unexplored waters. Cornwall in England yielded its vital tin ore. Then their ships were off for a clockwise voyage around the entire continent of Africa. Even North America may have been a port of call!

In the first century B.C., Diodorus of Sicily wrote that "in the deep off Libya [Africa] an island of considerable size ··· fruitful, much of it mountainous ··· Through it flow navigable rivers." He went on to note that the Phoenicians had discovered it by chance, after they had "planted many colonies throughout Libya ··· amassed great wealth and assayed to voyage beyond the Pillars of Hercules [Straits of Gibraltar] into the sea that men call the ocean." Since the Canary and the Madeira islands have no navigable rivers, and the Azores are too far northward, the first landfall west of Africa would be the Antilles Islands and the Americas.

There were many such Greek and Roman accounts of these lands of plenty in the distant west. For example, Plutarch in A.D. 70 recorded that "Far west in the ocean in the latitude of Britain, lie islands beyond which stretches a great continent. Greek language is spoken there." Pausanias, in A.D. 150, wrote that "West of the Atlantic are a group of islands whose inhabitants are red-skinned and whose hair is like a horse."

CAULDRON

THE NORA STONE WITH PHOENICIAN SCRIPT INSCRIPTION.

EXAMPLES OF CARTHAGINIAN COINS FOUND IN AMERICA, WITH PUNIC GODDESS AND HORSE AND PALM TREE OF CARTHAGE.

In the sixteenth century, French missionaries were astounded by their discovery of thousands of ancient mining pits, shafts, and tunnels in northern Michigan and on Isle Royal in Lake Superior. One shaft extended a full thirty feet. This was digging on a grand scale, quite unlike the surface copper nugget finds made by local Indians. More recently a considerable number of exploratory pits for copper samples have been found along the waterways of the Northeast, many with finds of amulets and stone inscriptions similar to those of Iberian times. Along some of these navigable rivers and the North American coastline, Punic coins have been unearthed, all dating around 300 BC. This was the period of the greatest Phoenician exploration and expansion. The Punic Wars with the Romans ended in 241 B.C. with the destruction of all that was the Carthaginian and Phoenician empire. Any accounts of extended voyages became part of the rubble, and hints of far west explorations could only be told secondhand by Grecian scribes and the victorious Romans.

Any Phoenician visitor to North America falls short of the Micmac legend. If, indeed, they were on this side of the Atlantic, it was for the purpose of finding raw materials rather than saving the Indians. Motivated by profit, these purple-garmented, hard-headed businessmen would have it no other way.

THE IRON AGE

About 800 B.C. and thereafter, large numbers of related tribesmen were joining forces north of the Alps. Although a common culture, language, and religion bound them into a loose union, it was their inventiveness, fierce independence, daring, lust for battle and the luxuries of life that produced a mighty empire. These peoples were the Celts (Selt or Kelt, as you wish).

To them goes the credit for introducing the Iron Age around 700 B.C. As with the smelting of bronze, the iron ore was superheated by jetting an airstream from the bellows into the fuel. Impurities were removed by cooling the hot, spongy mass, hammering, and then reheating before the final forging took place. Here was a metal, stronger than bronze, that could be honed to a sharp cutting edge.

ALL MUSCLE AND FURY, THE CELTIC WARRIOR WAS A FEARSOME SIGHT WITH HIS HAIR STIFFENED WITH LIME, SOMETIMES NAKED, OR IN CHAIN MAIL, AND SHOUTING INSULTS.

GOLD TORC, OR SACRED NECKPIECE, FROM SNETTISHAM, ENGLAND

SILVER WINE CUP, HERTFORDSHIRE

With it they invented many of the forged woodworking tools that we take for granted~iron-rimmed wheels, plows, rotary flour mills and wheels. It is of no surprise that the Celtic priority list included wrought-iron spears, swords, shields, helmets, and chain mail.

The Celts multiplied and prospered. Hordes of their fearless warriors~short and tall, dark-haired and blond, male and female~invaded other cultures and carried off the spoils of war and tributes from the conquered. Second only to a good fight was their craving for riches. Plundered jewelry, gaudy tunics and cloaks, fast horses, and fine wines were not to be denied. These status symbols were in addition to the severing of any enemy head for display over their doorways. All in all, the Celts were not the kind of folks that one would care to have as neighbors.

Yet there was among them a priestly group of individuals called the Druids. They served as religious instructors, schoolteachers, philosophers, prophets, and judges. Monk-like, they lived humbly in isolated small stone caves. These one-man dwellings were corbelled without mortar. Otherwise known as "beehives" today, they were built by laying one flat stone on another, allowing each topping row in the wall to overlap by several inches.

In this way a domed ceiling was formed, making the heavy lintel capstones of Neolithic days unnecessary.

CORBELLED STONE

By 200 B.C., the Celts had over~ run most of Europe from Spain and the Black Sea and from the Mediterranian to the North Sea. Like thunderclouds on the horizon, the armies were moving on Rome itself. Just sixteen years after the Punic Wars, the Romans would begin another round of some thirty battles with the Gauls (as they called the Celts). In the end, the discipline in the Roman ranks won out over their individualistic, less-coordinated enemy. By 52 B.C., the legions were mopping up most of the Celtic remnants in Europe.

Now the Druids were marked men. As Caesar had written, "these Gauls were completely addicted to religious observance." While Caesar would admit that his gods were not all that different, he knew that the Druids were the driving influence behind the Celtic offensives. They were to be shown no quarter. Indeed, when the British Celts finally surrendered in A.D. 78, every Druid priest was systematically put to death.

Spain seemed about as distant a hideaway as the Druids would find in Europe, and there were many old and sympathetic friends among the intermixed Punic colonists and the Celts. The transplanted Carthaginians, those old enemies of the Romans, had knowledge of the earlier Phoenician trade routes and ships, with the know-how to sail them. With the Roman Legions on their way for a final seek and search, America might just have seemed the ultimate retreat for the hard-pressed priests. There was little to lose and much to gain by such a westward voyage.

There is evidence that they did just that. The isolated corbelled "beehive caves" to be found in considerable numbers in the hills of New England, are strikingly similar to the Druids' European dwellings. In contrast to the linteled chambers

DRUID WITH FRIEND.

of the Megalithic builders, they are smaller, one-man retreats that average from four to six feet in diameter and four to five in floor-to-ceiling height. Flat stones pave the floors. These caves were always dug into the side of a hill, completely underground. Many face toward the sunrises and sunsets of the equinoxes and winter solstice ~ much to the liking of any sun-worshiping Druid. They may have been minitemples rather than dwellings.

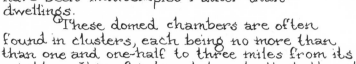
EXPLORING A BEEHIVE AT SHUTESBURY, MASSACHUSETTS

These domed chambers are often found in clusters, each being no more than than one and one-half to three miles from its neighbor. It is of interest to note that the structures seem to radiate out as spokes from the central hub of Mystery Hill in New Hampshire.

There are some two hundred examples that are tucked away in the New England countryside, in addition to those to be found on both sides of the Hudson River. And in the Connecticut River Valley, a dull conversation may suddenly be brought to life by their mention. It seems everyone has a favorite theory. One of the most interesting is that they were built in colonial days as a winter depository for the dead until spring thaws softened the ground for a proper grave. However, the winters were no more severe in the rest of the Northeast where no similar structures are found.

Another possible use might be as ice storage caves. But since most are distanced from any early settlement, up the side of a hill and well above any water supply, hauling heavy blocks of ice on a slant would appeal to few of our forefathers.

Many hold to the root-cellar theory, not taking into account that these are isolated structures, often well away from any field or homestead. The stone floors would invite a damaging frost, and the local wildlife would find a ready stock of food for their winter comfort. Since none of the beehives were mortared, as did the colonists for a strong, well-sealed wall, rains and meltoffs would make a soggy soup of spoiled vegetables.

A recent newspaper article about the nearby corbelled beehives reported the views of several university archeologists. One said " I'm skeptical of any Old World Civilization you may have heard of settling here." He went on to say that "farmers were just doing jazzy things with leftover rocks." In another magazine story, another local archeologist felt they were colonial in origin, but also mentioned that she had seen but one of these strange caves! The ancient stoneworks in America seem to be the archeologists' unwanted stepchildren. There has been little enthusiasm to launch a full-scale investigation on these "jazzy" structures that seem to fit so comfortably into the colonial farmer pigeonhole. Yet the possibilities of an earlier origin remain and grow and cannot be proven or disproven from an armchair.

THE ACADEMIC MORTARBOARD SHOULD HAVE NO CEMENT BLOCKS BENEATH IT!

STONE INSCRIPTIONS ~ Meanwhile, controversy continued to swirl around the mysterious megaliths of America. Suspicions, theories, denials, forgeries, and, now, discoveries tumbled about like leaves in a windstorm until the long silent stone monuments could speak for themselves through epigraphy. The science of deciphering ancient inscriptions is old, but its application to America's

POSSIBLE SUN SYMBOLS FROM EUROPEAN NEOLITHIC SLAB BURIAL CHAMBERS

stone markings is as young as 1975. Many of the fieldstones with apparent plow marks or age fissures, located hard by the stone structures, suddenly became a key to their final solution.

To retrace our steps, the ancient Egyptians, lacking any sort of alphabet, used pictographs to represent sounds and words. About four thousand years ago, the Phoenicians were finding it helpful to jot down the consonants in their speech. Their recordings used no vowels and appeared as a series of abbreviations. For example, the word "building" would be written as "bldg." The Greeks liked the idea and added vowels to make a complete alphabet. It remained for the Romans to make improvements and produce an alphabet that is still in use.

Meanwhile, the Phoenicians held to their vowel-poor "punic" inscriptions, terse statements that were more akin to those on a gravestone than a story of completed sentences. These written sounds were brought to their Iberian colonies from Carthage. When the Celts invaded those lands of present-day Spain and Portugal, they intermixed their own ideas with those of the Phoenicians and original Iberians. The result was a curious series of horizontal and vertical grooves, much like tally marks, that began at the corner of a stone. This was Ogam (the origin of the word is unknown) and on its way to becoming an alphabet. It remained for these prehistoric markings to spread northward to Ireland, where the stone grooves took on vowels to complete the alphabet as the Romans had done previously.

If all this sounds like alphabet soup, to the epigrapher such inscriptions were brief memorials to a famous person or god, an important happening or a religious site. It is indeed remarkable that the Old World markings have their engraved counterparts here in America. Barry Fell, a Harvard marine biologist and epigraphist, has spearheaded the translation efforts by decoding the scripts of combined cultures ~ native Iberians, Libyans, Phoenician Carthaginians, Iberian Celts and Irish Celts ~ and comparing their combined recordings to those on this side of the Atlantic. His conclusions are startling, for they place the Phoenicians, Iberian Celts, and Irish Celts squarely on North American soil. The verification of Fell's work is ongoing, but if confirmed, words like "Mystery Hill" and "root cellars" may never be heard again.

OGAM "DOT AND DASH" INSCRIPTIONS ON A STANDING STONE, EARLY HISTORIC. WATERFORD, IRELAND

THE MYSTERY HILL 'G' STONE, ACCORDING TO PROFESSOR FELL, IS A LIBYAN DEDICATION TO THE CELTIC SUN GOD BEL.

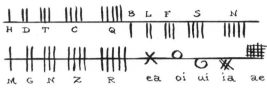

PHOENICIAN SCRIPT (PUNIC OR SEMITIC STYLE)

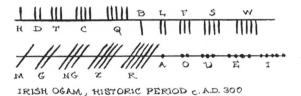

IBERIC INSCRIPTION ON A STONE AXE FOUND IN NEW JERSEY

| | | | | | | | | | | |
|H|D|T|C|Q|B|L|F|S|N|

| | | | | | X | O | * | 田 |
|M|G|N|Z|R|ea|oi|ui|ia|ae|

EARLY VOWELLESS OGAM AS USED IN AMERICA- CELT IBERIAN FROM 800 B.C. (FELL, SAGA AMERICA.)

| | | | | | | | | | |
|H|D|T|C|Q|B|L|F|S|W|

| | | | | A | O | U | E | I |
|M|G|NG|Z|R|

IRISH OGAM, HISTORIC PERIOD c. A.D. 300

SA S SE SI SO SU SV YA YE YI

PORTION OF 85 CHARACTER "TALKING LEAVES" OF CHEROKEE INDIANS. CREATED IN 1821 BY CHIEF SEQUOYAH. EACH MARK REPRESENTS A SOUND SYLLABLE. NOTE PHOENICIAN RESEMBLANCE.

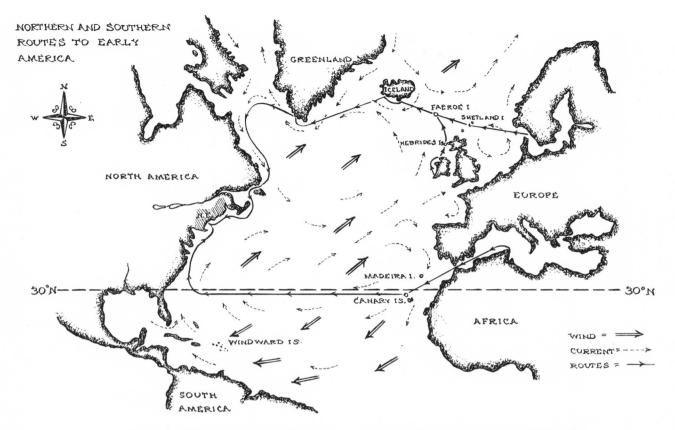

GREENLAND

ICELAND

FAEROE I.

SHETLAND I.

HEBRIDES IS.

EUROPE

NORTH AMERICA

MADEIRA I.

30°N —————————————————————————————— 30°N

CANARY IS.

AFRICA

WINDWARD IS.

SOUTH
AMERICA

WIND = ⟶
CURRENT = --→
ROUTES = →

EARLY NAVIGATION~ OR~WHERE ARE WE?

Granted, Old World prehistoric explorers may have set foot on the tribal
lands of the American Indian, but there remains the question as to how so daring an
adventure such as a transatlantic voyage could be made. As for the Neolithic peoples,
we do know that dugout canoes~some as long as forty feet~were in use. Since sails
were unknown at that time, a paddle across the ocean is questionable at best. However,
the Stone Age did not stop abruptly with the introduction of the Bronze Age. Megalithic
traditions certainly continued until the Celts occupied their lands. Ireland wasn't invaded
until 400 B.C.~ well within the scope of Phoenician activities on the high seas. If
their deep-water vessels were ranging the western coasts of Europe and far into
the Atlantic in search of raw materials and new markets, the transitional Stone-to-
Bronze-Age peoples or their stone know-how may have been brought to North America.

Until A.D. 1400, ships carried but a single sail to fill with wind. As long
as the breezes came from the stern, any craft could make reasonable headway~ say,
six or seven knots. Bucking or "beating" into the wind was
another story, for side drift could severely alter a
ship's course. The bow sail was unknown, and so
tacking into the eye of the wind on a zigzag
course must wait for later days. Any voyage
must wait for favorable winds from behind
before casting off.

Considering the limits of a single
mainsail, there were but two routes that
could be taken to America. The northern-
most course, although the prevailing winds
were westerly and contrary, had the advantage of scattered islands along the way. Not
only did they serve as route markers, but

SIDE DRIFT

1°

POINTING MORE THAN 1° INTO THE WIND
CAUSED DRIFT AND DECREASED WAY.

they also gave safe haven until a more favorable easterly wind would be at the sailor's back. The North Atlantic currents, which moved upward toward the British Isles and then swirled around and below Iceland and Greenland, were an added bonus. Returning home, the currents offered few problems, for the prevailing winds were more than enough to speed the ship along her course. Generally, the early seagoers from England, Ireland, Scotland, and the Scandinavian countries found this northern pathway to their liking.

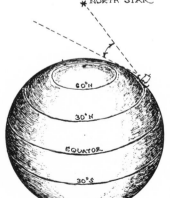

SOUNDING LEAD

The more southerly route, made famous by Columbus, took advantage of the prevailing northeasterly winds below 30°N latitude. It was an easy hitch to the Canary Islands for fresh provisions. Then the course would be set due west toward the Bahamas. Winds and currents there favored a cruise up the North American coast.

THE GNOMON. THE POLE-TO-POLE LONGI-TUDES WERE UNKNOWN UNTIL THE 18TH CENTURY CHRONOMETER CAME INTO USE.

To find one's position on that vast expanse of brine, up to and including the Viking voyages, the sounding lead had limited usefulness. When near a landfall, the navigator cast out the weighted line. Markings on the line gave the depth of the bottom. Sticky tallow, packed into a depression in the bottom of the lead, picked up samples from the ocean floor. It was of little help on the high seas.

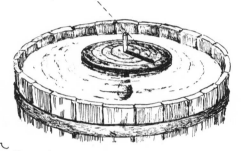

Only a latitude determination could place the ship on one of the imaginary lines running east and west and parallel to the equator. (Not until the eighteenth century was there a way to fix the lines of longitude that ran from north to south, pole to pole.) To stay on the same latitude and not wander off course, the early Greeks introduced the gnomon. Looking like an inverted child's top, the rounded wooden disk was marked with a series of concentric circles. At the center was a perpendicular stick that cast a shadow on one of the marked circles. If the sun cast a shadow that was longer or shorter than the previous day, the ship's bow must be changed northward or southward to return to the chosen latitude.

If fog and rain blanked out the sun, a clearing night could still be used to check the latitude. Since the North Star, or Polaris, remained at a constant height above the horizon for any chosen latitude. The navigator needed only to keep the angle between that star and the horizon the same. A rough estimate could be made by extending the arm and using the thumb and fingers for the measurement. Obviously, the ship was on course if the angle remained constant.

* NORTH STAR

60°N
30°N
EQUATOR
30°S
60°S

HORIZON

SIGHTING NORTH STAR FROM 30° N. LATITUDE

We have just skimmed over some 12,000 years of prehistoric possibilities. Perhaps the ancient Indian legends were on target. The pale-skinned and bearded holy man, with his long and flowing white robe, may have been a sun-worshipping Neolithic priest. Megalithic practices continued throughout the Bronze Age, for the new metal alloy remained a luxury for most and an unknown for many in Europe. Evidences of their pagan religion may be seen in America's standing stones, dolmens, cromleches, and temple chambers. The sailors who furled the square-rigged sail in the legend would logically be the seawise Phoenicians, here to search out new sources of tin and raw materials for their trading adventures.

The Celtic Druids would also be likely candidates for that time-dimmed legendary visit. Hounded by the revengeful Romans, they came with the help of Iberia's Phoenician descendants who continued in the deep-water traditions of their peoples. The Druid missionaries left a legacy of beehive temples, solitary stone dwellings, and inscribed stones. Greek and Roman scribes document such prehistoric westward voyages, and recent deciphering of the stone markings are keeping alive such possibilities. When all the pieces of the puzzle are in place, these earliest unsung explorers may be making long-overdue headlines.

EARLY HISTORIC EXPLORATIONS

By A.D. 400, the Christian religion had captured the imagination and enthusiasm of the Celts, and nowhere was the conversion from paganism more evident than in Ireland. Almost in penitence for their old sacrifices to the gods, cravings for wealth and finery and love of battle, a strong monastic movement was sweeping the island. The new ideals of purity, simplicity, self-denial and intense devotion to the teachings of Christ could best be practiced in the isolation of a monastery or as solitary small groups living in their humble corbelled stone chambers. Still, the old Celtic ways persisted. It had been the goal of one warrior to kill an enemy every day of the week. After joining the new religion, he vowed to kill two on Saturday so that he not profane the Lord on the Sabbath!

St. Brendan, a founder of one of the monasteries that dotted the Irish landscape, had the same inquisitive and restless spirit that touched off many an exploration into the unknown. Sometime

TRANSITIONAL STONE WITH OGAM MARKINGS (UPPER LEFT) AND LATER LATIN INSCRIPTION. CALDY ISLAND, IRELAND

CHAPEL OF CORBELLED STONES, KILMALKEDAR, IRELAND
6TH OR 7TH CENTURY

after A.D. 500, he began his search for the "Land of Promise of the Saints." With fourteen monks he set sail for the North Atlantic waters. His adventures were later recorded in Latin. The old Ogam marks were useless for narrative writing. The Roman alphabet brought the seven-year odyssey _Navigatio Brendani_ to life and into the historic period.

Brendan had many supernatural adventures, but like the old Indian legends, a fanciful telling simply embellished the underlying truths. One island that was seen at the outset had many flocks of sheep that were larger than oxen. Another nearby was called a "Paradise of birds." No doubt these were the Faeroes. They then came upon an island where "the mountain seemed a burning pyre" while "shooting flames into the sky." Iceland and its volcanos had been discovered. Further to the west they were amazed by a great mass in the sea with "the colour of silver, and was hard as marble," while the column itself was of the clearest crystal." This was the voyagers' first glimpse of an iceberg, carried southward by the Greenland current.

Forty days west of the Faeroes, the monks encountered whales, "pygmies and dwarfs black as coal" (Eskimos?) and a "sea-cat" with enormous eyes, whiskers,

VOYAGE OF ST. BRENDAN THE ABBOT (CONJECTURAL)

and tusks (a walrus?). They were probably off Greenland and Newfoundland. Ahead were the fogs off the Newfoundland Banks. Later, there is a remarkable account of a coral sea, "so clear they could see what was at the bottom." The Bahama Islands could fit the description. Setting sail again, the monks at last arrived at the "Land Of Promise." Reading between the lines, the landfall would be a mainland~ perhaps Florida. One of Brendan's companions remained behind and might also have been the white-robed holy man of the North American Indian legends.

The Irish religious community was inspired by St. Brendan's account of his travels, and many sought the isolation of the stepping stone islands to the west. There they could meditate in quiet and peace. The Ireland they left~ and all of Europe for that matter~ had precious little of that in the ninth and tenth centuries. The Vikings had landed, plundering and destroying their monasteries, churches, and even grave sites. The "North Men Pirates" next turned their attention to the islands to the northwest. The Faeroes, Iceland, and then Greenland were taken over and colonized. When- ever a dragon ship sail was seen on the horizon, the monks beat a hasty retreat in their hide-sheathed vessels to the west.

The thirteenth-century Viking Landnámabok (The Book of the Settle- ments) noted "But before Iceland was settled from Norway, there were men whom the Norse Men style 'papar.' These were Christians, and people con- sider that they must have been from the British Isles, because there were found left behind them Irish books, bells and croziers, and other things besides, from which it might be deduced that they were Vestmenn-Irish- men."

Farther to the west, the

MEETING A SIREN AT SEA WAS ONE OF ST. BRENDAN'S ADVENTURES. (FROM A LATER GERMAN VERSION OF 1499)

16

Icelandic sagas recalled a "White-Men's Land" or "Greater Ireland" that the Norsemen happened upon in the late tenth and early eleventh centuries. There, Christians who spoke a language thought to be Irish were either heard about or seen. From the geographical hints given, that land could only be Greenland or North America. Brendan's "Land of Promise" lay somewhere ahead. There could be no turning back to mother Ireland and the heavy hand of the Viking invaders.

Many believe that the monks found their haven in the hills of New England. A hasty mass exodus from Greenland could account for the several hundred corbelled stone caves in those states. They had built many such chambers in the past for their isolated living.

THE NORTH MEN ARE COMING! THE ABBOT HOLDS A CROSIER AS A SYMBOL OF HIS OFFICE.

The old pagan slab stone temples were there for the taking and only needed purification before being converted to Christian temples of worship. St. Patrick had done so with the Irish megalithic structures, and his followers in America would do likewise. In 1975, Barry Fell discovered a Christogram on the wall of a large Vermont stone slab chamber. This marking was a combination of the Greek letters Chi and Rho that were translated as "Christos." An exciting find it was, for the fancy, P-shaped mark had been superimposed on an earlier Celtic grid dedication to the sun god. To further sanctify the temple, the Greek word ANTP, meaning "grotto" or "cavern" was engraved above the sacred monogram. Below were the marks of A or Alpha, IC XP for Iessos Christos, and traces of an Omega. Christianity had reached North America.

CHRISTOGRAM, MARKED OVER THE EARLIER PAGAN SUN GOD GRID. VERMONT STONE CHAMBER. (FELL, SAGA AMERICA)

Compared with the sturdy wooden vessels of the Phoenicians, the Celtic ships, with their hide skins sewn over a wicker framework, would seem to be flimsy floaters. Such was hardly the case, for these curraghs were seeing deep-sea service in the British Isles before the invasion of the Romans. The keel and ribs were of light timber for sturdiness, while the rest of the hull was woven of osier and gave a degree of flexibility.

In 1976, skipper Timothy Severin and his four experienced crewmen set sail from southwest Ireland in a replica of St. Brendan's vessel. She was thirty-six feet long with a framework of ash laths tied with thongs. Forty-nine oxhides were stitched together as a covering. The route was that of the famous voyage to the Promised Land. There were anxious times with gales and a four-inch puncture from hostile ice floes. But they made the voyage to Newfoundland after one year and six weeks, proving that the Irish monks

THE RIBBING WAS LASHED WITH LEATHER THONGS.

THE CURRAGH WAS PROPELLED BY A SINGLE SAIL.

17

were certainly able to complete a westward passage in their skin boats. It would be equally satisfying to know that these monks who fled Greenland could have dropped anchor off the Maine or Massachusetts coast, thereby becoming a part of the Micmac Indian folklore.

As new discoveries are made and our understanding of the earliest explorers gains momentum and acceptance, we may find this ancient scenario changing. Unlike the venerable stone pictographs and inscriptions, our interpretations must remain flexible and not engraved permanently in granite. Most of us are part of a great army of inquisitive amateurs, anxious to add to the growing body of knowledge that will lead to the truth of the matter. After all, most of the important finds have been made by farmers, hikers, climbers, picnickers, and woodcutters.

The Middletown Archeological Research Center has offered several suggestions. Spring and fall were made for exploring the explorers. The leafy coverings of summer and the snows of winter make discovery difficult. Chances are best around the eastern and western crests of hills where the horizon is in full view and a stream or lake is not far distant.

Inscribed stones may be found along eroded riverbanks, in stone walls, or on stone steps or hearths. Chain link scrapes and plow markings may cloud the issue. If in doubt, there are experts who are ready and willing to lend a hand. Do send a photograph or rubbing, description, and location to the archeological or epigraphic centers noted in the back of this book. Meanwhile, there are two precautions to take. First, any digging without supervision will only destroy evidence that could otherwise add to our knowledge. Second, please shy away from publicity or specific details about the site. The twisted mind of the vandal is tuned in for destruction when worthwhile or treasured artifacts are in his path.

LOCATIONS OF A FEW OF THE STONE STRUCTURES FOUND IN THE UNITED STATES

STANDING STONE   I
STANDING STONE CIRCLES   ⊕
TABLE ROCKS   ⊤⊤
STONE CHAMBERS   ⌂
INSCRIBED STONES   ▲
STONE COMPLEX   ▦
(ALL OR MOST OF ABOVE)

2 THE VIKING EXPLORERS

The chilled, tempestuous North Sea had long isolated the Scandinavian countries from the armies that had periodically swept through Europe. Yet there was trouble brewing in the lands of the Norwegian, Swedish, and Danish peoples. A population explosion in the eighth century left younger sons with a bleak future, for only the oldest married son could take over the family farm. The mountainous countryside had yielded all of the tillable land it could for homesteading, and the demand for food was rapidly outpacing the supply. By the end of the century, fleets of swift-sailing Viking ships were probing across the North Sea — the start of a new era in trading and adventuring. The old ocean barriers had become a super highway for daring young men seeking their fortunes.

For almost four hundred years, all of Europe reeled under the hit-and-run commando raids by those who had gone a-viking. Ransoms and protection-from-raid monies, plunder and sale of captives brought unimagined wealth. From Ireland to the Volga, the terrorized inhabitants prayed to the heavens "From the fury of the Northmen deliver us, O Lord!"

Throughout those years of bloodshed, the need for land remained basic. Viking towns sprang up on the overrun landscape. Reaching out westward into the Atlantic, one island after another was colonized — the Orkneys, the Shetlands, the Faeroes, the Hebrides, Iceland, and then Greenland. These stepping stones inevitably led to America and a head-on collision between the conquerors of Iron Age Europe and the Stone Age North American Indians.

WEAPONS ~ Constant companions for conquest or exploration.

THE SLASHING BLADE THAT SWEPT A 3~FOOT ARC MADE THE SWORD THE VIKINGS' FAVORITE SIDEARM.

IN A.D. 922, THE ARABIAN HISTORIAN IBN FADLIN DESCRIBED VIKING TRADERS NEAR THE VOLGA RIVER. "NEVER HAVE I SEEN PEOPLE WITH MORE PERFECT PHYSIQUE THAN THESE. THEY ARE TALL AS DATE PALMS, HAVE REDDISH HAIR AND FAIR SKINS. THEY WEAR NEITHER SHIRTS NOR COATS WITH SLEEVES. THE MEN WEAR CLOAKS WITH ONE END THROWN OVER THE SHOULDER, LEAVING A HAND FREE. EVERY MAN CARRIES AN AXE, A SWORD, AND A DAGGER, AND IS NEVER SEEN WITHOUT THEM."

19

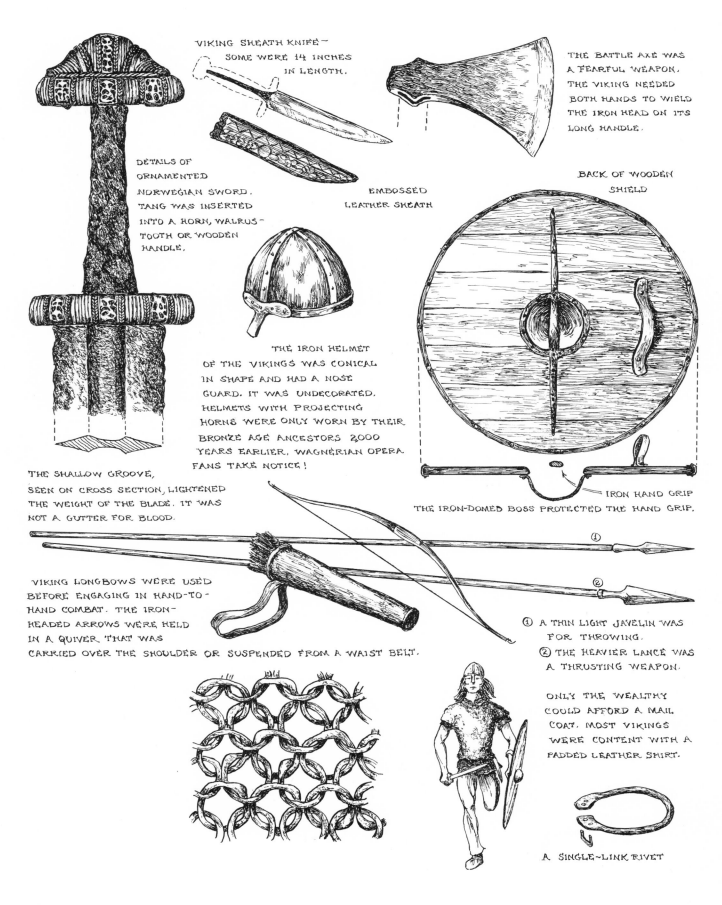

VIKING SHEATH KNIFE—
SOME WERE 14 INCHES
IN LENGTH.

THE BATTLE AXE WAS
A FEARFUL WEAPON,
THE VIKING NEEDED
BOTH HANDS TO WIELD
THE IRON HEAD ON ITS
LONG HANDLE.

DETAILS OF
ORNAMENTED
NORWEGIAN SWORD.
TANG WAS INSERTED
INTO A HORN, WALRUS—
TOOTH OR WOODEN
HANDLE.

EMBOSSED
LEATHER SHEATH

BACK OF WOODEN
SHIELD

THE IRON HELMET
OF THE VIKINGS WAS CONICAL
IN SHAPE AND HAD A NOSE
GUARD. IT WAS UNDECORATED.
HELMETS WITH PROJECTING
HORNS WERE ONLY WORN BY THEIR
BRONZE AGE ANCESTORS 2000
YEARS EARLIER. WAGNERIAN OPERA
FANS TAKE NOTICE!

THE SHALLOW GROOVE,
SEEN ON CROSS SECTION, LIGHTENED
THE WEIGHT OF THE BLADE. IT WAS
NOT A GUTTER FOR BLOOD.

IRON HAND GRIP
THE IRON-DOMED BOSS PROTECTED THE HAND GRIP.

①

②

VIKING LONGBOWS WERE USED
BEFORE ENGAGING IN HAND-TO-
HAND COMBAT. THE IRON-
HEADED ARROWS WERE HELD
IN A QUIVER THAT WAS
CARRIED OVER THE SHOULDER OR SUSPENDED FROM A WAIST BELT.

① A THIN LIGHT JAVELIN WAS
FOR THROWING.
② THE HEAVIER LANCE WAS
A THRUSTING WEAPON.

ONLY THE WEALTHY
COULD AFFORD A MAIL
COAT. MOST VIKINGS
WERE CONTENT WITH A
PADDED LEATHER SHIRT.

A SINGLE-LINK RIVET

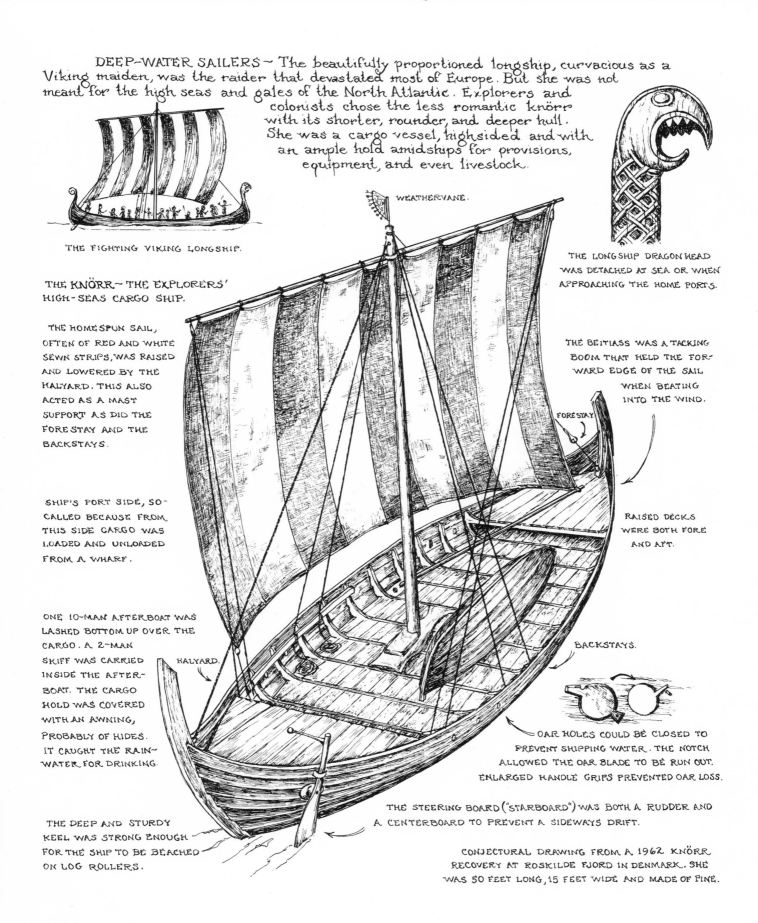

DEEP-WATER SAILERS ~ The beautifully proportioned longship, curvacious as a Viking maiden, was the raider that devastated most of Europe. But she was not meant for the high seas and gales of the North Atlantic. Explorers and colonists chose the less romantic knörr with its shorter, rounder, and deeper hull. She was a cargo vessel, highsided and with an ample hold amidships for provisions, equipment, and even livestock.

THE FIGHTING VIKING LONGSHIP.

WEATHERVANE.

THE LONGSHIP DRAGON HEAD WAS DETACHED AT SEA OR WHEN APPROACHING THE HOME PORTS.

THE KNÖRR ~ THE EXPLORERS' HIGH-SEAS CARGO SHIP.

THE HOMESPUN SAIL, OFTEN OF RED AND WHITE SEWN STRIPS, WAS RAISED AND LOWERED BY THE HALYARD. THIS ALSO ACTED AS A MAST SUPPORT AS DID THE FORESTAY AND THE BACKSTAYS.

THE BEITIASS WAS A TACKING BOOM THAT HELD THE FOR-WARD EDGE OF THE SAIL WHEN BEATING INTO THE WIND.

FORESTAY

SHIP'S PORT SIDE, SO-CALLED BECAUSE FROM THIS SIDE CARGO WAS LOADED AND UNLOADED FROM A WHARF.

RAISED DECKS WERE BOTH FORE AND AFT.

ONE 10-MAN AFTERBOAT WAS LASHED BOTTOM UP OVER THE CARGO. A 2-MAN SKIFF WAS CARRIED INSIDE THE AFTER-BOAT. THE CARGO HOLD WAS COVERED WITH AN AWNING, PROBABLY OF HIDES. IT CAUGHT THE RAIN-WATER FOR DRINKING.

HALYARD.

BACKSTAYS.

OAR HOLES COULD BE CLOSED TO PREVENT SHIPPING WATER. THE NOTCH ALLOWED THE OAR BLADE TO BE RUN OUT. ENLARGED HANDLE GRIPS PREVENTED OAR LOSS.

THE DEEP AND STURDY KEEL WAS STRONG ENOUGH FOR THE SHIP TO BE BEACHED ON LOG ROLLERS.

THE STEERING BOARD ("STARBOARD") WAS BOTH A RUDDER AND A CENTERBOARD TO PREVENT A SIDEWAYS DRIFT.

CONJECTURAL DRAWING FROM A 1962 KNÖRR RECOVERY AT ROSKILDE FJORD IN DENMARK. SHE WAS 50 FEET LONG, 15 FEET WIDE AND MADE OF PINE.

SHIP'S GEAR ~ In addition to the usual oars, ropes, spars, sail, harpoons, fishhooks, and carpenters' tools, equipment aboard would include:

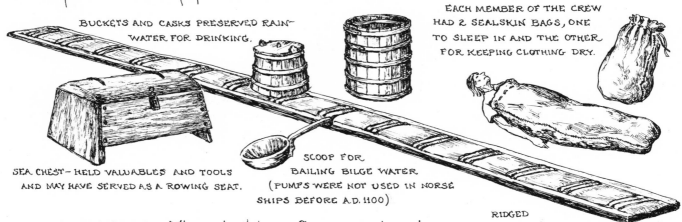

BUCKETS AND CASKS PRESERVED RAIN-WATER FOR DRINKING.

EACH MEMBER OF THE CREW HAD 2 SEALSKIN BAGS, ONE TO SLEEP IN AND THE OTHER FOR KEEPING CLOTHING DRY.

SEA CHEST ~ HELD VALUABLES AND TOOLS AND MAY HAVE SERVED AS A ROWING SEAT.

SCOOP FOR BAILING BILGE WATER (PUMPS WERE NOT USED IN NORSE SHIPS BEFORE A.D. 1100)

RIDGED GANGPLANK

NAVIGATION ~ There had been few navigational improvements since the Phoenicians explored the seas. The Norsemen, however, had a few modest additions to help them on their westward voyage to America.

Floki Vilgerdsson, a Norwegian, located the Icelandic colony with the help of three ravens. The first was released and rose high above the ship. After circling and sighting no westward islands, it flew back to Norway. After several days, a second bird was released. It circled above the watchful crew, saw no land in any direction, and returned to the ship. The last raven was released after several more days of sailing. This time it circled and struck out to the west. Floki knew his destination was near, and he followed the direction of the bird's flight until the shores of Iceland were in view. It was primitive navigation, perhaps, but it was hardly "for the birds!"

THE RAVEN IS A LARGER COUSIN OF THE CROW.

The time-honored gnomon, with its floating disk of concentric circles, was altered to become a notched bearing dial. At noon, when the sun had reached its highest point ~ just before the shadow began to reverse its direction ~ the disk was moved so that the shadow fell on north. The course marker was followed; in this example it was due west.

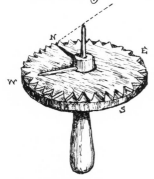

SHIP'S BEARING DIAL. HERE, SHADOW OF SUN FALLS ON NORTH AT NOON, COURSE IS SET DUE WEST. (NATIONAL MUSEUM, COPENHAGEN)

The Norsemen were able to navigate their northern route despite the sun and stars being blotted out by fog and clouds. The sunstone, used to find the longitude, was a transparent crystal, probably cordierite. It changed from yellow to a dark blue when its molecular alignment was at right angles to the polarized light plane of the sun. The angle of the obscured noon sun to the horizon remained constant if the same longitudinal course was to be continued.

A weathervane pivoted atop the mast or from the ship's bow. It indicated the wind's direction, and had a series of streamers or metal pendants that jangled in the breeze.

Sailing instructions gave the number of sailing days for each twenty-four-hour period that the ship was out of sight of the land. Winds, currents, and landfall topography was briefly described, as well as dangers from shoals and icebergs. Latitudes were given. There were no maps, and information was by word of mouth.

BRONZE-GILT WEATHER-VANE, HEGGEN, NORWAY

THE NORSE SAGAS~ For the Scandinavian peoples, the end of the first millennium was in sharp contrast to their years of enthusiastic plundering, profitable slave trading, and the old pagan beliefs. Christianity had gained a firm foothold in the north countries. With the missionaries came the Latin alphabet. Until then, the rune alphabet, much like that of the Germanic Celts, had to do. Its use, like the old ogam, was largely confined to inscriptions on stone. Along with the newly accepted alphabet came the convenience of pen and ink. The beginnings of written history had reached the north countries~ and just in time to document the colonization efforts in Iceland, Greenland AND the earliest recorded explorations of North America.

RUNE STONE FROM A VIKING TRADING POST. HEDEBY, W. GERMANY

The sagas, or "tellings," often combined history with legend. Two of the tellings were concerned with the Viking probes westward toward the New World. "Eirik's Saga," or "Saga of Erik the Red," was recorded before 1334. The Graendendinga Saga, or "The Tale of the Greenlanders," c. 1385, was as told by Leif Erikson himself. The only known copy holds a place of honor in the Royal Library at Copenhagen. Make no mistake, these two sagas hold a wealth of factual accounts, faithfully repeated until they could be recorded. Unlike some of the earlier documentations, they are free of fanciful legends, and both have meaty descriptions of navigational observations, new landfalls and eyewitness impressions. The uncharted and nameless sightings must be interpreted through the eyes of the early explorers, along with a familiarity of sailing terms and techniques, a knowledge of the North American shoreline topography, and a generous amount of common sense.

SECTION FROM A SAGA MANUSCRIPT

The sagas tell us that Leif Erikson's father, Erik the Red, had sailed westward from Iceland in 982 to discover Greenland. This huge island, the largest in the world, was as wild and rugged as its discoverer. It was a desolate piece of real estate with a few stunted birches and willows, along with some stretches of grass that had braved the permafrost. Hard by the shoreline was a massive glacier with ice caps that were two miles thick in places. This was no paradise and hardly a land of greenery; but for the land-hungry Norwegians, there was ample room to homestead and to scratch out a living.

In 985, the first wave of over one thousand pioneers crowded aboard twenty-five ships, along with their worldly goods and livestock, for their own piece of Greenland. Only fourteen ships arrived safely. The remaining eleven, each terrifying more than forty hopefuls, were scattered and lost upon the high seas. Some may have been able to return to Iceland before the prevailing southwest winds. Others were probably lost at sea. There remains a third possibility, for it was almost inevitable, then and now, that the powerful Labrador Current would sweep any floundering vessel in the southwest seas off Greenland down to the Strait of Belle. The discovery of a Norse settlement there makes such a happening all the more intriguing.

In 1963, Helge Ingstad searched out the only known Viking site in America. This lawyer/explorer had a single objective in mind ~ to find Leif Erikson's long-lost Vinland. The hunt brought him to the northern tip of Newfoundland. At L'Anse aux Meadows

GREENLAND

ICELAND

LABRADOR CURRENT

NEWFOUNDLAND (LABRADOR)

N

THE NORSE SETTLEMENT AT L'ANSE AUX MEADOW

BELLE I.

L'ANSE AUX MEADOWS

STRAIT OF BELLE I.

NEWFOUNDLAND I.

where he uncovered eight sod building remains, including a smithy. Radiocarbon dating* from charcoal placed the years between A.D. 860 / A.D. 1070, well within the early period of Viking explorations. Recovered artifacts were unquestionably Scandinavian in origin. The site is now a Canadian National Park, and ongoing research has made several conclusions possible.

First, this place is no Chamber of Commerce's dream come true, and it certainly doesn't fit the description of Vinland as described in the sagas by Leif. Arctic blasts bear down on L'Anse aux Meadows, unprotected by any mountain wind-screens or forests. Only dwarf balsam fir, birch, and willow have braved the elements. The icy Labrador Current chills the temperature to 15°C. in July and dips it down to -12°C. in January. Who but shipwrecked Norse colonists, glad still to be alive, would consider staying and surviving as best they could?

This was a small settlement. There were three dwelling remains, and archeologists estimate that each might hold twenty to thirty people, or sixty to ninety colonists in all. Two ships would be needed to carry this number and may have been part of the Greenland-bound fleet.

This was a temporary site. The maximum life of Norse sod buildings was twenty-five years, and there was no evidence that any had been rebuilt or replaced; further, none of the structures had the stone foundations to be found in more permanent dwellings. There is even evidence that two or more of the buildings were abandoned and burned.

Women were among those who lived briefly on this North American toehold. A soapstone whorl, used as a flywheel on a wooden shaft for twisting woolen fibers into yarn, gave evidence that they were part of a colonizing and not an exploratory effort.

If, then, two shiploads of Greenland-bound hopefuls were cast up on a forbidding northern tip of Newfoundland and then made do with temporary shelters, what became of them? Famine and disease may have claimed some lives, but there could be a happier end to their adventure. Parks Canada excavations have shown that Late Archaic Indians—not Eskimos—were on the site at the time of the Norse. It is entirely possible that the colonists moved with the Beothuks as the natives were known, to a more agreeable site to the south. Intermarriage would have been inevitable.

Later explorers describe a most unusual tribe of Indians that lived on Newfoundland Island. These Beothuks were recorded as being a tall, white-skinned people with black, brown, or yellow hair. They wore hoods and clothing of caribou in the Viking manner. Although peace-loving, the men carried swords of chipped stone. It was also reported that their winter storehouses had gable-ended roofs in the Scandinavian tradition. Their birch bark canoes had keels much like the Norse vessels and were sailed, paddled, or rowed with ten-foot oars of two pieces of wood fitted together.

SPINNING WHORL- ACTUAL SIZE

BRONZE PIN, ACTUAL SIZE, FOUND AT L'ANSE AUX MEADOWS

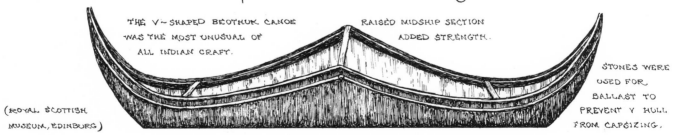

THE V-SHAPED BEOTHUK CANOE WAS THE MOST UNUSUAL OF ALL INDIAN CRAFT.

RAISED MIDSHIP SECTION ADDED STRENGTH.

STONES WERE USED FOR BALLAST TO PREVENT V HULL FROM CAPSIZING.

(ROYAL SCOTTISH MUSEUM, EDINBURG)

* CARBON DATING BEGINS WHEN A TREE DIES AND NOT WHEN IT BECOMES FIREWOOD.

Unfortunately, the Beothuks had an annoying habit of raiding the traps and nets of later fishermen. That made them fair game for the musket. Then, in the eighteenth century, the French offered a scalp bounty to the Micmacs of Nova Scotia for Beothuk hair. The last of the tribe died in 1829, along with any evidence or legends that might have cast some light on any Scandinavian ancestry.

BJARNI HERJOLFSSON'S GLIMPSE OF AMERICA ~

Fourteen of the ships that had sailed off to Erik the Red's Greenland in 985 were much more fortunate. They arrived safely at the embryo colony, and among their number was the father of a young Icelandic trader. The happenstances thereafter led to the first recorded Norse view of America ~ the "well wooded and with low hills" land that Leif Erikson would later call Vinland. The Groenlandinga Saga details the adventures and misadventures of Bjarni Herjolfsson and give important sailing directions to that new land. To better take part in his odyssey, numbers have been added to the original telling. These are the clues that help to sort out the locations of the three North American sightings.

"Bjarni arrived in Iceland at Eyrar in the summer of the year that his father had left for Greenland. The news came as a shock to Bjarni, and he refused to have his ship unloaded. His crew asked him what he had in mind; he replied that he intended to keep his custom of enjoying his father's hospitality over the winter - 'so I want to sail my ship to Greenland, if you are willing to come with me.'

"They all replied that they would do what he thought best. Then Bjarni said, 'This voyage of ours will be considered foolhardy, for not one of us has ever sailed the Greenland Sea.'

"However, they put to sea as soon as they were ready and sailed for three days until land was lost to sight below the horizon①. Then the fair wind failed and northerly ② winds and fog ③ set in, and for many days they had no idea what their course was. After that they saw the sun again and were able to get their bearings; they hoisted sail④ and after a day's sailing ⑤ they sighted land⑥.

"They discussed amongst themselves what country this might be. Bjarni said it could not be Greenland. The crew asked him if he wanted to land there or not; Bjarni replied, 'I think we should sail in close.'

"They did so, and soon they could see that the country was well wooded and with low hills ⑥. So they put to sea again, leaving the land on the port quarter; and after sailing for two days ⑦ they sighted land once more. Bjarni's men asked him if he thought this was Greenland yet; he said he did not think this was Greenland, any more than the previous one ~ 'for there are said to be huge glaciers in Greenland.'

"They closed the land quickly and saw it was flat and wooded ⑦. Then the wind failed and the crew all said they thought it advisable to land there but Bjarni refused. They claimed they needed both firewood and water; but Bjarni said 'You have no shortage of either.' He was criticized for this by his men.

"He ordered them to hoist sail and they did so. They turned the prow out to sea and sailed before a south-west wind ⑧ for three days before they sighted a third land. This one was high and mountainous, and topped by a glacier. Again they asked Bjarni if he wished to land there, but he replied, 'No, for this country seems to me to be worthless.'

"They did not lower sail at this time, but followed the coastline and saw that it was an island⑧⑨. Once again they put the land astern and sailed out to sea before the same fair wind ⑨. But now it began to blow a gale ⑨, and Bjarni ordered his men to shorten sail and not go harder than the ship and rigging could stand. They sailed for four days ⑨⑩, until they sighted a fourth land.

"The men asked Bjarni if he thought this would be Greenland or not.

"'This tallies most closely with what I have been told about Greenland,' replied Bjarni. 'And here we shall go into land.'

THE FIRST RECORDED AMERICAN LANDFALL BY BJARNI HERJOLFSSON
A.D. 985

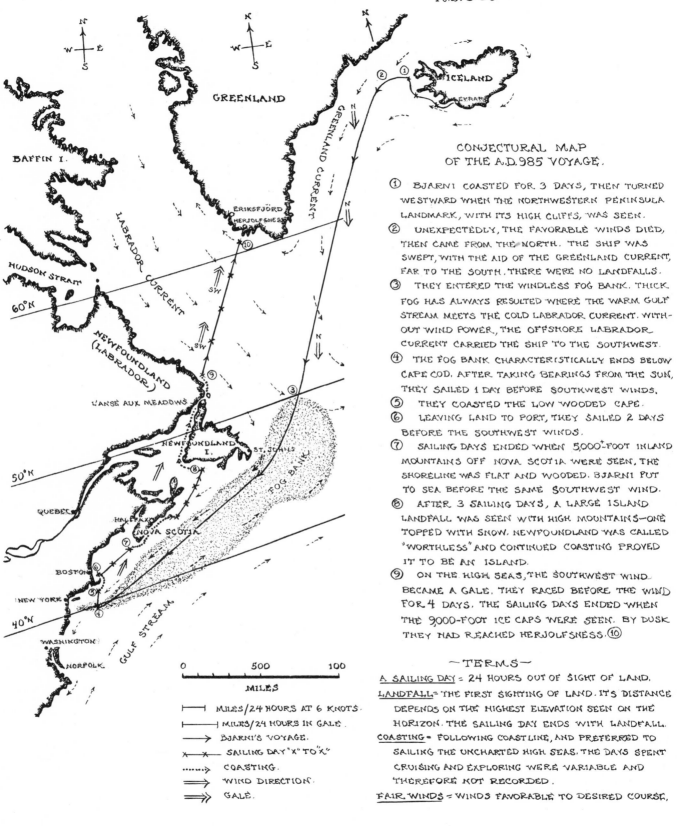

CONJECTURAL MAP
OF THE A.D. 985 VOYAGE.

① BJARNI COASTED FOR 3 DAYS, THEN TURNED WESTWARD WHEN THE NORTHWESTERN PENINSULA LANDMARK, WITH ITS HIGH CLIFFS, WAS SEEN.

② UNEXPECTEDLY, THE FAVORABLE WINDS DIED, THEN CAME FROM THE NORTH. THE SHIP WAS SWEPT, WITH THE AID OF THE GREENLAND CURRENT, FAR TO THE SOUTH. THERE WERE NO LANDFALLS.

③ THEY ENTERED THE WINDLESS FOG BANK. THICK FOG HAS ALWAYS RESULTED WHERE THE WARM GULF STREAM MEETS THE COLD LABRADOR CURRENT. WITHOUT WIND POWER, THE OFFSHORE LABRADOR CURRENT CARRIED THE SHIP TO THE SOUTHWEST.

④ THE FOG BANK CHARACTERISTICALLY ENDS BELOW CAPE COD. AFTER TAKING BEARINGS FROM THE SUN, THEY SAILED 1 DAY BEFORE SOUTHWEST WINDS.

⑤ THEY COASTED THE LOW WOODED CAPE.

⑥ LEAVING LAND TO PORT, THEY SAILED 2 DAYS BEFORE THE SOUTHWEST WINDS.

⑦ SAILING DAYS ENDED WHEN 5,000+ FOOT INLAND MOUNTAINS OFF NOVA SCOTIA WERE SEEN. THE SHORELINE WAS FLAT AND WOODED. BJARNI PUT TO SEA BEFORE THE SAME SOUTHWEST WIND.

⑧ AFTER 3 SAILING DAYS, A LARGE ISLAND LANDFALL WAS SEEN WITH HIGH MOUNTAINS—ONE TOPPED WITH SNOW. NEWFOUNDLAND WAS CALLED "WORTHLESS" AND CONTINUED COASTING PROVED IT TO BE AN ISLAND.

⑨ ON THE HIGH SEAS, THE SOUTHWEST WIND BECAME A GALE. THEY RACED BEFORE THE WIND FOR 4 DAYS. THE SAILING DAYS ENDED WHEN THE 9,000-FOOT ICE CAPS WERE SEEN. BY DUSK THEY HAD REACHED HERJOLFSNESS. ⑩

~ TERMS ~

A SAILING DAY = 24 HOURS OUT OF SIGHT OF LAND.

LANDFALL = THE FIRST SIGHTING OF LAND. ITS DISTANCE DEPENDS ON THE HIGHEST ELEVATION SEEN ON THE HORIZON. THE SAILING DAY ENDS WITH LANDFALL.

COASTING = FOLLOWING COASTLINE, AND PREFERRED TO SAILING THE UNCHARTED HIGH SEAS. THE DAYS SPENT CRUISING AND EXPLORING WERE VARIABLE AND THEREFORE NOT RECORDED.

FAIR WINDS = WINDS FAVORABLE TO DESIRED COURSE.

MILES

0 — 500 — 100

├──┤ MILES/24 HOURS AT 6 KNOTS.
├──┤ MILES/24 HOURS IN GALE.
⟶ BJARNI'S VOYAGE.
×—× SAILING DAY "X" TO "X"
······⟩ COASTING.
⟹ WIND DIRECTION.
⟹ GALE.

"They did so, and made land as dusk was falling at a promontory which had a boat hauled up on it. This was where Bjarni's father, Herjolf, lived, and it has been called Herjolfsness for that reason ever since."

When contrary winds and currents conspired to send Bjarni into strange New World waters, his outstanding seamanship brought his crew safely back to a Greenland he had never seen. His accurate account of this odyssey of a lifetime gave some hint as to the location of Vinland. Once the windless pea soup fog bank had been left astern, he was able to determine a rough latitude with his gnomon and bearing dial. It was obvious that the ship was far south of her goal. Therefore the prow was aimed to the north. A day's sailing brought the wanderers to a land that Leif Erikson would later call Vinland~Cape Cod.

After coasting along the southeastern arm of the land, he probably left present Provincetown on his port and headed northward on the high seas. Throughout the return voyage the winds remained "fair"~ favorable southwest winds blowing toward the northeast. In two days, or three hundred miles between landfalls, the inland mountains of Nova Scotia were spotted on the horizon. They coasted the "flat and wooded" land along the southeastern coast to present Halifax. The inland hills were too distant to be seen from shipboard.

Still sailing before the same southwesterly winds, they put to sea for three days, or about four hundred and fifty miles. The landfall was "high, mountainous, and topped by a glacier." Since he knew that the Greenland settlements were on its southwestern coast, he steered around the western coast of New-foundland. There were no signs of habitation. In a trader's terms, it was therefore "worthless" to Bjarni. He followed along the western range of mountains that usually retain some winter snows, and found it to be a large island. Frederick Pohl has pointed out that "coasting" would indicate the island to be sizable, and only by sailing between it and the mainland could Bjarni be sure that it really was an island.

With the southwest wind at their backs, they found the Labrador mainland to be continuous and unbroken. They put to sea and sailed before gale winds. This passage was rapid, covering over two hundred miles a day before the driving blasts. Almost miraculously, they came upon Bjarni's father's home at Herjolfsness.

Bjarni was certainly no explorer, and reaching Greenland before the ports were locked in early winter ice out-weighed the wishes of his inquisitive crew. It remained for Leif Erikson to follow the sailing directions in reverse, to locate Bjarni's first land and to provide further clues as to the whereabouts of Vinland.

THE HOUSES OF THE GREENLAND VIKING SETTLEMENTS AND AT L'ANSE AUX MEADOWS WERE OF SOD. THE WALLS WERE FACED INSIDE AND OUTSIDE WITH SOD BLOCKS, AND SANDWICHED BETWEEN WAS A FILLER OF GRAVEL. BOTH WERE A GOOD INSULATION, AND THE GRAVEL HELPED TO DRAIN WATER FROM THE ROOF.

THE ROOF WAS OF 2 LAYERS OF SOD~THE OUTER LAYER GRASS SIDE UP AND THE INNER WITH GRASSY SIDE DOWN. SUCH HEAVY SHINGLING HAD NEED OF A SUBSTANTIAL FRAMEWORK OF WOODEN PLANKS OR INTERWOVEN BRANCHES. ONE OR MORE ROWS OF INTERIOR POSTS SUPPORTED THE ROOF. STONE WALLS WERE A LATER DEVELOPMENT AT GREENLAND.

LEIF ERIKSON EXPLORES VINLAND

Discoveries such as Bjarni's are stumbled upon by accident. In contrast, explorations are searches by intent from inquiring minds. Leif Erikson was America's first recorded explorer. His father, Erik the Red, had set the example by discovering, exploring, and then colonizing Greenland. Now fate called upon his twenty-five-year-old son to probe the unknown lands to the west. The sagas leave no doubt that Leif was a born leader~ tall and commanding without being overbearing and with a curiosity tempered by caution. A man of his own convictions, he brought Christianity to Greenland against his father's wishes. In short, Leif had both common sense and uncommon vision.

The Saga of the Greenlanders continued with the exploration of North America, and provided more clues about the location of Leif's Vinland. The year was 1003 or about eighteen years after Bjarni chanced upon those lands to the west.

THOR'S HAMMER, THE WEAPON THE GOD USED TO FIGHT EVIL, WAS WORN AS AN AMULET FOR PROTECTION. (DANISH)

"Some time later, Bjarni Herjolfsson sailed from Greenland to Norway and visited Earl Eirik, who received him well. Bjarni told the earl about his voyage and the lands he had sighted. People thought he had shown great lack of curiosity, since he could tell them nothing about these countries, and he was criticized for this. Bjarni was made a retainer at the earl's court, and went back to Greenland the following summer.

"There was now great talk of discovering new countries. Leif, the son of Eirik the Red of Brattahlid, went to see Bjarni Herjolfsson and bought his ship from him, and engaged a crew of thirty-five...

THE CHRISTIAN CROSS REPLACED THE PAGAN CHARMS IN GREENLAND WHEN LEIF INTRODUCED THE NEW RELIGION. (SWEDISH)

"They made their ship ready and put out to sea. The first landfall they made was the country that Bjarni had sighted last. They sailed right up to the shore and cast anchor, then lowered a boat and landed. There was no grass to be seen, and the hinterland was covered with great glaciers, and between glaciers and shore the land was like one great slab of rock. It seemed to them a worthless country.

"Then Leif said, 'Now we have done better than Bjarni where this country is concerned — we at least have set foot on it. I shall give this country a name and call it HELLULAND.'

"They returned to their ship and put to sea, and sighted a second land. Once again they sailed right up to it and cast anchor, lowered a boat and went ashore. This country was flat and wooded, with white sandy beaches wherever they went; and the land sloped gently down to the sea.

"Leif said, 'This country shall be named after its natural resources: it shall be called MARKLAND.'

"They hurried back to their ship as quickly as possible and sailed away to sea in a north-east wind for two days until they sighted land again. They sailed toward it and came to an island which lay to the north of it.

"They went ashore and looked about them. The weather was fine. There was dew on the grass, and the first thing they did was to get some of it on their hands and put it to their lips, and to them it seemed the sweetest thing they had ever tasted. Then they went back to their ship and sailed into the sound that lay between the island and the headland jutting out to the north.

"They steered a westerly course round the headland. There were extensive shallows there and at low tide their ship was left high and dry, with the sea almost out of sight. But they were so impatient to land that they could not bear to wait for the rising tide to float the ship; they ran ashore to a place where a river flowed out of a lake. As soon as the tide had refloated the ship they took a boat and rowed to it and brought it up the river to the lake, where they anchored it. They carried their hammocks ashore and put up booths. Then they decided to winter there and built some large houses.

"There was no lack of salmon in the river or the lake, bigger salmon than they had ever seen. The country seemed to them so kind that no winter fodder would be needed for livestock: there was never any frost all winter and the grass hardly withered at all.

"In this country, night and day were of more even length than in either Greenland or Iceland: on the shortest day of the year, the sun was already up by 9 a.m., and did not set until after 3 p.m.

28

"When they had finished their houses, Leif said to his companions, 'Now I want to divide our company into two parties and have the country explored; half the company are to remain here at the houses while the other half go exploring ~ but they must not go so far that they cannot return by the same evening, and they are not to become separated...'"

ONE OF THE EXPLORING PARTY WAS GERMAN-BORN TYRKER, A FORMER EMPLOYEE OF ERIC THE RED WHEN THE FAMILY LIVED IN ICELAND. ERIC WAS BANISHED FROM THE ISLAND FOR THREE YEARS, FOLLOWING A SKIRMISH WITH A RIVAL FAMILY. WHEN ERIK SAILED WESTWARD TO DISCOVER GREENLAND, HE ENTRUSTED HIS WIFE AND YOUNGSTERS TO THE CARE OF TYRKER. A BOND OF AFFECTION GREW BETWEEN LEIF AND HIS FOSTER FATHER, AND NOW THEY WERE EXPLORING VINLAND TOGETHER. TYRKER WANDERED OFF ON HIS OWN TO FIND VINES AND GRAPES, FROM WHICH LEIF NAMED THE COUNTRY. APPARENTLY TYRKIR HADN'T FOUND A CATCH OF THE FERMENTED FRUIT. HE WAS ONLY OVERJOYED TO REDISCOVER A CHILDHOOD MEMORY AND SHORTEN THE WINTER BY MAKING WINE.

A VIKING DRINKING HORN WITH GILDED BRONZE MOUNTS. DANISH ORIGIN.

"At first Tyrker spoke for a long time in German, rolling his eyes in all directions and pulling faces, and no one could understand what he was saying. After a while he spoke in Icelandic.

"'I did not go much farther than you' he said. 'I have some news. I found vines and grapes.'

"'Is that true, foster-father?' asked Leif.

"'Of course it is true,' he replied. 'Where I was born there were plenty of vines and grapes.'

"They slept for the rest of the night, and next morning Leif said to his men, 'Now we have two tasks on our hands. On alternate days we must gather grapes and cut vines, and then fell trees to make a cargo for my ship.'

"This was done. It is said that the tow-boat was filled with grapes. They took on a full cargo of timber; and in the spring they made ready to leave and sailed away. Leif named the country after its natural qualities and called it VINLAND."

Leif's logbook, at first glance, would seem to localize his Vinland with some certainty. Yet such unexplored lands offered no signposts ~no previous maps or previous settlements~ and the Vikings could only mention any unusual topography and the direction of the winds and courses that brought them there. It is not surprising that some fifty historians have placed Vinland at thirty different sites along the North American coastline ~ all the way from Labrador on down to the tip of Florida. Two nineteenth-century investigators even theorized that the long-sought Leif shelters may have been back in Greenland where Leif began his journey! After sifting through these educated guesses of the past several centuries, however, it will be found that most have narrowed the search down to New England. More specifically, the sandy, tree-studded shores of Cape Cod have come in for top billing. There are many evidences that point to such a conclusion.

HELLULAND~ Bjarni's third land and Leif's first landfall was quite "worthless." There was no grass, a "great glacier" covered the interior, while the shore "was like one great slab of rock." And so bleak Labrador was called Helluland (Land of Flat Rocks or "Slab-Land"). Indeed, the early mariners who sailed the region in the seventeenth century had a common saying, "God made most of the world in five days, Labrador on the sixth, and spent the seventh day throwing rocks at it." The fierce and jagged rocks that lined the coast

29

are made all the more inhospitable by the chilled Labrador Current that carries the Arctic Sea icefloes with it. In this land of deep freeze, the temperature rarely rises above 47°F in July and usually drops to -75°F in winter. Today, we'd probably name it "Hellovaland."

MARKLAND ~ It seems likely that Leif then coasted southward along the eastern coast of Newfoundland Island. The western shores had been described and considered "worthless" by Bjarni, and Leif had no desire to land or even mention such an island in his log. But Bjarni's second land was distinctive. The explorers landed on the white, sandy beaches that are still characteristic of southeastern Nova Scotia. The flat and forested land beyond prompted Leif to call it MARKLAND or "Wood-land."

VINLAND ~ After leaving Nova Scotia with the favorable northeast wind at their backs and the Labrador Current to hurry them along, the explorers saw Bjarni's first land after two days on the high seas. The observations that followed were strikingly similar to Cape Cod as we know it today ~ without the hordes of summer tourists, of course!

Vinland was named for the profusion of vines and grapes that grew there. So highly was the purple fruit prized for making wine that the afterboat was filled for the return trip to Greenland. Wild grapes have a struggle to grow north of the Passamaquoddy Bay in Maine, and it was a rare explorer who didn't mention grapes as an outstanding feature of New England.

The same "kind" countryside that grew grapes was so far south that the grass remained green enough throughout the winter to sustain grazing cattle. The tall beach or marsh grass would fit such a description. Without any frost "all winter," any point north of Cape Cod would be an unlikely candidate. All but surrounded by the moderating temperature of the sea, Leif could have had a frost-free stay, or at least nothing to compare with the permafrost of Greenland. Virginia would be the nearest place where frost would usually be absent, and there is nothing in the sagas that hints that this exploration could be so far southward.

The latitude of Vinland has actually been calculated from an interesting bit of historical sleuthing. Leif and his crew were surprised that the days and nights were more equal in length in Vinland than Greenland, and that the sun was already in the heavens by 9:00 A.M. and still bright after 3:00 P.M. on the shortest day of the year. Clocks had not yet been invented, and so the ancient Icelandic law divided the twenty~four~hour day into eight sections, each with three hours. These hours were then matched with the position of the sun's shadow on the bearing dial. This was done on the shortest day of the year, December 21st, to standardize the bearing hours for the rest of the year. At noontime, the sun was directly overhead at its

THE VINLAND BEARING AT SUNSET.

highest point. Its shadow was due south, just before it began moving westward. The indicator arm was positioned on the shadow to give other degree references. When the shadow had shifted westward to S60°W, a three-hour section had passed. On that shortest day in the more northerly latitudes of Ireland, Greenland, and Labrador, it was, then, 3:00 P.M., and the sun was just setting. In Vinland, the sun was still in the heavens at that hour.

Another saga, the Flat Island Book or Flateyjarbók, gave more specifics. It stated that on the shortest day of the year, the sun set at "Eyktarstad," or in other words, 4:30 P.M., when the families back home ate their late afternoon meal. That time was known to Leif because the dial shadow had moved that number of degrees farther to the west~ or one and one-half hours later than when darkness fell in Iceland and Greenland. Careful calculations by researchers have determined that sunset on December 21st at 4:30 P.M. could only occur between the latitudes of 41° and 42° N. Cape Cod is located at about 41°42′ N and on December 21st the sun sets there at 4:30 P.M.

30

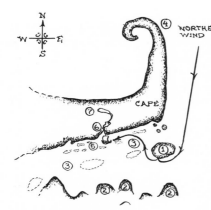

LEIF'S IMPRESSION OF VINLAND

Leif painted a word picture of his first sightings of the Vinland region. Sailing before the northeast wind, they anchored in the lee of an island ① that was north of land ②. A sound ③ lay between that island and the headland ④ to the north. They steered a westerly course, became grounded on extensive low-tide shallows, ⑤ then explored a river ⑥ that flowed out of a lake. ⑦ The river was deep enough to row the ship into the lake.

For the Vikings to know that the cape's headland was to the north, they must have coasted it before arriving at the island to the south. From there, the more southerly "land" of Nantucket and the string of islands might have seemed part of the mainland, for they were neither coasted nor explored. The landmarks of Cape Cod's hook and Nantucket on the horizon seem obvious enough, but a glance at a modern map shows no likely island.

Over the past thousand years, nature has remodeled the southern shores of Cape Cod. DeCosta, in his Pre-Columbian Discovery of America, points out that "in earlier times an island existed northward from Nantucket at the entrance of Nantucket Sound." This, with a large point of land, which has also since disappeared, was described by Gosnold when he explored the cape in 1602. It was large enough to have named landmarks of "Point Care" and "Point Gilbert." John Smith, sailing the area in 1614, called it Isle Nauset. It was formed of sand drift, and it was recorded that the Nantucket Islanders cut their wood there. Later, Thornton's 1685 map called it "Old Rose & Crown."

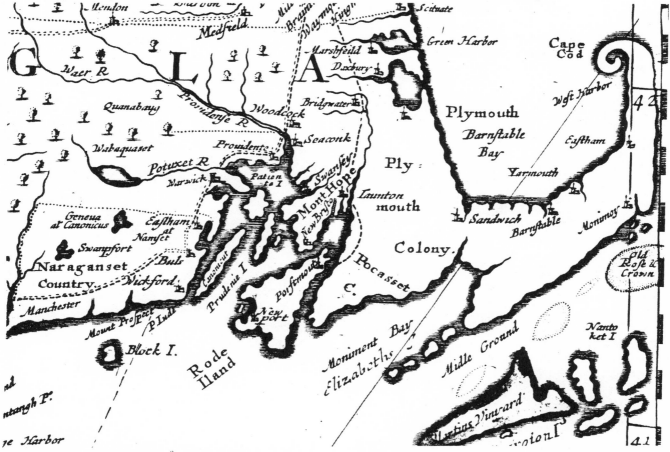

SECTION OF JOHN THORNTON'S "A NEW MAP OF NEW ENGLAND," c.1685. NOTE OLD ROSE AND CROWN ISLAND/SHOAL AND THE OTHER NANTUCKET SOUND SHOALS THAT AT LOW TIDE MAY HAVE MADE THE SEA SEEM "ALMOST OUT OF SIGHT."

31

LEIF'S ELUSIVE WINTER CAMP ~ W. B. Prescott

once said that "we are all continuously faced with a series of great opportunities brilliantly disguised as insoluble problems." Although reason would accept Cape Cod as the long-lost Vinland, hard proof seemed an impossibility. After all, the building boom on that vacation-land seems determined to wipe out any thousand-year-old traces. Metal detectors had scoured any likely spot for Viking relics and proved to be an exercise in futility. Even at the carefully searched and sifted Norse settlement at L'Anse aux Meadows in Newfoundland, the only metal object found to date was a two-and three-quarter-inch bronze pin. It seemed that if ever there was an "insoluble problem," Leif's winter campsite must be a prime example.

When exploring the explorers, one must take a mind's journey back to those earlier days, walk in their shoes, and think as they did. Viking author Frederick Pohl had hiked many a sand dune and pitch-pine stand on the cape to recapture some of those historic days. He had reasoned that Follins Pond, connected to the ocean by Bass River, might be the "lake" of Leif's telling. In 1951, he chanced upon a gully by the south shore of the pond, which would have pleased any Viking who wished to dry-dock his ship.

The usual way to shore a relatively light Norse vessel was to lay down a track of debarked poles to the water's edge. On these, log rollers without bark were positioned. The long, straight, and sturdy keel gave minimal surface contact on the rollers to make the job easier. Once ashore, the ship was propped upright with slanted poles that rested against the waterline planking, or strake, that extended from stem to stern. To protect the ship from snows and freezing rains, and to prevent the drying winds from shrinking the strakes and separating the caulking, a shed was built. As with most homes of the period, the walls were built of layered sod, which supported the roofing framework.

SHIP WAS SHORED ON ROLLERS.

"SHORED UP" WITH SIDE PROPS

THE SOD SHORING SHED

There were several features about the gully that intrigued Mr. Pohl. For one thing, there was a U-shaped mound of earth toward the inner part, almost hidden by the profusion of brush and brambles. The gully's floor was sizable~ about one hundred and sixty feet in length and thirty-five feet in width~ with a slight slope to the water's edge. There the shore had been cleared of stones and boulders to apparently provide a smooth landing surface. It was time to put suspicions to the test, and the Massachusetts Archeological Society agreed to bring in the manpower for a thorough search.

Pohl and the archeologists had no illusions that such surface equipment as the log rollers and pole tracks could have survived the centuries. As the topsoil was laid bare, one discovery followed another. Down the center and on to the shore lay a line of flat stones. Those nearest the pond were two feet deeper

32

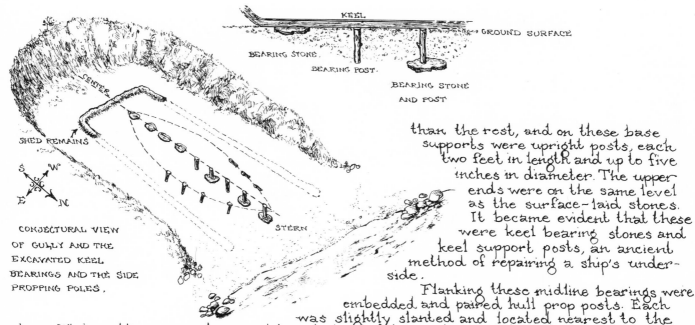

KEEL

BEARING STONE

GROUND SURFACE

BEARING POST

BEARING STONE
AND POST

CENTER

SHED REMAINS

S W
E N

STERN

CONJECTURAL VIEW
OF GULLY AND THE
EXCAVATED KEEL
BEARINGS AND THE SIDE
PROPPING POLES.

than the rest, and on these base supports were upright posts, each two feet in length and up to five inches in diameter. The upper ends were on the same level as the surface-laid stones.

It became evident that these were keel bearing stones and keel support posts, an ancient method of repairing a ship's underside.

Flanking these midline bearings were embedded and paired hull prop posts. Each was slightly slanted and located nearest to the shore. Their outlines curved inward to a distinct point at the last keel bearing. Since all ships then and now are beached bow first, this represented a pointed stern. It need not be mentioned that all vessels have pointed bows. Fortunately, the wooden underground supports had been preserved by moisture from the gully drainage. It was not so fortunate that the same drainage had contaminated the site enough to prevent accurate carbon dating.

It was time to draw some conclusions~ and they were startling. The remnants of the shoring shed was of earth and not stone construction, much like the sod walls excavated at L'Anse aux Meadows. Because the surface bearing stones and the planted bearing posts were on the same level, the keel was straight and not curved. Measurements gave an overall ship length of seventy feet. The ship was pointed fore and aft, and the prop poles were sixteen feet at the widest. Since vessels were propped to the strengthened waterline strake, the outward swell above that planking to the gunwale would add an additional foot on each side for a vessel of this size. The widest width would therefore be about eighteen feet. Later and more complicated calculations found that the bearing stones and posts could support no more than twenty-two tons. Pohl found that while a Norse ship would weigh about fourteen tons, any post-Columbian seagoer of these dimensions and draft would range between sixty to seventy tons. In short, we have a clear description of a Viking period ship that had repairs made to the stern half of the keel and planking.

HOW THOSE REPAIRS WERE MADE

WEDGES ON SURFACE KEEL
BEARING STONES RAISED THE
SHIP ENOUGH TO REMOVE ROLLERS.

WITH WEDGES REMOVED,
THE KEEL RESTED ON
THE BEARING STONES.

THE SIDE POSTS WERE REPOSITIONED.

THE 40 OR SO LOG ROLLERS MUST BE REMOVED
TO GIVE ROOM ENOUGH FOR HULL REPAIRS.

UNDER THE STERN, A HOLE WAS DUG AND THE BEARING STONE LOWERED. A STURDY POST WAS THEN WEDGED BETWEEN IT AND THE KEEL.

ONE BY ONE, THE 4 BEARING STONES AND POSTS WERE POSITIONED. THE ENLARGED HOLE ALLOWED FOR REPAIRS

THE KEEL WAS THEN WEDGED UP. THE ROLLERS REPLACED, AND THE SHIP WAS READY FOR LAUNCHING.

Could this be Leif's shoring shed and the site of his long-lost winter shelters? Mr. Pohl reasoned as much and pointed out that when Leif's brother Thorvald later used the base for exploring, he had the misfortune to have his ship's keel fractured on a sandbar. Although repairs were made on the spot, a close inspection and caulking would be needed upon his return to the shoring shed. If the excavated gully at Follins Pond held that building, then the placement of the bearing stones and posts would mean that the stern half of the keel had been replaced. Reworking would be necessary before the return to Greenland.

Sad but true, a bulldozer has since plowed a roadway to a new housing development just above the gully. A line of stockade posts have been located to one side of the road, but "progress" had destroyed most of what was suspected to be Leif's dwelling.

THE FIRST RECORDED INDIAN CONTACT ~ Leif's brother Thorvald felt that "the country had not been explored extensively enough." The saga continued with his adventures and on to the unfortunate skirmish with the Indians somewhere north of Cape Cod. The year was A.D. 1004.

"Thorvald prepared his expedition with his brother Leif's guidance and engaged a crew of thirty. Then the ship was ready to put out to sea and there are no reports of their voyage until they reached Leif's Houses in Vinland. There they laid up the ship and settled down for the winter, catching fish for their food.

"In the spring Thorvald said they should get the ship ready, and that meanwhile a small party of men should take the ship's boat and sail west along the coast and explore that region during the summer.

THORVALD'S EXPLORATIONS AND HIS SKIRMISH LOCATION AS SUGGESTED BY SEVERAL HISTORIANS.

CAPE BRETON I.

NOVA SCOTIA

MOUNT DESERT I.
(PORTLAND)
SAILING DOWN EAST

POINT ALLERTON BELOW BOSTON
GALE
PAMET R.
DIGHTON

SHIP'S BOAT EXPLORED WESTWARD.

"They found the country there very attractive, with woods stretching almost down to the shore and white sandy beaches. There were numerous islands there, and extensive shallows. They found no traces of human habitation or animals except on one westerly island, where they found a wooden stack-cover. That was the only man-made thing they found; and in the autumn they returned to Leif's Houses.

"Next summer Thorvald sailed east with his ship and then north along the coast. They ran into a fierce gale off a headland and were driven ashore; the keel was shattered and they had to

34

stay there for a long time while they repaired the ship.

"Thorvald said to his companions, 'I want to erect the old keel here on the headland and call the place KJALARNES.'

"They did this and then sailed away eastward along the coast. Soon they found themselves at the mouth of two fjords, and sailed up to the promontory that jutted out between them; it was heavily wooded. They moored the ship alongside and put out the gangway, and Thorvald went ashore with all his men.

"'It is beautiful here,' he said. 'Here I should like to make my home.'

"On their way back to the ship they noticed three humps on the sandy beach just in front of the headland. When they went closer they found that these were three skin-boats, with three men under each of them. Thorvald and his men divided forces and captured all of them except one, who escaped in his boat. They killed the other eight and returned to the headland, from which they scanned the surrounding country. They could make out a number of humps farther up the fjord and concluded that these were settlements.

"Then they were overwhelmed by such a drowziness that they could not stay awake, and they all fell asleep—until they were awakened by a voice that shouted, 'Wake up, Thorvald, and all your men, if you want to stay alive! Get to your ship with all your company and get away as fast as you can!'

"A great swarm of skin-boats was then heading towards them down the fjord.

"Thorvald said, 'We shall set up breastworks on the gunwales and defend ourselves as best we can, but fight back as little as possible.'

"They did this. The Skraelings shot at them for a while, and then turned and fled as fast as they could.

"Thorvald asked his men if any of them were wounded; they all replied that they were unhurt.

"'I have a wound in the armpit,' said Thorvald. An arrow flew up between the gunwale and my shield, under my arm—here it is. This will lead to my death.

"'I advise you now to go back as soon as you can. But first I want you to take me to the headland I thought so suitable for a home. I seem to have hit on the truth when I said that I would settle there for a while. Bury me there, and put crosses at my head and feet, and let the place be called KROSSANES for ever afterwards.'

"With that Thorvald died, and his men did exactly as he had asked of them. Afterward they sailed back and joined the rest of the expedition and exchanged all the news they had to tell.

"They spent the winter there and gathered grapes and vines as cargo for the ship. In the spring they set off on the voyage to Greenland;

THE VIKING EXPLORERS FOLLOWED THE COASTLINE WHENEVER POSSIBLE. THEY ALWAYS PREFERRED TO CAMP ASHORE IN TENTS. COOKING COULD ONLY BE DONE ON LAND, AND DRIED FISH AND COLD CURED MEATS AT SEA WERE NOT GOURMET DINING. FURTHER, SLEEPING ON THE HARD AND CRAMPED SHIP'S DECK UNDER SCANT COVER HAD LITTLE TO RECOMMEND IT.

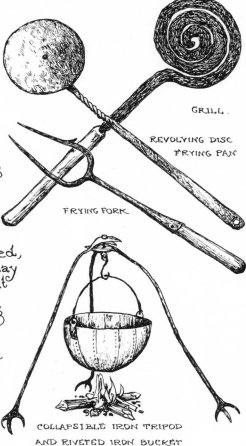

GRILL.

REVOLVING DISC
FRYING PAN

FRYING FORK

COLLAPSIBLE IRON TRIPOD
AND RIVETED IRON BUCKET

PEGGED, COLLAPSIBLE TENT FRAME

THE ABOVE CAMPING GEAR IS SIMILAR TO THAT FOUND ON BURIED VIKING SHIPS.

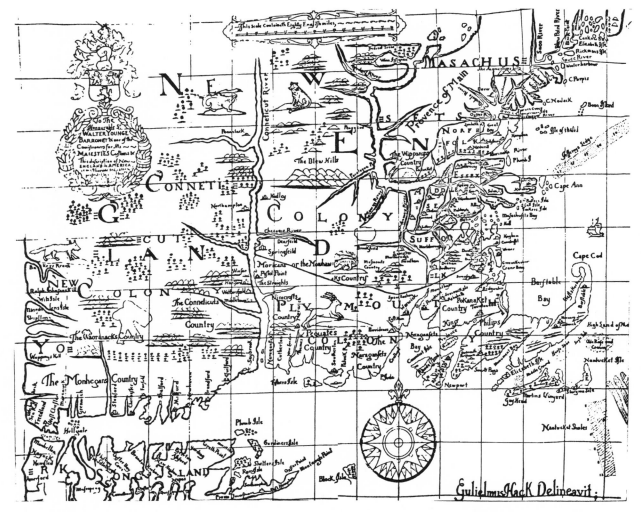

THE HACK MAP OF 1690. THE SUMMER EXPLORATION WITH THE SHIP'S BOAT PROBABLY PROBED UP NARRAGANSETT BAY AND ALONG THE COAST THAT INCLUDED LONG ISLAND. THORVALD'S KROSSANES, WHERE HE LOST HIS LIFE, MAY HAVE BEEN AT ONE OF THE MANY PROMONTORIES TO BE FOUND ABOVE CAPE COD.   (COURTESY OF PLYMOUTH HALL, PLYMOUTH)

they made land at Eiriksfjord, and had plenty of news to tell Leif."

With the fine summer weather at hand, an exploring party left Vinland to search westward along the islands and mainland that bordered Nantucket and Long Island sounds. No Indians were sighted ~ only a wooden "stack cover" on one of the many islands. Bark-domed wigwams do resemble a covered haystack. Tribal families regularly journeyed to the ocean or lakes for the spring and summer fishing season. They retreated to another wigwam before winter set in, deep in the protection of the forest.

The following summer, the explorers extended their discoveries by sailing eastward below Cape Cod and then northward above its tip ~ and into the teeth of a "fierce gale." Dashed toward the upper arm of the cape. The ship's keel fractured after becoming hogged on a sandbar. Extraordinary skill and no little time was spent replacing the broken back of the ship. As a monument to a successful rebuilding, the

BARK WIGWAM SHOWING FRAMEWORK AND COVERING.
(WILBUR, LAND OF THE NONOTUCKS)

broken half of the keel was raised near Provincetown. This landmark gave the promontory its name of Kjalarnes or "Keel Cape."

Now seaworthy, the ship was steered on an easterly course, or as the Maine mariners would say, "Goin' down-east." They sailed along the northeasterly coastline of New England until a "promontory" caught their eye. This land jutted out between two fjords (the dictionary definition is "a long, narrow, often deep inlet from the sea between steep cliffs and slopes"). Writers have suggested many candidates for this landing spot-even as far northward as Lake Melville in Labrador! Wherever it was, it was "beautiful," and seemed an ideal place for a Norse colony. Unfortunately, an Algonquin tribe thought so too. Nine of their number were found asleep under three overturned canoes.

Later, the explorers described these canoes as "skin-boats," for they knew nothing of the native Americans or their method of sheathing a craft with white birchbark. They had only their recollections of a more cumbersome boat made of hide that was stretched over a framework and used on the protected waters of the Norwegian fjords. The sleeping men were not Eskimos. It would be impossible for three men to sleep under a kayak. The other kind of Eskimo hide boat was the umiak – large, heavy and flat-bottomed enough to carry a family and all their possessions. It would be much too awkward for the lone Indian survivor to launch it and make his escape before the Norsemen were upon him. Further, it is known that Eskimos lived no farther south than Labrador. And while on the subject of birchbark canoes, explorer Jacques Cartier observed of some Indians that "they have no other dwelling but their boats, which they turn upside down, and under them they lay themselves all along upon the bare ground."

Mistrust of strangers is not peculiar to any one people or period in history. The sleeping braves, however, presented no danger, and signs of friendship with a shared meal could have had a good many benefits. If a colony was to be considered at such a favorable spot, friendly Indians could make the difference between success and failure. It would prove so in the centuries that followed. As guides, they would have been of great help to further explorations. As neighbors, they would willingly share their hunting and farming skills with newcomers and set up a lively trade in furs and garden produce. At the very least, the nine tribesmen might serve as hostages if the clan proved to be hostile.

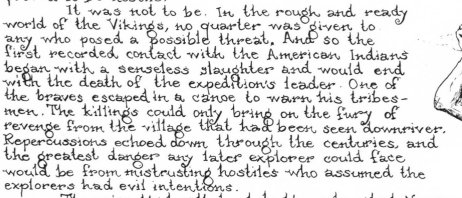

It was not to be. In the rough and ready world of the Vikings, no quarter was given to any who posed a possible threat. And so the first recorded contact with the American Indians began with a senseless slaughter and would end with the death of the expedition's leader. One of the braves escaped in a canoe to warn his tribesmen. The killings could only bring on the fury of revenge from the village that had been seen downriver. Repercussions echoed down through the centuries, and the greatest danger any later explorer could face would be from mistrusting hostiles who assumed the explorers had evil intentions.

The voice that called out to the exhausted Norsemen was no supernatural warning from the heavens. Just

as on shipboard, a watch would be posted—especially after the countryside had been warned at their intrusion. The "great swarm" of approaching canoes must have been an awesome sight. The spine-chilling whoops and thud of the arrows certainly made death seem very near. The Indians, thereafter, were called Skraelings, meaning shouters, shriekers, or warwhoopers. The crew could only crouch behind the row of gunwale shields, swords and axes ready should there be an attempt at boarding. In a way, justice was served when an arrow found its mark in Thorvald's lung.

THE "BREAST-WORKS ON THE GUNWALES" WERE SHIELDS TIED IN PLACE. THE RAIDING LONGSHIPS OF THE PAST NEVER DISPLAYED SHIELDS ON THE HIGH SEAS, WHERE WAVES AND A SWINGING BOOM MIGHT SWEEP THEM AWAY.

The northern tribes have many a legend about "terrifying North Men" who came to their lands in "immense canoes." In one, the tale of "The Liver-Colored Giants And Magicians," a young wife was startled—to say the least—by a part human, part beast, part demon. Her fear increased as he came closer, for "it was the size and form of an old man, stark naked and with a hideous countenance. His lips and shoulders seemed to be gnawed away." In short, he or it was no candidate for a Viking-of-the-year contest.

The good woman tried kindness and attentiveness in the hope that he would not "kill and devour her." The creature was won over and was soon chopping down "great trees into firewood with his axe" as though they had been straw. The legend had a happy ending when this newfound friend defended the woman's family from another rampaging North Man. The theme of kindness and understanding, unfortunately, was also lost on the Karlsefni expedition that followed Thorvald's.

KARLSEFNI'S EXPLORATIONS AND ATTEMPTED COLONIZATION ~

One year after Thorvald Erikson's death, his brother Thorstein sailed off for Vinland, only to be carried far out in the Atlantic by contrary winds. He finally reached Greenland's western settlement and died shortly thereafter. About 1019, Icelander Thorfinn Karlsefni visited Greenland and married Thorstein's widow Gudrid the following year. Intrigued with Vinland's possibilities, he set sail about 1020 with one hundred and sixty men and women, including Gudrid and Leif's sister Freydis. After a more extensive exploration of North America, he hoped for a permanent Norse colony near Vinland. The following account is from "Eirik the Red's Saga."

"There were great discussions at Brattahlid that winter about going in search of Vinland, where, it was said, there was excellent land to be had. The outcome was that Karlsefni and Snorri Thorbrandsson prepared their ship [there were three shiploads of colonists] and made ready to search for Vinland that summer…

"They sailed first up to the Western Settlement, and then to Bjarn Isles. From there they sailed before a northerly wind and after two days at sea they sighted land and rowed ashore in boats to explore it. They found there many slabs of stone so huge that two men could stretch out on them sole to sole. There were numerous foxes there. They gave this country a name and called it HELLULAND.

"From there they sailed for two days before a northerly wind and sighted land ahead; this was a heavily-wooded country abounding with animals. There was an island to the south-east, where they found bears, and so named it Bjarn Isle; they named the wooded mainland itself MARKLAND.

"After two days they sighted land again and held in towards it; it was a promontory they were approaching. They tacked along the coast, with the land to

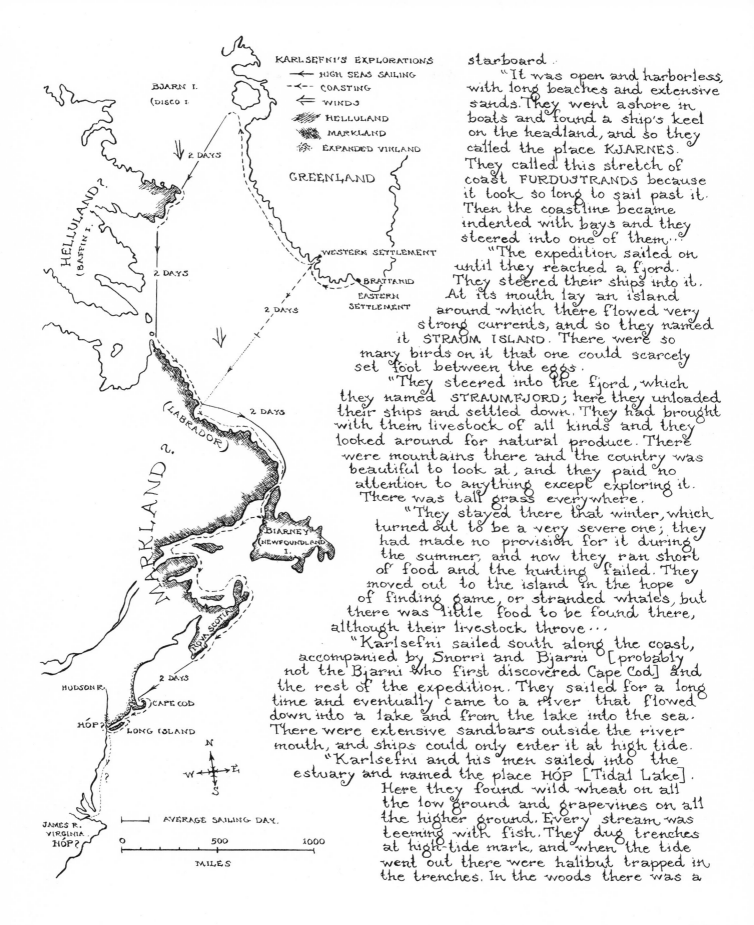

starboard.

"It was open and harborless, with long beaches and extensive sands. They went ashore in boats and found a ship's keel on the headland, and so they called the place KJARNES. They called this stretch of coast FURDUSTRANDS because it took so long to sail past it. Then the coastline became indented with bays and they steered into one of them...

"The expedition sailed on until they reached a fjord. They steered their ships into it. At its mouth lay an island around which there flowed very strong currents, and so they named it STRAUM ISLAND. There were so many birds on it that one could scarcely set foot between the eggs.

"They steered into the fjord, which they named STRAUMFJORD; here they unloaded their ships and settled down. They had brought with them livestock of all kinds and they looked around for natural produce. There were mountains there and the country was beautiful to look at, and they paid no attention to anything except exploring it. There was tall grass everywhere.

"They stayed there that winter, which turned out to be a very severe one; they had made no provision for it during the summer, and now they ran short of food and the hunting failed. They moved out to the island in the hope of finding game, or stranded whales, but there was little food to be found there, although their livestock throve...

"Karlsefni sailed south along the coast, accompanied by Snorri and Bjarni [probably not the Bjarni who first discovered Cape Cod] and the rest of the expedition. They sailed for a long time and eventually came to a river that flowed down into a lake and from the lake into the sea. There were extensive sandbars outside the river mouth, and ships could only enter it at high tide.

"Karlsefni and his men sailed into the estuary and named the place HÓP [Tidal Lake]. Here they found wild wheat on all the low ground and grapevines on all the higher ground. Every stream was teeming with fish. They dug trenches at high-tide mark, and when the tide went out there were halibut trapped in the trenches. In the woods there was a great number of animals of all kinds.

"They stayed there for a fortnight, enjoying themselves and noticing nothing untoward. They had their livestock with them. But early one morning as they looked around they caught sight of nine skin-boats; the men in them were waving sticks which made a noise like flails, and the motion was sunrise.

"Karlsefni said, 'What can this signify?'

"'It could well be a token of peace,' said Snorri. 'Let us take a white shield and go to meet them with it.'

"They did so. The newcomers rowed towards them and stared at them in amazement as they came ashore. They were small and evil-looking, and their hair was coarse; they had large eyes and broad cheekbones. They stayed there for a while, marvelling and then rowed away south round the headland.

"Karlsefni and his men had built their settlement on a slope by the lakeside; some of the houses were close to the lake, and others were farther away. They stayed there that winter. There was no snow at all, and all the livestock were able to fend for themselves.

"Then early one morning in spring, they saw a horde of skin-boats approaching from the south round the headland, so dense it looked as if the estuary were strewn with charcoal; and sticks were being waved from every boat. Karlsefni's men raised their shields and the two parties began to trade.

"What the natives wanted most to buy was red cloth; they also wanted to buy swords and spears, but Karlsefni and Snorri forbade that. In exchange for the cloth they traded grey pelts. The natives took a span of red cloth for each pelt, and tied the cloth around their heads. The trading went on like this for a while until the cloth began to run short; then Karlsefni and his men cut it up into pieces which were no more than a finger's breadth wide; but the Skraelings paid just as much or even more for it.

"Then it so happened that a bull belonging to Karlsefni and his men came running out of the woods, bellowing furiously. The Skraelings were terrified and ran to their skin-boats and rowed away south round the headland.

"After that there was no sign of the natives for three whole weeks. But then Karlsefni's men saw a huge number of boats coming from the south, pouring in like a torrent. This time all the sticks were being waved anti-clockwise and all the Skraelings were howling loudly. Karlsefni and his men now hoisted red

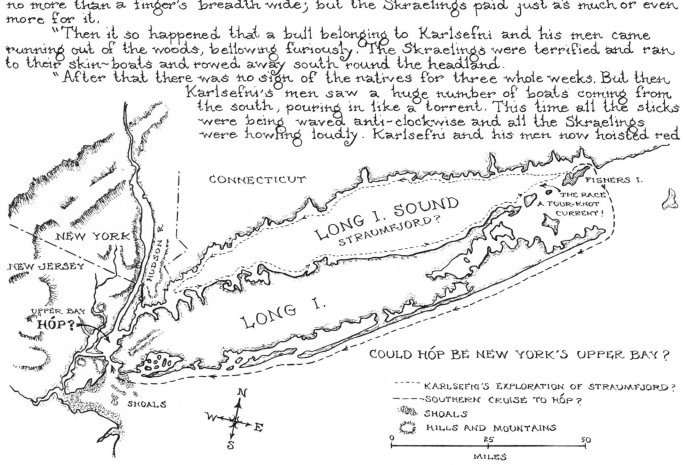

COULD HÓP BE NEW YORK'S UPPER BAY?

-------- KARLSEFNI'S EXPLORATION OF STRAUMFJORD?
----- SOUTHERN CRUISE TO HÓP?
SHOALS
HILLS AND MOUNTAINS

0   25   50
MILES

40

shields and advanced towards them.

"When they clashed there was a fierce battle and a hail of missiles came flying over, for the Skraelings were using catapults. Karlsefni and Snorri saw them hoist a large sphere on a pole; it was dark blue in color. It came flying in over the heads of Karlsefni's men and made an ugly din when it struck the ground. This terrified Karlsefni and his men so much that their only thought was to flee, and they retreated farther up the river. They did not halt until they reached some cliffs, where they prepared to make a resolute stand.

"Freydis came out and saw the retreat. She shouted, 'Why do you flee from such pitiful wretches, brave men like you? You should be able to slaughter them like cattle. If I had weapons, I am sure I could fight better than any of you.'

FREYDIS ~ A ONE-WOMAN ARMY

"The men paid no attention to what she was saying. Freydis tried to join them but she could not keep up with them because she was pregnant. She was following them into the woods when the Skraelings closed in on her. In front of her lay a dead man, Thorbrand Snorrason, with a flintstone buried in his head, and his sword beside him. She snatched up the sword and prepared to defend herself. When the Skraelings came rushing towards her she pulled one of her breasts out of her bodice and slapped it with the sword. The Skraelings were terrified at the sight of this and fled back to their boats and hastened away.

"Karlsefni and his men came over to her and praised her courage. Two of their men had been killed and four of the Skraelings, even though Karlsefni and his men had been fighting against heavy odds.

"They returned to their houses and pondered what forces it was that had attacked them from inland; they then realized that the only attackers had been those who had come in the boats, and that the other force had just been a delusion.

"The Skraelings found the other dead Norseman, with his axe lying beside him. One of them hacked at a rock with the axe, and the axe broke; and thinking it worthless now because it could not withstand stone, they threw it away.

"Karlsefni and his men had realized by now that although the land was excellent they could never live there in safety or freedom from fear, because of the native inhabitants. So they made ready to leave the place and return home. They sailed off north along the coast. They came upon five Skraelings clad in skins, asleep; beside them were containers full of deer marrow mixed with blood. Karlsefni's men reckoned that these five must be outlaws, and killed them.

"Then they came to a headland on which there were numerous deer; the headland looked like a huge cake of dung, for the animals used to spend the winters there.

"Soon afterwards Karlsefni and his men arrived at Straumfjord, where they found plenty of everything.

"Karlsefni set out with one ship in search of Thorhall the Hunter [who had sailed north of the keel point Kjalarnes in search of Vinland when the others headed south to Hóp], while the rest of the company stayed behind. He sailed north past Kjalarnes and then bore west, with the land on the port beam. It was a region of wild and desolate woodland; and when they had travelled a long way they came to a river which flowed from east to west into the sea. They steered into the river mouth and lay to by its southern bank.

"They returned to Straumfjord and spent the third winter there. But now quarrels broke out frequently; those who were unmarried kept pestering the married men.

"It was in the first autumn that Karlsefni's son, Snorri, was born; he was three years old when they left.

"They set sail before a southerly wind and reached Markland, where they came upon five Skraelings ~ a bearded man, two women and two children. Karlsefni and his men captured the two boys, but the others got away and sank down into the ground.

"They took the boys with them and taught them the language and baptized them. The boys said that their mother was called Vaetild and their father Ovaegir. They said that the land of the Skraelings was ruled by two kings, one of whom was called Avaldamon and the other Valdida. They said that there were no houses there and that people lived in caves or holes in the ground. They said that there was a country across from their own land where the people went about in white clothing and uttered loud cries and carried poles with patches of cloth attached. This is thought to have been HVITRAMANNALAND.

"Finally they reached Greenland, and spent the winter with Eirik the Red."

MAPPING KARLSEFNI'S DISCOVERIES ~
Thorvald's broken keel, erected at the tip of Cape Cod, served as a landmark of Leif's Vinland. It was not until Karlsefni's expedition reached that beacon that his voyage can be traced with any certainty. The whereabouts of Bjarn Isles and the two-day sail from there to Helluland make plotting difficult. If Disco Island to the north was their Greenland departure, then two days before a north wind would make Baffin Island the first landfall. Helluland would then become that island. Markland must necessarily include the vast territory of Labrador, Newfoundland Island (Biarney or Bear Island), the Gulf of St. Lawrence, and all of Nova Scotia. This viewpoint holds that the expedition planned a comprehensive exploration of Helluland, Markland, and Vinland and then the selection of a new Norse colony at the most favorable site.

Gathorne-Hardy finds it hard to believe that three shiploads of colonists, crammed with 160 men, women, livestock, and homesteading necessities would sail to the northern wastelands, where it was already known that a new colony would be "unprofitable." Vinland beckoned to the southwest, and the proper course had been well established by Bjarni, Leif, and Thorvald. He feels that the mysterious Bjarn Isles were hard by the Western Settlement (present-day Godthåb).

This second theory, however, would bring the colonists less than halfway to their first landing at Helluland~Labrador. The author points out that the word "two" was written as ii and "five" as u. Time and wear may have blurred one into the other. A five-day sailing would make sense, for Karlsefni's passage to Helluland (Labrador) would then follow the same course, distance, and destinations as the earlier Vikings.

Be that as it may, the two-day sailing from the southern tip of Markland or Nova Scotia would bring the party to Cape Cod and Kjalarnes. Rounding the arm of the cape and coasting along the southern shore, they were so taken by the seemingly endless stretches of white, sandy beaches that the shoreline was called Furdustrands or "Astonishing Strands." The saga makes no mention of any stopover at Leif's shelters but they did coast on to the many bays that lay farther westward. "They steered into one of them," and Narragansett Bay would certainly be one to invite exploration.

At this point, the historical detective finds himself adrift in a sea of possibilities. Somewhere to the west was an island with swift currents, a long, narrow inlet that resembled a fjord, and finally there was the long sail southward along the coast to Hóp's tidal lake, well guarded by sandbars outside the river's mouth. Practically all the authorities place Thorvald's keel marker and Astonishing Strands at Cape Cod. Haugen points to the southern New England shore as Hóp's location. Hermannsson believes Hóp to be "somewhere south of Cape Cod, in Barnstable, Buzzard's Bay or thereabouts." Rafn prefers Mount Hope Bay for Hóp, and De Costa places Straumfjord on the shore opposite Martha's Vinland with Hóp also at Mount Hope Bay. Horsford looks for Hóp at Boston's Back Bay and Hovgaard claims Karlsefni never reached Leif's Vinland at Cape Cod, but rather found Hóp at the Sop's Arm inlet at White Bay or the east coast of Newfoundland. Gathorne-Hardy's Straumfjord would be Long

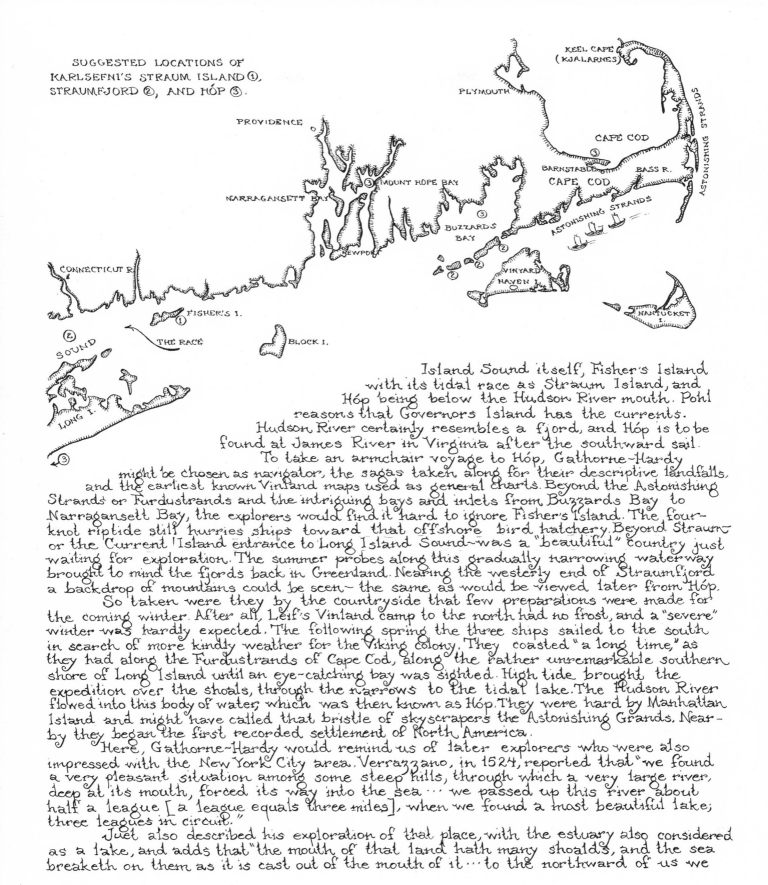

SUGGESTED LOCATIONS OF
KARLSEFNI'S STRAUM ISLAND ①,
STRAUMFJORD ②, AND HÓP ③.

Island Sound itself, Fisher's Island with its tidal race as Straum Island, and Hóp being below the Hudson River mouth. Pohl reasons that Governors Island has the currents. Hudson River certainly resembles a fjord, and Hóp is to be found at James River in Virginia after the southward sail.

To take an armchair voyage to Hóp, Gathorne-Hardy might be chosen as navigator, the sagas taken along for their descriptive landfalls, and the earliest known Vinland maps used as general charts. Beyond the Astonishing Strands or Furdustrands and the intriguing bays and inlets from Buzzards Bay to Narragansett Bay, the explorers would find it hard to ignore Fisher's Island. The four-knot riptide still hurries ships toward that offshore bird hatchery. Beyond Straum or the Current Island entrance to Long Island Sound—was a "beautiful" country just waiting for exploration. The summer probes along this gradually narrowing waterway brought to mind the fjords back in Greenland. Nearing the westerly end of Straumfjord a backdrop of mountains could be seen~ the same as would be viewed later from Hóp.

So taken were they by the countryside that few preparations were made for the coming winter. After all, Leif's Vinland camp to the north had no frost, and a "severe" winter was hardly expected. The following spring the three ships sailed to the south in search of more kindly weather for the Viking colony. They coasted "a long time," as they had along the Furdustrands of Cape Cod, along the rather unremarkable southern shore of Long Island until an eye-catching bay was sighted. High tide brought the expedition over the shoals, through the narrows to the tidal lake. The Hudson River flowed into this body of water, which was then known as Hóp. They were hard by Manhattan Island and might have called that bristle of skyscrapers the Astonishing Grands. Nearby they began the first recorded settlement of North America.

Here, Gathorne-Hardy would remind us of later explorers who were also impressed with the New York City area. Verrazzano, in 1524, reported that "we found a very pleasant situation among some steep hills, through which a very large river, deep at its mouth, forced its way into the sea ⋯ we passed up this river about half a league [a league equals three miles], when we found a most beautiful lake; three leagues in circuit."

Juet also described his exploration of that place, with the estuary also considered as a lake, and adds that "the mouth of that land hath many shoalds, and the sea breaketh on them as it is cast out of the mouth of it ⋯ to the northward of us we

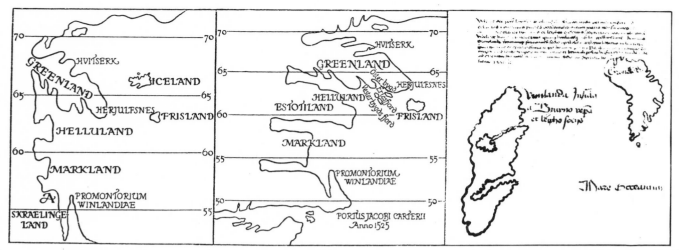

saw high hills ... This is a very good land to fall with, and a pleasant land to see."

Some historians feel that the lack of snow would place Hóp farther to the south. Yet Leif's frost-free Cape Cod shelters were even more to the north. It seems that the North American climate was milder between A.D. 950 and 1200. Thereafter came the Little Ice Age, and before 1400, southern Greenland had a permanent freezing of the ground. The meager crops that were possible before were later impossible to grow. The survivors of the colony packed up, bag and baggage, for greener pastures. Many or all are believed to have sailed off to a kinder Vinland to establish a permanent colony — but we're getting ahead of the story.

Karlsefni's aborted colonial effort had some real pluses, if only for later historians. His extensive travels along the North American coastline gave a sweeping impression of a large land mass from which projected Helluland, Markland, and Vinland itself. No logbook, charts, or sketches are known, but cartographers feel certain that an early map existed in the twelfth century. Similarities of names, locations, landforms, and orientation in the few-known fifteenth and sixteenth-century New World maps point to such a common source. The Stefansson map of 1590 is considered closest to that earliest graphic recording. Another, the 1605 Resen version, has identical geographics, although the indented gulfs have become deeper and more narrowed. Indeed, Resen twice cites an ancient Icelandic map "some centuries old" as an authority for his work. It is of interest that the Resen map extends farther southward than that of Stefansson, and it would seem to be a reasonable representation of Cape Cod as "Promontorium Winlandiae" and the Long Island Sound to its southwest.

Cartographers shy away from drawing too many conclusions from these early maps. That earliest Icelandic map, now lost, may have been an impression drawn from word of mouth or written sources. If so, any interpretations can be made only in a general way. Then again, maps of later centuries were an attempt to incorporate the old Viking landfalls into a "modern" map with the known geography of the Old World latitudes, and certainly longitudes of land outlines and orientation of the North American coast were but educated guesses in the fifteenth century.

A case in point is the more recently discovered Vinland Map, now the prized possession of Yale University. This was a contemporary version of the 1436 world map by Andrea Bianco, the Venetian shipmaster and navigator. As George Painter points out in <u>The Vinland Map and the Tartar Relation</u>, the huge island of Vinland represents a generalized and degenerate simplification of the saga narratives. Because of this, an interpretation of the swiggles and bumps is difficult at best.

In spite of any such words of caution, the Vinland Map of 1440 does raise suspicions that the unexplored and unknown areas were simply rounded off as one

* THE AUTHENTICITY OF THE VINLAND MAP REMAINS IN QUESTION BECAUSE OF CONFLICTING ANALYSES OF THE INK.

44

YALE'S VINLAND MAP WITH
LOCATIONS THAT ARE
ENTIRELY CONJECTURAL!

great island that was considerably larger than Greenland. Karlsefni's expedition apparently thought that
Long Island was a mainland projection, and it wasn't
until 1614 that explorer Adrian Block found it to
be just that~ an island.

We've considered a number of Vinland theories
and conclude that the only agreement among the
historians is that they disagree. Yet their reasoning
presents real possibilities, and few discoveries
have been made without preconceived ideas. Hard
proof may then be unearthed, such as a Viking
sword, axe, or cooking pot, or even that long-
lost original Vinland map.

Throughout the ancient Indian legends runs
the ongoing conflict between the forces of good
and evil. It began when the great and kindly
god of the Algonquins, Cautantowit, had remade
the world and fashioned man and woman after the
evil spirits had unleashed a devastating flood. Lesser
and personal gods, or manitos, continued to offer
protection and guidance. There were many such good
spirits ~ Roger Williams, the founder of Rhode Island,
counted a total of thirty-eight ~ which included the gods of
fire, thunder, sun, moon, north, south, east, and west, and of women and the home.
Yet malicious spirits were forever lurking, ready to bring their own brand
of misery to the unwary tribesperson.

At first, the natives met the Viking strangers with a friendly curiosity
and no little awe, for they could well be in the presence of supernatural beings.
If so, and even if they had not heard of Thorvald's massacre of their sleeping
kinsmen to the north, it became evident that here was an invasion by the evil
spirits. Generosity had long been an Indian virtue, and suspicions grew when
they were given increasingly narrow strips of red[1] cloth in exchange for their pelts.
Then came the bellowing bull[2] the likes of which no Algonquin had ever seen. The
four-legged devil and its evil masters had become unwanted neighbors. The natives
attacked, only to be confronted by Freydis. They stopped in their tracks when this
she-devil, pregnant and slapping her breast with a sword, screamed at them
like a thing possessed. Until they could call on their medicine men to counter
with some potent magic, a retreat from these fearful beings made sense.

The Indian legends, with their mixture of fact and fancy, are open to
so many interpretations that here the sagas must speak for them. Strange people with
different traditions, then and now, are often viewed with suspicion. There was a touch of
prejudice when it came to Skraelings, for they were no more "small and evil looking"
than the Vikings were large and evil looking. Still, the tellings, like the Norse explorers
themselves, were in a straight-from-the-shoulder and a no-nonsense manner. They
told it as they saw it.

It was said that the Skraelings first paddled to the Viking camp at Hóp
waving "sticks" in the direction of the sun's arc, or clockwise, as a sign of friendship. Once
they had become enemies, these sticks were swung in an opposite direction, contrary to
nature. The flail-like racket was no doubt from these "lightning sticks," otherwise known as
"whizzing sticks" or "bull-roarers." These sacred implements were associated with rain, wind,
and lightning. A narrow, rectangular slat of wood between six inches and two feet in

---

[1] RED WAS THE FAVORED INDIAN COLOR. THEY WERE SO TAKEN BY IT THAT THEY SMEARED THEIR BODIES WITH POWDERED RED OCHRE
AND WERE KNOWN BY LATER EXPLORERS AS "RED MEN."

[2] SAILING WITH LIVESTOCK IN AN OPEN VIKING VESSEL WAS NEITHER DIFFICULT NOR UNUSUAL. ACCORDING TO FREDERICK POHL, THE
CATTLE, SHEEP, AND PIGS OF 1000 YEARS AGO WERE BUT HALF THE SIZE AND A QUARTER OF THE WEIGHT AS TODAY'S FARM ANIMALS.

WHIZZING STICK, ABOUT 7 INCHES LONG, WITH PAINTED RED EDGE   (FIELD MUSEUM, CHICAGO, ILLINOIS)

length was attached by a thong to a stick or a toggle. When it was whirled rapidly in a uniform motion over the head, it gave a distinctive whizzing sound.

The catapults, which terrified the hard-pressed Vikings, have been identified. Henry Schoolcraft's Indian Tribes of the United States, 1851, describes this Balista or Demon's Head. "Algonquin tradition affirms, that in ancient times during the fierce wars which the Indians carried on, they constructed a very formidable instrument of attack, by sewing up a large round boulder in a new skin. To this, a long handle was tied. When the skin dried, it became very tight around the stone; and after being painted with devices, assumed the appearance and character of a solid globe on a pole. This formidable instrument, to which the name of balista may be applied, is figured (plate 15, fig. 2) from the description of an Algonquin chief. It was borne by several warriors, who acted as balisteers. Plunged upon a boat, or canoe, it was capable of sinking it. Brought down among a group of men on a sudden, it produced consternation and death."

One historian came up with a different and rather novel catapult idea. "We know with practical certainty" that the large sphere on a pole was a hornet's nest! He postulates that an animal skin was tied around the nest at night. In battle, the tie was loosened and flung from the end of a flexible pole. Those of us who have had the misfortune of meeting a swarm of angry hornets on their own terms can well imagine the chaos caused by these vicious little dive bombers. Although it would seem that Karlsefni would have been more specific if such were the case, and such an unusual weapon would appear in later Indian skirmish accounts, the warriors would have had thousands of unbeatable allies for their attack.

The Vikings were up to their old tricks. On the retreat back to Straum-fjord, the five sleeping Indian "outlaws" were dispatched in the usual manner. Considering that the aborted Hóp colony was near New York City, those unfortunates met their maker somewhere along the southern Long Island shore.

A lengthy passage about Thorhall the Hunter was not included from the "Eirik the Red" saga, and it deserves some explanation. He was Erik's summer huntsman, an older man

— BALISTA —
(AFTER SCHOOLCRAFT'S DRAWING IN INDIAN TRIBES OF THE UNITED STATES, 1851)

of great size and strength and with experience enough to captain one of the expedition's ships. His sour disposition and contrary nature made him a poor traveling companion. When Karlsefni decided to sail southward from Straumfjord, Thorhall chose to take his ship northward to explore the Vinland beyond the Astonishing Strands and Keel Cape at Cape Cod's tip. Understandably, only nine men agreed to ship aboard with him. It was an unfortunate decision, for a storm carried the vessel eastward and clear across the Atlantic. They were washed ashore at Ireland, where they were roughly treated and enslaved. There, according to traders, Thorhall died.

Karlsefni's search for him along the "wild and desolate woodland" coast probably brought the vessel as far as the western shores of Nova Scotia or Markland. Pohl points out that there are but two west-flowing rivers along the entire North American seaboard. The Annapolis River and the Apple River are both to be found on the western shores of Nova Scotia.

Snorri, the son of Gudrid and Karlsefni, made history as the first recorded birth in America. Other deliveries may well have followed, for the defiant Freydis was certainly pregnant at Hóp, and other wives may have been expecting. There were a number of unmarried men who were anxious to add to the population at Straumfjord that third and last winter. The wedded women were badgered for favors, if it may be put that delicately. Any further hopes for colonization were riddled by mistrust and dissension.

The return voyage brought the ships back to Markland where the kidnapping of the two Skraeling boys took place. It appears that the Vikings were bent on spreading ill will along the entire North American coastline! Karlsefni's observations and the boys' statement are of considerable interest. A bearded man escaped the raid. Since the Algonquin men took great pains to pluck any and all hair from their faces, anyone who dared to hide his chin in fur might well be of a different culture. Many are the ancient Indian legends that recall the bearded holy men, white skinned and white robed, who came among them as missionaries. Indeed, the boys spoke of "a country across from their own land where people went about in white clothes and uttered loud cries and carried poles with patches of cloth attached." The white robes, loud chants, and the religious banners make the legends all the more real.

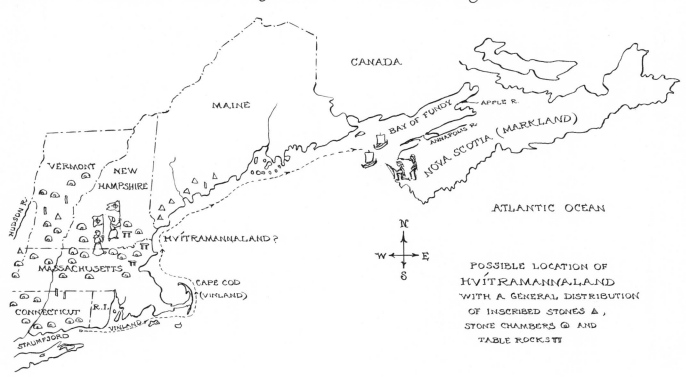

POSSIBLE LOCATION OF
HVÍTRAMANNALAND
WITH A GENERAL DISTRIBUTION
OF INSCRIBED STONES △,
STONE CHAMBERS ◉ AND
TABLE ROCKS π

47

The boys mentioned that their people had no houses, but rather "lived in caves or holes in the ground." If this hasn't a familiar ring to it, it might be worthwhile to recheck the "Before the Vikings" section. New Hampshire, Vermont, Massachusetts, Connecticut, and New York to the Hudson River have just such slab stone dwellings, which are reminiscent of the neolithic religious rites. There is also the profusion of corbelled stone chambers, known as beehive caves, which are associated with the Celtic Druid priests and the Irish Christian monks. It should be remembered that the Algonquin people had no stone-building traditions and had little inclination to be cramped below the ground in caves.

Hvitramannaland ("White Man's Country" or "Ireland the Great") was said to be a "country across from their own land..." Hawk's Saga adds that the boys "reported that another country lay on the other side, opposite to their own..." If this implies that such a country was across the water, then we must continue to focus on New England. It lies across the Bay of Fundy to the west, with its concentration of ancient stone structures.

Another saga, the Landnámabók or History of the Settlement of Iceland, contains a brief but interesting note about Vinland. It tells of one Ari Marsson, who was cast up upon the shores of Hvitramannaland, "which some call Ireland the Great, it lies westward in the sea near Wineland the Good." Since we consider Wineland (Vinland) to be in the Cape Cod area, Ireland the Great might be regarded as being in the New Hampshire and upper Massachusetts region.

LATER NORSE COLONIES~ The Greenland settlements fell on hard times. Historia Norvegiae, an anonymous writing from about 1170, tells of an invasion of Eskimo hunters. They were "very small people who they call Skraelings [the Norse term for any "savages"]...They have no iron at all, and use walrus tusks for arrowheads and sharp stones for knives." The 1379 Icelandic say that the Skraelings raided the Greenlanders, killing eighteen men and carrying off two boys as slaves." Erik the Red's colonial adventure, weakened by the Little Ice Age of 1200, which lasted for some one hundred and fifty years, was being frozen out of existence. Trade with this Norse outpost all but ceased, and, by the end of the 1400s, the isolated colony had vanished from their island icebox.

AN ESKIMO "PYGMY" BATTLES A GREENLANDER AS VISUALIZED BY OLAUS MAGNUS IN HISTORIA DE GENTIBUS SEPTENTRIONALIBUS, 1555. THE LARGE COMPASS CARD WAS SAID TO HAVE BEEN SET UP ON A ROCKY ISLAND BY FIFTEENTH-CENTURY DANISH PIRATES AS A SEA MARK.

The final fate of Greenland's survivors is unknown. Either they made an unrecorded exodus back to Iceland, or, more likely, they sailed off in a body to "Vinland the Good." The Icelandic Annals mention several Vinland visits by Eric, Bishop of Greenland. In 1117 and 1121, he sailed to his American diocese to check on his flock and perhaps lessen any Indian hostility by conversions to Christianity.

The 1440 Vinland Map at Yale has a Latin legend that R. A. Skelton translates as "Eric [Henricus], legate of the Apostolic See and Bishop of Greenland and the neighboring regions, arrived in this truely vast and rich land [Vinland], in the name of almighty God, in the year of our most blessed father Pascal, remained a long time in both summer and winter, and later returned northeastward [?~ ad orientem hiemalé] toward Greenland, and then proceeded in most humble obedience to the will of his superiors." George D. Painter adds that the visit implies the existence of a twelfth-century Norse American settlement in Vinland and "deserves serious consideration."

48

THE OLD STONE TOWER
NEWPORT, RHODE ISLAND.

CHESTERTON MILL, 3 MILES
FROM THE OLD ARNOLD HOME-
STEAD, ENGLAND.

Any interpretations of the Viking Sagas and the known Vinland Maps, however reasonable, require hard archeological evidence before they can become fact. Even when a discovery yields an object of suspicious Norse origin, a critical analysis may still be unable to provide absolute proof of its ancestry.

THE STONE TOWER OF NEWPORT — Controversy has swirled around this Rhode Island landmark for centuries. In 1946, five runic markers were discovered, chiseled into one of the stones. Barry Fell has identified the inscription as HNKRS, an ancient Norse word for "stool." He reminds us that, to this day, the Scandinavians still use the word (now spelled "stol") for the seat or throne of a bishop's church. To him, the late styling of the rune letters indicates that the church was built in the fourteenth century, perhaps as a replacement for a more permanent church.

NEWPORT TOWER "NORSE" RUNES MARKING THE CHURCH "OF THE BISHOP'S STOOL."

(FELL, SAGA AMERICA)

The stone tower has other features that may be of a religious nature. Its eight pillars are located exactly on the cardinal points of the compass. Well above the eastern arch is a fireplace. One of its flues runs northward, and the other passes to the south. It was an old religious custom never to permit altar fires to go out, and the ancients looked to the east for light and knowledge. The fireplace is so high above the floor that it would seem to serve better as an altar rather than for cooking or heating. Perhaps holy objects were placed in recesses that were built into the walls nearby.

According to some authorities, the tower was built with the Norse linear measure and is in the style of thirteenth- and fourteenth-century Old World buildings. Further, explorer Verrazzano's map of the North American coast is offered as proof that this was no seventeenth-century English colonial structure. Drawn in 1524, the tower was recorded as a "Norman Villa."

Newport may have been, therefore, the center of Vinland's permanent colony. If so, the Greenland refugees would have logically left their unforgiving island for such a kinder, well-established settlement.

A somewhat modest discovery added another tie to a Newport colony. At Karlsefni's Greenland house site, a lump of anthracite was found. Helge Ingstad, the

THE SOUTHERN PART OF NEW ENGLAND, 1634, BY WILLIAM WOOD. NOTE "OLD PLYMOUTH" AT NEWPORT (ACTUALLY ON AN ISLAND) ~ COULD "OLD" REPRESENT AN EARLIER NORSE COLONY?

49

discoverer of the Norse L'Anse aux Meadows site, has said that Greenland, Iceland, and Norway have only bituminous coal ("soft coal" that burns with a smoky, yellow flame) but no traces of anthracite ("hard coal" that burns with a clean flame). He goes on to say that the only anthracite outcrop of coal on the entire eastern coast of North America is near Newport!

On the other hand, there are those who believe the Newport tower was built for the first English colonial governor of Rhode Island. Benedict Arnold (not the Revolutionary War traitor of one hundred years later, of course) took office in 1663, and his will mentioned "my stone-built wind mill." The governor was said to have come from Warwickshire, England, where a nearby windmill of similar construction may be seen. Apparently, the arches made it easier for carts to be moved underneath for loading and unloading. Further, the mortar between the stones has been analyzed and found to be similar to that used in some of the earlier Newport buildings. A limited archeological dig at the base of the tower yielded nothing earlier than a few colonial artifacts. More extensive work might have undermined the base, and probably the city fathers were glad enough to see the Norse controversy laid to rest!

"THE SKELETON IN ARMOR" ~ In 1831, a skeleton with a brass breast plate, brass belt, and a quiver of brass-headed arrows was unearthed in Fall River, Massachusetts. Unfortunately, before experts could examine the evidence, it was lost in a fire. Seven years later, when Henry Wadsworth Longfellow visited Newport, he was intrigued by the "Norse" tower and the nearby skeleton discovery. Imagination and poetic license were combined to flesh out the skeleton in the form of a heroic Viking. His "Skeleton in Armor" caught the public's fancy, even though the subject was likely an Algonquin brave who was prepared to meet the Great Spirit in all his finery.

THE DIGHTON WRITING ROCK ~
Pictographs are infrequently found in New England. One of the most notable examples in America may be seen on the eastern bank of Taunton River at Assonet Neck, about eight miles below and on the opposite side of the river from Taunton. The Roman letters and figures near the center have been attributed to the Phoenicians, Libyans, Norse, Portuguese, English, and even the Japanese and Chinese.

THE DIGHTON ROCK INSCRIPTION, FROM A DRAWING MADE FOR THE RHODE ISLAND HISTORICAL SOCIETY IN 1834.

But there is no doubt that the remainder are of American Indian origin.

Our first president agreed. In 1789, a copy of it was shown to George Washington, who "smiled and said he believed that the learned Gentlemen were mistakened; and added, that he had so often examined the rude way of writing practiced by the Indians of Virginia, he had no doubt the inscriptions were made, long ago, by some natives of America."

THE KENSINGTON STONE was discovered in 1831 in Alexandria, Minnesota. When it was removed from under the roots of an ancient tree, the translators gave a startling interpretation. The date was 1362, and the inscription told of a party of Swedes and Norwegians "on a journey of exploration from Vinland to the west." Some experts felt the runic characters were unorthodox and perhaps a forgery, although there were second thoughts when axes, swords, and spearpoints were found in that general area. These artifacts are considered undoubtedly genuine and do closely resemble those used during the Viking expeditions.

There remains a goodly number of North American rune-inscribed stones that have yet to be translated and artifacts that await authentication. Some

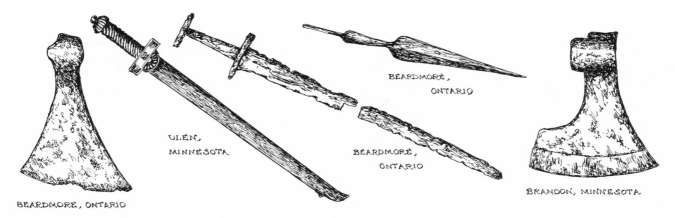

SUSPECTED VIKING WEAPONS FOUND IN THE AREA OF THE KENSINGTON STONE IN MINNESOTA

ULEN, MINNESOTA

BEARDMORE, ONTARIO

BEARDMORE, ONTARIO

BEARDMORE, ONTARIO

BRANDON, MINNESOTA

may be proved to be outright fakes and forgeries, some to be genuine but of a later period than that of the Vikings, and others to fit nicely into the Norse days of exploration. Our theories about the Norse sagas serve as reasoned guideposts and leads for proper archeological investigation. Under those centuries of ground cover may rest the final proof of the locations of such as Straum Island and Hóp. And really, the surface has only begun to be scratched.

3 FROM SINGLE SAIL TO FULL-RIGGED SHIP

The Viking knörr, that deepwater combination of merchantman and explorer gradually underwent changes in the northern waters. While the single square sail, the clinker hull with its overlapping strakes, and the single steering oar continued in use throughout the 1200s, an early newcomer was a stubby bowsprit. From it, bow lines or bowlines ran to the outer sail edges. When steering into the wind "close-hauled," the lines prevented flapping or "luffing." Reef points were added to reduce the sail surface when strong winds were gusting. With the Crusades in progress, it was also found helpful to build fore, stern, and top "castles" for protection, shelter, and lookout posts. Cruising the Mediterranean Sea could be a risky business in those days.

In the southern waters, the Crusaders saw the triangular lateen sail rig everywhere. This rig was more efficient, when sailing windward, than the square sail, but it performed poorly with a stern wind. Most of the vessels were caravels with two or three such sails, although there were a few two-masted square-sail ships that were direct descendants from the Roman days. All were carvel-built with hull planks laid edge to edge instead of the overlapping clapboard effect. It was inevitable that the best of these two sailing worlds be combined to give a later full-rigged ship.

900~1200   SQUARE SAIL

TO 1200   LATEEN SAIL

1200s   NORTHERN

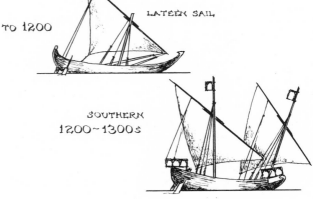

SOUTHERN
1200~1300s

CARAVEL

51

During the 1300s, the northern vessels discarded the old starboard("steerboard") rudder in favor of a pivoting stern rudder. To center it aft, the stern was altered from the sharpness of the knörr to become flat and square. At the same time, the hull was built deeper to give less side drift and to hold the course when sailing into the wind. The "cog," as it was called, soon made the double-ended ship obsolete in the north seas.

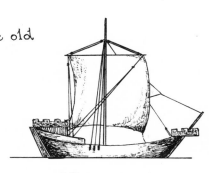

A 14TH-CENTURY COG

The 1400s began with a marriage of the most admirable features that both northern and southern ships had to offer. The advantages of the North Atlantic vessels ~ the propelling power of the square sails, the deep draught hulls, and the stern rudders ~ were combined with the Mediterranean's efficient lateen sails for sailing windward and their smooth carvel-planked hulls. Almost overnight it seemed that the old castle flagstaffs grew into full-grown masts fore and aft. The mainmast square sail that had stood alone for centuries was now flanked by a square sail at the foremast and at the stern mast (mizzenmast) with a lateen rig. These additions were of great help when tacking across the eye of the wind. Before the first fifty years were spent, a spritsail had blossomed from under the bowsprit, and canvas was reaching high in the sky on some as the fore and main topsails. The full-rigged ship had arrived and was ready for new westward discoveries.

COLUMBUS' <u>SANTA MARIA</u> OF 1492 ~ A FULL-RIGGED CARRACK WITH A MAIN BUT NO FORE TOPSAIL

The ship's hull became more streamlined, and the flimsy little castles were discarded. Permanent superstructures took their place topside with a long overhanging forecastle ("foc'sle") and an aft castle that extended forward to the mainmast. This new version was called the "carrack," and was the type of ship that carried John Cabot off to discover (or rediscover) Newfoundland in 1497. For the next four hundred years, there were but few changes in the basic design.

AN EXPANDING WORLD

Europeans had caught the exploring fever again. Less than a century after the Vikings had found Vinland to the west, the Crusader armies were sailing eastward to free the Holy Land from the Moslems. For two hundred years, waves of armored Christians coursed down the familiar Mediterranean waterway with varying degrees of success, then returned home with samplings of Near East luxuries. Raisins, dates, preserved fruits, and candied melons became more commonplace, for the traders of Venice and Genoa were doing their level best to keep up with the demand. But by the late 1400s, the Turks had effectively blocked off the Mediterranean. The Near East indulgences, which were fast becoming necessities, had been reduced to expensive rarities.

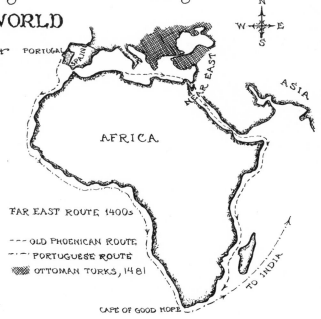

FAR EAST ROUTE 1400s

- - - OLD PHOENICAN ROUTE
- · - · PORTUGUESE ROUTE
▨▨▨ OTTOMAN TURKS, 1481

CAPE OF GOOD HOPE

TO INDIA

In 1271, trader Marco Polo began his remarkable overland journey to the Far East. His Book of Marco Polo had captured the imagination of all Europe for hundreds of years thereafter. Any country that could discover a sea route to the riches of India and China would have gained a monopoly in spices and other luxuries. With it, the blockaded Near East would be but an unimportant bypass. Such was the goal of a new breed of professional navigator/mapmaker/geographers who were ready and willing to offer their favorite passage-to-India theory to any king who would take the gamble.

Portugal began the search by sending probes along the west African coastline. Their efforts were rewarded with ivory, cinnamon, pepper, some gold~ and slaves. As for the latter, forced servitude of the blacks was rationalized as being a small price to pay for being converted to Christianity and the heavenly rewards that must surely follow. The same thinking would be applied to the North American "savages" to justify later kidnappings and enslavement. At any rate, Portugal's yield of African desirables still fell short of those in the fabled Far East. When their explorations finally succeeded in rounding the Cape of Good Hope, it was just a matter of sailing to eastward and India itself.

There might be another way to the Indies. Since the world must be round (a flat earth could hardly make sense to any thinking mariner who had seen a ship or landfall gradually appear over the horizon), the same objective might be reached by sailing westward. Certainly there were precedents for considering the far Atlantic waters. The Phoenicians had not only circumnavigated the continent of Africa, but had also discovered distant lands to its west. There were the wondrous sightings there by the early Christian Irish monks, as well as the Helluland, Markland, and Vinland of the Viking sagas. But after the passage of several centuries, it could only be assumed that these were a part of Asia or perhaps an indefinite landmass that only needed to be sailed around to reach the Far East.

Christopher Columbus thought as much. He squandered a good many years trying to convince the rulers of Portugal, Spain, and France that such was the case. Columbus even sent his brother Bartholomew off to England with the same proposal. The scheme was rejected there as well~ with many later regrets. Finally, with Queen Isabella's blessing, he sailed under the Spanish flag in 1492, taking a southern and then a westerly course. Although he hadn't realized it, the great American continent got in his way, and the Caribbean Islands that he called the West Indies were really not the outer islands off India. No matter~ Spain could lay claim to those discoveries and to much of the South and Central American vastness that lay beyond.

5 JOHN CABOT FOR ENGLAND

John Cabot* of Venice, a geographer and navigator like Columbus, believed that a northwesterly route to Asian riches was just as possible as sailing to the southwest. England seemed the most likely prospect for such an exploratory adventure. King Henry VII had missed his chance when approached by Columbus' brother, and he was more than ready to see that his country had a piece of the Asian pie.

Cabot was shrewd enough to move to Bristol with his family in 1495. There he started something of a grassroots campaign, for that seaport was influential as well as prosperous. His new neighbors

CABOT'S CARRACK MATTHEW (CONJECTURAL)

* CABOT'S NAME WAS ANGLICIZED FROM GIOVANNI CABOTO. THE FAMILY NAME MEANT "COASTER" OR "COASTAL SHIPPING."

53

were familiar with the old Viking Iceland-to-Greenland sailing latitudes. At least twelve years before Columbus crossed the Atlantic, Bristol fishermen had been tapping the rich fishing banks off Newfoundland. They may have landed at North America itself, but they were a close-mouthed lot and had no wish to advertise their activities to foreign competition. And so, the people of Bristol realized the possibilities of Cabot's northwest passage and the wealth to be gained from shipping Indian and Chinese luxuries. The King agreed, and on or about May 20, 1497, Cabot and his eighteen-man crew set sail. Spring was that time of year when more easterly winds would be favorable for a westerly passage.

In contrast to Columbus's fleet of three ships, Cabot's lone carrack, Matthew, had a capacity of fifty tuns~a tun being a large cask that held two hundred and fifty-two gallons of wine. She was even smaller than the Niña by ten tuns. Still, she was a Bristol vessel and had the speed and sturdy construction that take on the wild Atlantic on her own terms. The saying "shipshape and Bristol fashion" has come down through the centuries to mean an excellence in all things nautical.

As with Columbus's flagship, the Santa Maria, there are no woodcuts to show how the Matthew actually looked. For that matter, we have no first-hand accounts from Cabot and no ship's log or even an idea of Cabot's appearance. Generally, one can assume that the Matthew carried a number of seagoing improvements that were common to late fifteenth-century merchant ships.

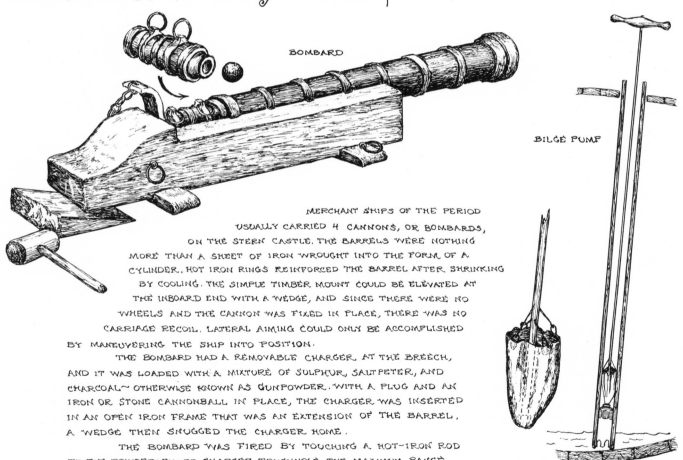

BOMBARD

BILGE PUMP

MERCHANT SHIPS OF THE PERIOD USUALLY CARRIED 4 CANNONS, OR BOMBARDS, ON THE STERN CASTLE. THE BARRELS WERE NOTHING MORE THAN A SHEET OF IRON WROUGHT INTO THE FORM OF A CYLINDER. HOT IRON RINGS REINFORCED THE BARREL AFTER SHRINKING BY COOLING. THE SIMPLE TIMBER MOUNT COULD BE ELEVATED AT THE INBOARD END WITH A WEDGE, AND SINCE THERE WERE NO WHEELS AND THE CANNON WAS FIXED IN PLACE, THERE WAS NO CARRIAGE RECOIL. LATERAL AIMING COULD ONLY BE ACCOMPLISHED BY MANEUVERING THE SHIP INTO POSITION.

THE BOMBARD HAD A REMOVABLE CHARGER AT THE BREECH, AND IT WAS LOADED WITH A MIXTURE OF SULPHUR, SALTPETER, AND CHARCOAL~OTHERWISE KNOWN AS GUNPOWDER. WITH A PLUG AND AN IRON OR STONE CANNONBALL IN PLACE, THE CHARGER WAS INSERTED IN AN OPEN IRON FRAME THAT WAS AN EXTENSION OF THE BARREL. A WEDGE THEN SNUGGED THE CHARGER HOME.

THE BOMBARD WAS FIRED BY TOUCHING A HOT-IRON ROD TO THE POWDER-FILLED CHARGER TOUCHHOLE. THE MAXIMUM RANGE WAS NOT OVER 900 FEET, AND ANY DEGREE OF ACCURACY WAS BUT HALF THAT DISTANCE.

PUMPS WERE LOCATED ON BOTH SIDES OF THE MAINMAST. THE PUMP WAS A BORED LOG AND CARRIED A LEATHER VALVE THAT WAS SHAPED LIKE AN INVERTED UMBRELLA. LATER, BRONZE PUMPS WERE FOUND TO BE MUCH MORE EFFICIENT.

54

THE FALCONET OR SWIVEL GUN WAS
LIGHT AND EASILY AIMED. THIS SMALL
CANNON COULD BE MOUNTED ON A GUNWALE
OR ABOVE ON THE CROW'S NEST. LIKE THE
BOMBARD, THE FALCONET HAD A BREECH~
LOADING CHARGER. THE BORE OF
ABOUT 2 INCHES COULD CARRY
AN IRON OR LEAD BALL, OR
SEND OUT A HAIL OF
SMALL PIECES OF IRON.

WHEN SAILING OFF TO
UNKNOWN LANDS FOR EXPLORATION,
IT WAS PRUDENT THAT BOTH LIGHT
AND HEAVY ARMAMENT BE ABOARD.

NAVIGATIONAL AIDS

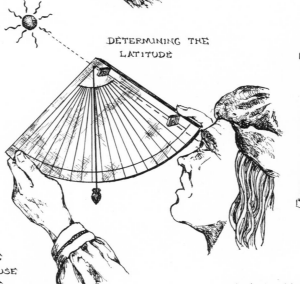

DETERMINING THE
LATITUDE

THE COMPASS WAS OF FIRST IMPORTANCE
TO MARINERS OF ANY AGE. IT HAD BEEN IN USE
FOR 250 YEARS BEFORE THE SAILING OF THE
MATTHEW . AN IRON MAGNET NEEDLE WAS
ATTACHED TO THE UNDERSIDE OF A CIRCULAR
COMPASS CARD. IT WAS FREE TO PIVOT ON A
BRASS PIN, SAFE IN ITS BOX OR BINNACLE.
A LODESTONE WAS USED TO REMAGNETIZE THE
COMPASS AT FREQUENT INTERVALS. ALTHOUGH
SEAMEN KNEW THAT THE DIFFERENCE
BETWEEN MAGNETIC AND TRUE NORTH VARIED
ALONG ANY SAILING LATITUDE, FINDING TRUE
NORTH MUST WAIT FOR A LATER DAY. THEN,
THE VARIATION OR DECLINATION BETWEEN THE
TWO WOULD BE CORRECTED WITH A
DECLINATION CHART.

THE QUADRANT WAS
THE OLDEST INSTRUMENT
FOR MEASURING THE
ANGLE BETWEEN THE NORTH STAR OR THE SUN (SQUINTING
THE SUN WAS A REAL DANGER TO EYESIGHT) ON THE HORIZON.
A WEIGHTED LINE HUNG FROM THE APEX OF A WOODEN
QUARTER CIRCLE. WHEN THE STAR OR SUN WAS SIGHTED
ALONG ONE SIDE, THE PLUMB LINE COULD BE READ ON
THE ANGLE SCALE BY A SECOND SEAMAN. THE SHIP'S
ROLL MADE THIS RECORDING SOMEWHAT INACCURATE,
BUT IT CERTAINLY WAS AN IMPROVEMENT OVER THE OLD
VIKING GNOMON OR THE OUTSTRETCHED HAND MEASUREMENT.

LOG GLASSES OR SAND GLASSES
SERVED TO TELL THE TIME OF DAY.
IT WAS TURNED EVERY HALF
HOUR AND A BELL WAS STRUCK.

The late fifteenth-century cartographers were under the spell of Marco
Polo's eyewitness reports and the mind-boggling wealth that he found in the lands
of the Grand Khan. Paolo Toscanelli, the foremost mapmaker and astronomer of
Florence, was deeply influenced by Polo's adventures when he drew his sailing
chart of the world for the King of Portugal. His instructions were to draw "an
exhibition to the eye, so that even slightly educated persons can grasp and
comprehend that route [westerly to the Orient]." He also sent along the same
map to Columbus, who used it to show the practicality of following the more
southerly latitudes to the empire of the Grand Kahn. He carried the same
chartings aboard when he set out on his first exploration, and with it he was all
the more convinced that he had landed on the outskirts of the Far East.

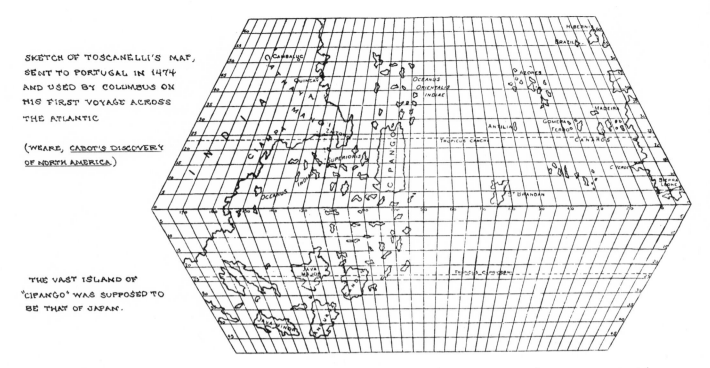

SKETCH OF TOSCANELLI'S MAP,
SENT TO PORTUGAL IN 1474
AND USED BY COLUMBUS ON
HIS FIRST VOYAGE ACROSS
THE ATLANTIC

(WEARE, CABOT'S DISCOVERY
OF NORTH AMERICA.)

THE VAST ISLAND OF
"CIPANGO" WAS SUPPOSED TO
BE THAT OF JAPAN.

No doubt John Cabot also had access to Toscanelli's concept of the world. Like Columbus, he assumed that just beyond his North American landfalls lay the promised lands of gold, silver, jewels, and spices. And like him, Cabot never realized that by claiming his first and only landing site in the name of King Henry VII, much of the vastness of North America was England's by right of discovery.

Cabot had made his own map and a globe to show the extent of his 1497 exploration of the high latitudes. Both have been lost. All of his notes, letters, logs, and reports to the king have vanished as well. It certainly seems strange that a voyage of such importance can only be relived through contemporary dispatches.

A letter, written by Lorenzo Pasqualigo in London on August 23, 1497, told his brothers in Venice the following news: " The Venetian, our country-man, who went with a ship from Bristol, is returned, and says that seven hundred leagues [a league equals three statute miles] from here he discovered main land (terra firma), the territory of the Grand Khan. He coasted for three hundred leagues and landed; saw no human beings, but he has brought here to the king certain snares which had been set to catch game, and a needle for making nets; he also found some felled trees, by which he judged there were inhabitants, and returned to his ship in alarm. He was three months on the voyage, and on his return saw two islands to starboard, but would not land. He (Cabota) says that the tides are slack there, and do not flow as they do here. This has greatly pleased the King of England. The king has promised him in the spring ten ships, armed to his order, and at his request has conceded him all the prisoners, except those confined for high treason, to man his fleet, the king has also given him money with which he may amuse himself until that time, and he is now in Bristol with his wife, who is also a Venetian, and with his sons. His name is John Calbot [sic], and he is called the great admiral. Great honour is paid him; he dresses in silk, and these English run after him like insane people, so that he can enlist as many of them as he pleases, and a number of our own rogues [Italians] besides. The discoverer of these places planted on this newly~found land a large cross, with one flag of England and another of St. Mark [the patron saint of Venice] on account of his being a Venetian, so that our banner has floated very far afield."

56

John Day, an English merchant of Andalusia, Spain, wrote to "The Lord Grand Admiral of Spain," presumably Columbus, in the winter of 1497~98. He also described the 1497 voyage of John Cabot and sent along "a copy of the land which had been found" and has since, most unfortunately, gone astray.

"From the said copy your Lordship will learn what you wish to know, for in it are named the capes of the mainland and the islands, and thus you will see where land was first sighted, since most of the land was discovered after turning back. Thus your Lordship will know that the cape nearest to Ireland is 1800 miles west of Dursey Head which is in Ireland, and the southernmost part of the Island of the Seven Cities[1] is west of Bordeaux River, and your Lordship will know that he [Cabot] landed at only one spot of the mainland, near the place where land was first sighted, and they disembarked there with a crucifix and raised banners with the arms of the Holy Father and those of the King of England, my master; and they found tall trees of the kind masts are made, and other smaller trees, and the country is very rich in grass. In that particular spot, as I told your Lordship, they found a trail that went inland, they saw a site where a fire had been made, they saw manure of animals which they thought to be farm animals, and they saw a stick half a yard long pierced at both ends, carved and painted with brazil[2], and by such signs they believe the land to be inhabited. Since he was with just a few people he did not dare advance inland beyond the shooting distance of a cross-bow, and after taking in fresh water he returned to his ship. All along the coast they found many fish like those which in Iceland are dried in the open and sold in England and other countries, and these fish are called in English 'stockfish'; and thus following the shore they saw two forms running on land one after the other, but they could not tell if they were human beings or animals; and it seemed to them that there were fields where they thought might also be villages, and they saw a forest whose foliage looked beautiful. They left England toward the end of May, and must have been on the way 35 days before sighting land;

THE MAST TREE, THE EASTERN WHITE PINE, GROWS STRAIGHT AND TALL TO OVER 100 FEET.

CARVED WOODEN SACRED COD, 1773, NOW HANGING IN THE HOUSE OF REPRESENTATIVES, STATE HOUSE, BOSTON
(WILBUR, TALL SHIPS OF THE WORLD)

MOHEGAN HARD-WOOD NETTING NEEDLE (MUSEUM OF NATURAL HISTORY, NEW YORK CITY)

[1] SEE TOSCANELLI'S WORLD MAP FOR THE ISLAND OF THE SEVEN CITIES, OTHERWISE KNOWN AS ANTILIA. THAT LEGENDARY ISLAND WAS THOUGHT TO BE A GUIDE TO THE RICHES OF CIPANGO (JAPAN), IN THE EARLY EIGHTH CENTURY WERE SUPPOSED TO HAVE FLED THERE WITH AN ARCHBISHOP AND SIX BISHOPS. EACH BUILT THEIR OWN CITY. THE NAME ANTILLES WAS GIVEN TO THE CARIBBEAN ISLANDS EARLY IN THE SIXTEENTH CENTURY.
[2] BRAZIL WAS THE COLOR OF BRAISE OR HOT COALS, AND MADE WITH DYEWOOD FROM THE FAR EAST. BRAZIL, IN SOUTH AMERICA, WAS SO NAMED BECAUSE OF A DYEWOOD FOUND THERE THAT PRODUCED A RED COLOR.

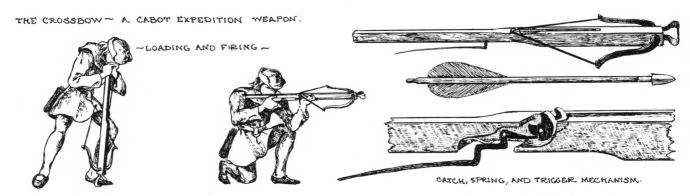

THE CROSSBOW ~ A CABOT EXPEDITION WEAPON.

~LOADING AND FIRING ~

CATCH, SPRING, AND TRIGGER MECHANISM.

THE CROSSBOW WAS SPANNED BY FIRST KNEELING WITH ONE FOOT IN THE STIRRUP, THEN ATTACHING THE BELT HOOK TO THE BOWSTRING. WHEN THE ARCHER STOOD UP, THE STRING WAS PULLED OVER THE NOTCHED CATCH IN THE STOCK. WHEN THE ARROW WAS PLACED IN ITS GROOVE, THE LONG TRIGGER WAS RELEASED.

LAYERS OF PRESSED HORN STRIPS OR THE STEEL SPRING GAVE THE BOW SUCH STRENGTH THAT SOMETIMES A LEVER OR WINDLASS WAS NEEDED TO DRAW BACK THE BOWSTRING. LOADING AND FIRING WAS A LENGTHY PROCESS, AND LATER EXPLORERS WERE TARGETS FOR 4 INDIAN ARROWS TO THEIR 1. ALTHOUGH THE CROSSBOW ARROW OR QUARREL COULD PENETRATE ARMOR ON THE BATTLEFIELDS OF EUROPE, IT WAS OF LITTLE USE AGAINST THE FLEET-FOOTED NATIVES. THE QUARREL WAS ACCURATE TO ABOUT 65 YARDS AND HAD A RANGE OF UP TO 350 YARDS WHEN SHOT AT A 45-DEGREE ANGLE.

the wind was east~north~east and the sea calm going and coming back, except for one day when he ran into a storm two or three days before finding land; and going so far out, his compass needle failed to point north and marked two rhumbs below. They spent about one month discovering the coast and from the above mentioned cape of the mainland which is nearest to Ireland, they returned to the coast of Europe in fifteen days. They had the wind behind them, and he reached Brittany because the sailors confused him, saying he was headed too far north. From there he came to Bristol, and he went to see the King to report to him all the above mentioned..."

John Cabot's modest discoveries of nets and needle, white pine trees and thick grass, an open fireplace, codfish in great plenty, and even animal manure fell a bit short of King Henry VII's Far East expectations! Nonetheless, His Majesty looked kindly on plans for Cabot to extend his explorations well beyond his

THE DOTTED OUTLINE NEAR THE THIRD FLAG MARKS A HOLE IN THE ORIGINAL.

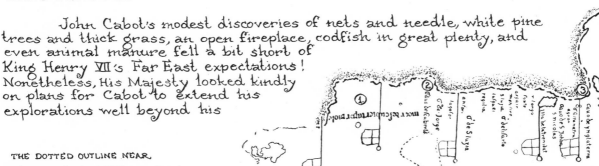

JUAN DE LA COSA'S MAP, A.D. 1500

SKETCHED FROM THE ORIGINAL, AND SHOWING COLUMBUS' CARIBBEAN DISCOVERIES AND THE MORE RECENTLY FOUND SOUTH AMERICAN MAIN-LAND BEYOND. CABOT'S DISCOVERIES IN NORTH AMERICA ARE MARKED BY ENGLISH FLAGS. I HAVE TAKEN THE LIBERTY TO HIGHLIGHT HIS COASTLINE AND HAVE NUMBERED THE MOST IMPORTANT LANDMARKS.

① MAR DESCUBIERTA POR YNGLESE = "SEA DISCOVERED BY THE ENGLISH" ~ CABOT'S MOST SOUTHWESTERLY VOYAGE.

② CAVO DESCUBIERTO = "THE DISCOVERED CAPE."

③ CAVO DE YNGLATERRA = "CAPE OF ENGLAND."

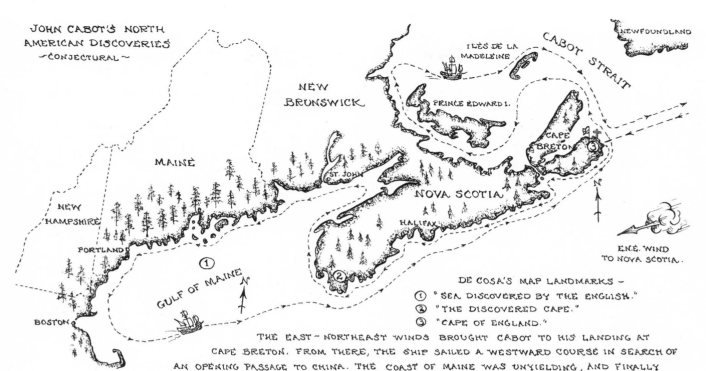

JOHN CABOT'S NORTH AMERICAN DISCOVERIES ~CONJECTURAL~

NEWFOUNDLAND

CABOT STRAIT

ILES DE LA MADELEINE

NEW BRUNSWICK

PRINCE EDWARD I.

CAPE BRETON

MAINE

ST. JOHN

NOVA SCOTIA

NEW HAMPSHIRE

HALIFAX

N

PORTLAND

E.N.E. WIND TO NOVA SCOTIA.

①

GULF OF MAINE

②

N

DE COSA'S MAP LANDMARKS ~
① "SEA DISCOVERED BY THE ENGLISH."
② "THE DISCOVERED CAPE."
③ "CAPE OF ENGLAND."

BOSTON

THE EAST~NORTHEAST WINDS BROUGHT CABOT TO HIS LANDING AT CAPE BRETON. FROM THERE, THE SHIP SAILED A WESTWARD COURSE IN SEARCH OF AN OPENING PASSAGE TO CHINA. THE COAST OF MAINE WAS UNYIELDING, AND FINALLY THE EXPLORERS RETURNED TO CAPE BRETON TO PROBE THE WESTERLY REACHES OF CABOT STRAIT. NO NORTHWEST PASSAGE WAS FOUND, BUT TWO ISLANDS ~ PRINCE EDWARD AND ILES DE LA MADELEINE~WERE PASSED ON THE STARBOARD. ONCE BACK AT THE LANDING LANDMARK AT CAPE BRETON, CABOT COULD RETRACE HIS COURSE FROM BRISTOL.

"Cape of the Mainland" and on to that elusive Far East passage. From the explorers accounts and maps, he knew the details of the one and only landing and the month-long coasting that followed.

Although none of the specifics have been passed down through history, a contemporary cartographer has come to our rescue. Juan de la Cosa was a man of considerable nautical experience, but not to be confused with the owner and master of the _Santa Maria_ who was on Columbus's first voyage. La Cosa served as a seaman aboard the _Niña_ on the second voyage in 1493 and acted as the chief pilot for a 1499 exploration of the South American mainland. His map of America was completed upon returning home. Fortunately, he also included Cabot's North American discoveries under the English flag.

In May of 1498, Cabot left Bristol with five ships to follow up his North American discoveries. There he planned to establish a trading colony with the requisitioned convicts he had aboard and "coarse cloth, caps, laces, points and other trifles," designed to gladden the savage heart. He would then sail on a southwesterly course to the equator, where the fabled island of C'pango (Japan) must be and "where he "believes all the spices of the world grow and where there are also gems." ①

Perhaps it was an omen of things to come when one of the ships was somehow damaged and limped into an Irish port. The remainder of the fleet sailed off into oblivion. There was an unconfirmed report by the Spanish explorer Ojeda, who had taken mapmaker La Cosa aboard as chief pilot. Apparently that 1499 expedition to the newly discovered Caribbean Islands "found some Englishmen in the immediate vicinity of Coquibacoa." ② Be that as it may, a contemporary writer summed up John Cabot's fate when he wrote that "he found his new lands only in the ocean's

① DISPATCH DECEMBER 18, 1497, FROM RAIMONDO DE SONCINO TO THE DUKE OF MILAN.

② ACCORDING TO SPANISH HISTORIAN NAVARETTE'S COLLECTION DE LOS VIAGES Y DESCUBRIMZENTOS.

bottom, to which he and his ships are thought to have sunk, since, after that voyage, he was never heard of more."

6 PORTUGAL LOOKS TO THE WEST

The Spanish were losing no time exploiting Columbus's newly found Caribbean islands. To protect their rights of discovery, the Spanish crown sent a delegation to Pope Alexander VI in 1493. As head of Christianized Europe~ and who, not so incidentally, was a Spaniard himself who owed much of his success to the backing of his mother country ~ he divided the world in half. Spain could claim all new lands one hundred leagues west of the Azores at 38° W. longitude. Portugal was to have a free hand in any new lands to the east. When Portugal objected the Line of Demarcation was arbitrarily shifted to three hundred and seventy leagues west of the Cape Verde Islands and 46° 37' W. With a few scratches of the pen, Portugal could then claim a sizable chunk of undiscovered South America~ Brazil.

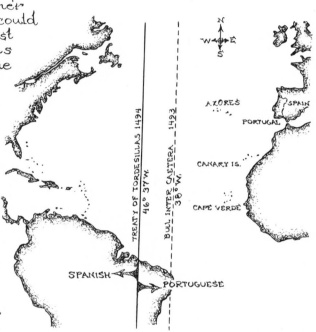

THE LINE OF DEMARCATION, 1494

The other European nations, all latecomers to the business of exploration, would eventually shrug off the worldwide monopoly. As Francis I, King of France, sarcastically remarked, "I should like very much to see the passage in Adam's will that divides the New World between my brothers, the Emperor Charles V [of Spain] and the King of Portugal."

Henry VII of England had sent Cabot off to discover a northwest passage despite any papal decree. After all, English and French fishermen had been making unrecorded sailings to the Grand Banks well before the turn of the century. The glowing descriptions of those cod-ladened waters by Cabot was bringing in a new influx of men who sought their fortunes in the icy Atlantic waters rather than searching out the gold and jewels much to the south.

Portugal viewed the discoveries by Cabot for England with some alarm. If her side of the Line of Demarcation violated, then England must be called to account for trespassing. While in those northerly seas, it might be worthwhile to look for that elusive northwest passage to the Orient. Vasco da Gama's spectacular Cape of Good Hope to India round trip had taken well over two years. A shorter westerly route, as well as the easterly rounding of Africa, would give Portugal an overwhelming trade monopoly. With Spain pressing her advantage to the southwest, the idea had a nice ring to it.

JOHN FERNANDES FOR PORTUGAL ~ 1500

The Portuguese Azores had become favorite way stations for ships trading along the African coast. Columbus had brought his tales of the fabulous West Indies when he stopped over on his first return trip to Spain. Returning from his Indian voyage in 1494, Vasco da Gama no doubt displayed his gold and silver trade goods to the islanders. Not the least of these was a sixty-pound gold idol, complete with emerald eyes and a ruby as large as a walnut in its breast.

Excitement ran wild in the Azores, and one farmer decided to seek his fortune to the northwest. John (João) Fernandes was able to muster enough neighbors to finance an expedition, and, with the king's grant in hand, sailed off in the wake of Cabot. His expectations certainly fell short of his discoveries, for all that was seen were the ice mountains of Greenland.

Had it not been for his renaming Erik the Red's old island "Labrador," his name would have been promptly forgotten. Perhaps, with tongue in cheek, he gave the name ~ which meant small farm landowner ~ to show the world that plain dirt farmers could make discoveries as well as the usual wealthy nobleman-turned-explorer. Half a century later, when geographers realized that Greenland had already been discovered and had a perfectly acceptable name, "Labrador was transferred to the old Viking Helluland, that chilled pile of rocks above Newfoundland Island."

GASPAR CORTE-REAL FOR PORTUGAL ~ 1500

Fernandes' small jab at the aristocracy was well timed. The same year he returned to Portugal, the youngest son of an unjust and much disliked ruler of the Azores made his bid for fame. As a gentleman of the court and a favorite of the king, he had no trouble taking over Fernandes' grant for the rights and privileges to any northwestern lands that he might discover. He sailed along the old Norse latitudes in the spring of 1500 and was turned back by the formidable ice floes that peppered the Labrador coast. Sailing southward into kinder waters, he rediscovered "a land that is very cool and with big trees." Corte-Real had happened upon the northern reaches of Newfoundland. The Norse had considered the island as part of their Helluland and was the location of their temporary L'Anse aux Meadows settlement.

THE KIDNAPPING OF
THE BEOTHUK INDIANS

Corte-Real returned the following year for further exploration. According to a letter written on October 9, 1501, to the Duke of Ferrara from his emissary in Lisbon, Alberto Cantino, "they found the sea to be frozen [turning west after three month's sailing] they caught sight of a very large country... numerous large rivers flowed into the sea... They made their way about a league inland [where] on landing they found abundance of most luscious and varied fruits, and trees and pines of such measureless height and girth, that they would be too big as a mast for the largest ship that sails the Sea."

A "three month sailing" was not unusual. As the megalithic peoples, the Irish monks, and the Vikings had found hundreds of years earlier, the prevailing westerly winds must be met head on. Fortunately, springtime brought more frequent easterly blows. If they remained favorable, the passage might take as short a time as two or three weeks. Bucking contrary winds could delay a ship for as long as Corte-Real's three months. When homeward bound with the wind at her stern, a ship might cross the Atlantic in as little as two weeks. One month, however, might be considered an average time.

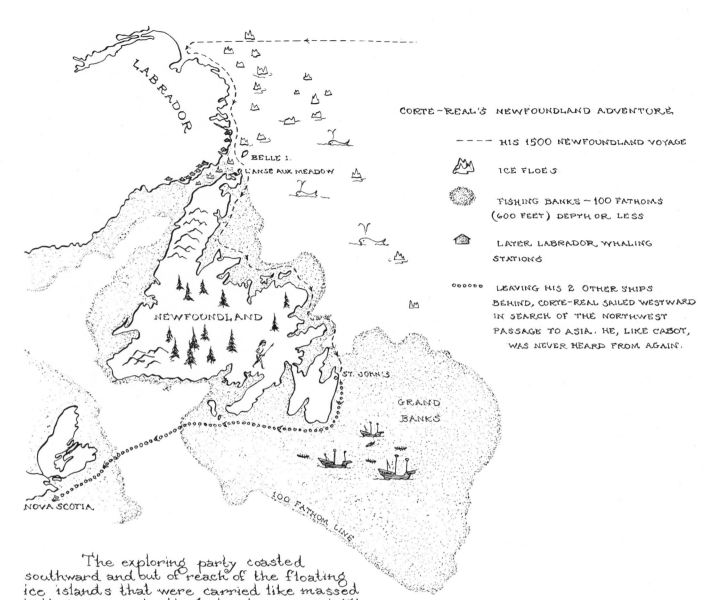

The exploring party coasted
southward and out of reach of the floating
ice islands that were carried like massed
battering rams by the Labrador current. They
were safe enough when Newfoundland was once again offshore. Only by coasting its
Atlantic coastline could they realize that their earlier island sighting was "a very large
country," indeed. At the southern tip of Newfoundland, they found late-summer edibles.
In spite of the rave notices about an "abundance of the most luscious and varied
fruits," a glance at a modern seed catalogue will show that the short growing season
of Newfoundland could produce no Garden of Eden. Explorers were apt to oversell
their discoveries to those who waited expectantly at home, especially when it was
assumed that the new lands were part of the spice-rich Orient.

A second Cantino letter gave the first descriptive account of the unfortunate
Beothuk Indians. One may recall their possible Indian and Viking ancestry as
mentioned under "The Viking Sagas."

"No corn grows here, but the people of that country say they live together
by fishing and hunting animals, in which the land abounds, such as very large deer,
[caribou] covered with extremely long hair, the skins of which they use for
garments and also make houses and boats thereof and again wolves, foxes, tigers,
[lynxes?] and sables. They affirm that there are what appears to me wonderful,
as many falcons there as there are sparrows in our country, and I have seen

some of them and they are very pretty. They forcibly kidnapped about fifty men and women of this country [actually fifty-seven] and have brought them to the king. I have seen, touched and examined these people, and beginning with their stature, declare they are somewhat taller than our average, with members corresponding and well formed. The hair of the men is long... and [they] have their faces marked with great signs... Their speech is unintelligible but nevertheless is not harsh but rather human. Their manners and gestures are most gentle; they laugh considerably and manifest the greatest pleasure... The women have small breasts and most beautiful bodies, and rather pleasant faces. They go quite naked except for their privy parts, which they cover with a skin of the above mentioned deer."

Damiã de Góis, a contemporary chronicler of Corte-Real, cast further light on the Beothuks, when he wrote that they hunt, not with bow and arrow, but with "pieces of wood burnt in the fire in the place of spears, which when they throw them make wounds as if pointed with fine steel... They live in rocky caves and thatched huts."

THIS BUSY NEWFOUNDLAND SCENE IS A 17ᵀᴴ~CENTURY IMPRESSION OF THE BEOTHUKS HUNTING AND FISHING. SINCE WILD GRAPES DID NOT GROW SO FAR NORTH, THE CARIBOU SEEMS MORE OF A HORSE THAN ANYTHING ELSE, AND LOG DUGOUT CANOES RATHER THAN THE UNUSUAL BEOTHUK BIRCHBARK OR HIDE-SHEATHED CANOES, THE INDIANS THEMSELVES ARE PROBABLY NOT ACCURATE.
(T. DE BRY, AMERICA, PART XIII, 1634.)

Archeological evidence from Newfoundland has added much to the sketchy Beothuk descriptions to be found in the Viking and Corte-Real reports. They lived in the traditions of their Late Archaic ancestors, for their island home had isolated them from mainland progress. They knew nothing of crafting raw clay into useful ceramic utensils. While others were planting crops of corn, beans, pumpkin and squash, the Beothuks subsisted just by hunting and fishing. It was almost as though they had stepped off the time machine five thousand years ago with one foot still in the early Stone Age days. Curiously, the other foot seemed to be firmly planted in more "modern" influences that smacked suspiciously of the Iron Age Vikings.

Perhaps the two worlds of these remarkable people might be better appreciated with a brief review of their Indian heritage.

NORTH AMERICAN INDIAN CULTURES

PALEO~AMERICAN INDIANS, 15,000 YEARS AGO ~ Warmer weather was melting the huge glacial ice sheet that covered much of North America. Their Asian ancestors crossed the Bering Strait ice bridge into Alaska to track down mastodons,

63

mammoths, and lesser game. Their handsome spear points were Paleolithic hallmarks, and have been found along the eastward trek and on into New Brunswick and Nova Scotia.

EARLY ARCHAIC INDIANS, 7,000 TO 5,000 YEARS AGO ~

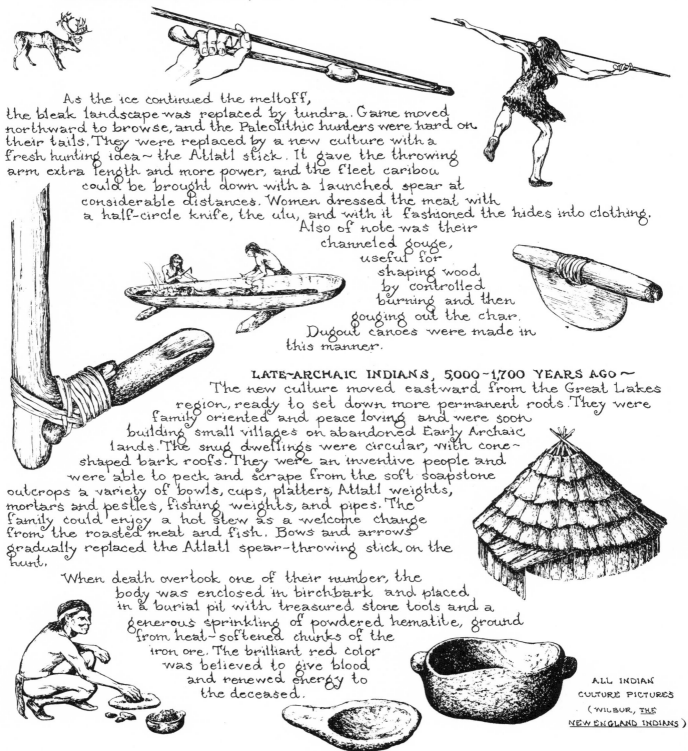

As the ice continued the meltoff, the bleak landscape was replaced by tundra. Game moved northward to browse, and the Paleolithic hunters were hard on their tails. They were replaced by a new culture with a fresh hunting idea ~ the Atlatl stick. It gave the throwing arm extra length and more power, and the fleet caribou could be brought down with a launched spear at considerable distances. Women dressed the meat with a half-circle knife, the ulu, and with it fashioned the hides into clothing. Also of note was their channeled gouge, useful for shaping wood by controlled burning and then gouging out the char. Dugout canoes were made in this manner.

LATE-ARCHAIC INDIANS, 5,000~1,700 YEARS AGO ~

The new culture moved eastward from the Great Lakes region, ready to set down more permanent roots. They were family oriented and peace loving and were soon building small villages on abandoned Early Archaic lands. The snug dwellings were circular, with cone~shaped bark roofs. They were an inventive people and were able to peck and scrape from the soft soapstone outcrops a variety of bowls, cups, platters, Atlatl weights, mortars and pestles, fishing weights, and pipes. The family could enjoy a hot stew as a welcome change from the roasted meat and fish. Bows and arrows gradually replaced the Atlatl spear-throwing stick on the hunt.

When death overtook one of their number, the body was enclosed in birchbark and placed in a burial pit with treasured stone tools and a generous sprinkling of powdered hematite, ground from heat~softened chunks of the iron ore. The brilliant red color was believed to give blood and renewed energy to the deceased.

ALL INDIAN CULTURE PICTURES
(WILBUR, THE NEW ENGLAND INDIANS)

64

for the journey to the spirit world. Because of their love of that color, their bodies were smeared with a mixture of the red pigment and oil or grease. Probably the term "Red Indian" caught on when the Corte-Real explorers came upon the Beothuks. So enthusiastic was their use of the color, their clothing, implements, ornaments, canoes, and bows and arrows were colored in the same manner.

CERAMIC~WOODLAND INDIANS, A.D. 300 TO EUROPEAN CONTACT~

As the new culture absorbed the Late Archaics, the old soapstone techniques gave way to fired clay ceramics. Gardens thrived around the villages~ so much so that envious neighbors took to the warpath to impose tributes and control choice hunting and fishing grounds. Tribal wars became a deadly game, and the men cast aside their peace-loving traditions to become experts with stone tomahawks, clubs, and arrows for their human targets. Protective stockades ringed the villages, and intertribal wars decimated the Indian population well before the explorers and their diseases added to the misfortunes of the North American Indians.

Such was the way of Indian life in the northeast, and, in many respects, similar throughout the continent. As for the Beothuks and early Norse influences, some evidence has been suggested under "The Viking Sagas" heading. They were reported by later explorers to be tall, white-skinned (under all that red paint!) with many being blond or light-haired. They built their winter homes in the manner of the Late Archaics, but with walls of posts that were flattened on two sides and were similar to the vertical siding boards of early Scandinavian dwellings. Storehouses were large, with gable-ended roofs in the Norse tradition. So, too, were their canoes somewhat like the Norse small boats that could be rowed and sailed as well as paddled. The Beothuk clothing, as described, seemed to be a combination adopted from the two cultures. Unfortunately, the peaceful Beothuks were exterminated by warring Algonquins and the French and English who later took over their fishing grounds and their island home. They left no legends or further evidence. Perhaps further archeological evidence will help solve the mystery of their two-culture background.

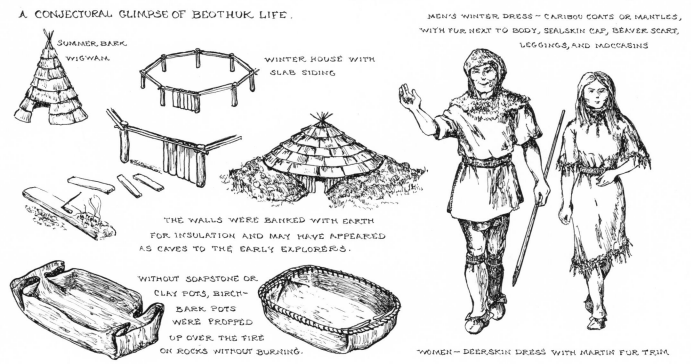

A CONJECTURAL GLIMPSE OF BEOTHUK LIFE.

SUMMER BARK WIGWAM

WINTER HOUSE WITH SLAB SIDING

THE WALLS WERE BANKED WITH EARTH FOR INSULATION AND MAY HAVE APPEARED AS CAVES TO THE EARLY EXPLORERS.

WITHOUT SOAPSTONE OR CLAY POTS, BIRCH-BARK POTS WERE PROPPED UP OVER THE FIRE ON ROCKS WITHOUT BURNING.

MEN'S WINTER DRESS ~ CARIBOU COATS OR MANTLES, WITH FUR NEXT TO BODY, SEALSKIN CAP, BEAVER SCARF, LEGGINGS, AND MOCCASINS

WOMEN ~ DEERSKIN DRESS WITH MARTIN FUR TRIM

65

The unsuspecting Beothuks were easy prey for kidnapping. When fifty-seven bewildered captives were herded aboard, they had no idea that they had begun a life of slavery. The Portuguese king was pleased, indeed, to have a fresh hunting ground available. His country had made a tidy profit from the African slave trade, but the blacks had become more wary and more difficult to take. But as he and later explorers would realize, the American Indian could no more exist in captivity than shoot down the moon with an arrow. Unlike the Africans, they withered and died when their freedom was lost.

►►►8 THE GRAND BANKS FISHERIES

Both Cabot and Corte-Real named the coastline from Nova Scotia to southern Labrador "Baccalaos," or Land of the Cod. While the few earlier fishermen who had chanced upon this concentration of sea treasure remained closemouthed, the explorers' accounts soon brought an influx of fishing fleets to those shores. French Normans and Bretons, Basques from the border country between France and Spain, Portuguese, and English were sailing for the Grand Banks. There was more than enough for all. While the Spanish were expanding their conquests of the southern lands discovered by Columbus in search of gold and jewels, the Banks were yielding a much less glamorous treasure. By the end of the century, Spanish plunder had become second best to the wealth to be netted under those chill northern waters.

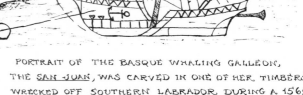

SIMPLIFIED SKETCH OF A BASQUE NEWFOUNDLANDER ~ FROM ARCHIVO DE PROTOCOLOS, OÑATE, SPAIN

EDGE DAMAGED BY SEA BORERS.

PORTRAIT OF THE BASQUE WHALING GALLEON, THE SAN JUAN, WAS CARVED IN ONE OF HER TIMBERS. WRECKED OFF SOUTHERN LABRADOR DURING A 1565 STORM, THE REMAINS HAVE YIELDED VALUABLE INFORMATION ON SHIP CONSTRUCTION. NOTE STERN CANNON. (PARKS CANADA ARCHEOLOGY)

At first, the Beothuks were little plagued by the off-shore fishing. The hardy fishermen would leave home port as early as January or February to drop anchor in the ice-choked, fog-shrouded waters. Hooks and nets were lowered from the ship or from the shallops that were carried aboard. The fish were then gutted, trimmed, and heavily salted for the return voyage. Arrival by June was a must, for spoilage of the "green" or wet-salted cod meant a cargo that matched its aroma. If all went well, there would be time enough for another trip that year.

When it was discovered that the cod swam the shallow coastal waters in June to lunch on their favorite small fish, the caplin, inshore fishing added to the haul. A nearby land base was then a must, for the fish could be better preserved by salting and then drying out in the sun. The curious Beothuks found the shore stations on their island to be as irresistible as a twentieth-century bargain basement. When the fishermen had retreated from the harshness of a Newfoundland winter, the Indians were able to carry off a fascinating array of barrels, boats, fishing gear, and sundry equipment. But they were pilfering from a crusty lot of no-nonsense seafarers who then considered the thieves fair hunting game.

When the whaling industry began its midsixteenth-century boom along the Labrador and Newfoundland coasts, the whalers tolerated permanent borrowing from their tryworks no better than the fishermen. A concentrated kind of frontier justice prevailed, and it was the beginning of the end for the mystery tribe of Newfoundland.

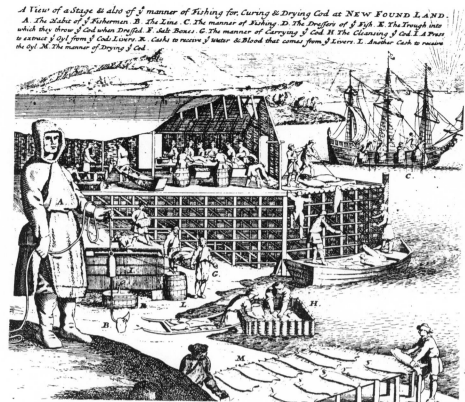

A View of a Stage & also of ye manner of Fishing for, Curing & Drying Cod at NEW FOUND LAND.
A. The Habit of ye Fishermen. B. The Line. C. The manner of Fishing. D. The Dressers of ye Fish. E. The Trough into which they throw ye Cod when Dressed. F. Salt Boxes. G. The manner of Carrying ye Cod. H. The Cleansing ye Cod. I. A Press to extract ye Oyl from ye Cods Livers. K. Casks to receive ye water & Blood that comes from ye Livers. L. Another Cask to receive the Oyl. M. The manner of Drying ye Cod.

FROM AN INSET TO "THE MAP OF NORTH AMERICA," BY H. MOLL, LONDON, 1720

Across the Cabot Strait, the Micmacs of Nova Scotia had a more optimistic future than that of their Beothuk neighbors. In spite of having the longest contact with European explorers, their more numerous and better-organized tribesmen were able to keep their Stone Age traditions intact. They were also fortunate that French fishermen and traders had taken a liking to Cape Breton and the surrounding country that Cabot had recently discovered. In a day when the tune was exploitation, and the Indians were expected to dance to it, France came to North America with a refreshing idea. Both natives and the French could mutually benefit by a brisk trade in furs for European goods. They came as friends and partners in trade, not as superior beings who could manipulate the Indians at will and take what lands and possessions they saw fit.

Although the French took a dim view of slavery, their people did bring back a number of Indians to Europe as examples of life in North America. Such transplanting was only temporary, for they made the Atlantic crossing with the promise that they would be returned to their Micmac friends. The word of the French was kept in good faith, and the Indians that were chosen brought back wondrous tales of their friends abroad. Thomas Aubert of Rowen was one such early visitor to Nova Scotia and in 1509 brought back seven Micmac men to Normandy. They created a sensation, and it is entirely possible that the following Micmac legend is about one of their number.

"Shortly after the country was discovered by the French, an Indian named Silmoodāwā was taken to Plancheän [France] as a curiosity. Among other curious adventures, he was prevailed upon to exhibit the Indian mode of killing and curing game. A fat ox or deer was brought out of a beautiful park and handed over to the Indian; he was provided with all the necessary implements, and placed within an enclosure of ropes, through which no person was allowed to pass, but around which multitudes were gathered to witness the butchering operations of the savage. He shot the animal with a bow, bled him, skinned and dressed him, sliced up the meat, and spread it out on flakes to dry; then he cooked a portion and ate it, and in order to exhibit the whole process, and to take a mischievous revenge upon them for making an exhibition of him, he went into a corner of the yard and eased himself before them all."

AMERIGO VIEWS THE CHANGING CONCEPT OF THE NEW WORLD, HERE CALLED "AMERICA" FOR THE FIRST TIME IN THIS 1507 MAP. (MARTIN WALDSEEMÜLLER, COSMOGRAPHAE INTRODUCTO)

9 DEFINING THE NEW WORLD ~ VESPUCCI AND MAGELLAN

Cabot and Columbus were convinced that their widely separated north and south discoveries were the outer lands of Asia. While such was the mind-set of most Europeans, some cartographers were questioning the truth of the matter. Any available information didn't seem to jibe with what was known of the Far East. On his second voyage to the Caribbean, Columbus hoped to defuse those negative thinkers by having all those aboard swear that his discovered islands were indeed just offshore to India. A notary and four witnesses verified each oath that was made. He who would say otherwise was to have his tongue slit, and any officer who mentioned such doubts would also have a hefty fine. Common seamen could count on one hundred lashes. Even after sighting the South American mainland during his third voyage, Columbus stoutly maintained that he was all the more nearer to the promised land of spices and gold.

One such doubter was Amerigo Vespucci. As one of the long line of gifted Italians who mapped out exploration possibilities, he made four western voyages under the Portuguese and Spanish flags. After observing the extensive South American coast, Amerigo theorized that here was a previously unknown continent. From his notes, a German cartographer drew the concept of a huge island that blocked the way to India. Rather than leave that body nameless, he labeled it "America," which was the Latin for Amerigo. The idea caught the imagination of all Europe, and so the New World had a name of its own.

A Portuguese nobleman pondered this Asian obstruction, and thought it might be possible to find an opening at its southern reaches. Ferdinand Magellan became all the more convinced when he heard that Balboa had crossed the Isthmus of Panama in 1513 and gazed upon the great ocean that lay beyond. Magellan meant to be the first explorer to sail that body of water westward to the Indies, however near or far that might be. He had everything in his favor— influence in court, an excellent navigator, a fearless soldier and leader, as well

as a vision that could not be dimmed. Unfortunately, such qualities were lost on King Manuel, for an earlier misunderstanding had placed him in disfavor. Magellan's proposal was answered with a curt refusal. It was one of history's most notable blunders.

It was a frustrated Magellan who renounced his citizenship and sought out King Charles of Spain as his sponsor. By the summer of 1519 he had been appointed captain-general of a five-ship fleet, off to seek out an Atlantic-Pacific passage. Masterly seamanship

THE CROSS STAFF MEASURED THE ANGLE BETWEEN THE NORTH STAR AND THE HORIZON. THE FEWER THE DEGREES AND MINUTES ON THE STAFF SCALE, THE FARTHER SOUTH WAS THE SHIP.

SEA ASTROLABE ~ GRAVITY KEPT THE CENTER BAR PARALLEL TO THE HORIZON WHILE SIGHTING THE STAR OR SUN. THE ANGLE MARKINGS MEASURED THE ALTITUDE.

brought him through the treacherous strait that bears his name and on to the Philippines. Magellan had sailed beyond the scope of these pages, but his stranger-than-fiction problems would surely have discouraged a lesser man. The voyage was marred by murders, mutinies, beheadings, offenders quartered and impaled, marooned seamen, poisoned arrows, scurvy, and the seduction of native women. Since the wormy biscuits had long since given out, the crews tried to ward off starvation by eating sawdust, soaked and toasted leather, and even rats, a delicacy at half a ducat apiece.

The greatest tragedy of all came on April 27, 1521, when the captain-general lost his life in a Philippine intertribal war. After three years on the high seas, the one surviving ship limped into the Spanish home port with but eighteen of the original two hundred and forty-three still aboard.

The cargo of cloves sold for more than the cost of outfitting the expedition. It was of no benefit to the man who had inspired the first voyage around the world and had placed the Americas and the vastness of the Pacific Ocean in their proper perspective. Although the westerly route through the Strait of Magellan had proved too long, dangerous, and costly, spices and other Asian luxuries could be shipped directly from the new Pacific possessions to Mexico for distribution. When the news reached Portugal and King Manuel, he angrily ordered any and all of the Magellan family coat of arms be removed from the home town of Sabrosa. Thereafter, the blank walls stood as a fitting tribute to the crown's stupidity.

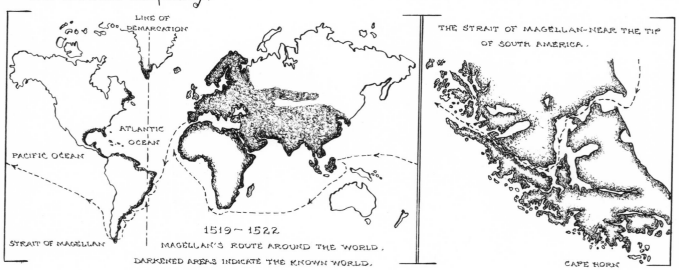

LINE OF DEMARCATION

ATLANTIC OCEAN

PACIFIC OCEAN

STRAIT OF MAGELLAN

1519 ~ 1522
MAGELLAN'S ROUTE AROUND THE WORLD.
DARKENED AREAS INDICATE THE KNOWN WORLD.

THE STRAIT OF MAGELLAN-NEAR THE TIP OF SOUTH AMERICA.

CAPE HORN

✝10 THE SPANISH CONQUESTS IN NORTH AMERICA

Almost overnight, Spain had become the envy of all Europe. Her flag now flew over the huge new continent that lay to the west of the Line of Demarcation and on to the far reaches of the Pacific Ocean. Such good fortune must surely be God's will, for Spain had become champion of the Roman Catholic faith. Since the Church was the very foundation of law and order, it followed that any who dared differ from those beliefs must also be enemies and a danger to the state. After leading a religious crusade to drive the infidel Moors from her countryside, Queen Isabella turned her energies to stamping out heresy through state tribunals. Untold numbers of the Reform Movement, Moslems and those of the Jewish faith were tortured, put to death, or exiled if they were more fortunate. Spain's enthusiastic manhunt during the Inquisition could now be extended to those unsuspecting pagan "savages" who had no idea that Spain had claimed their tribal lands. A new breed of explorers, the conquistadors, soon left no doubt of Spanish intentions. It was a matter of kill or convert, and only the daring and pitiless need apply for the job.

PART OF A SCENE FROM THE SPANISH CONQUEST OF THE NEW WORLD FROM T. DE BRY, <u>AMERICA</u>, PART VI, 1596 (BRITISH MUSEUM, LONDON)

A GOLDEN HEART PENDANT FROM THE WRECKED SPANISH GALLEON <u>TOLOSA</u>

Before Columbus had set sail for the New World, Isabella had united the various independent Spanish kingdoms under one crown. That left a surplus of young noblemen ready for something more adventuresome than the usual court functions. Fame, glory, and riches awaited on the other side of the Atlantic. It should be realized that there were some wise and compassionate leaders who among the many who ventured abroad. Certainly there were the dedicated priests who labored against the odds to bring salvation to the Indians. They did what they could to encourage the more humane commanders while condemning the ruthless.

Generally, they were overwhelmed by the stampede for riches. Back home most Spanish authorities were so heady with success that it was difficult to hear any voices of Christian concern that came from the American wilderness.

The southern route to the West Indies proved to be a relatively easy sail. There were few of the contrary winds that the Vikings, Cabot, and Corte-Real experienced on their northern explorations. From the Canary Islands, the northwest trades and currents carried the Spanish westward to the Caribbean. Treasure-ladened galleons would then be carried homeward by the Gulf Stream and the prevailing westerlies. In a short time, the crossing was becoming routine, and it almost seemed that the Spanish fleets would groove a path on the surface of the Atlantic.

ARMS AND ARMOR~ Every conquistador prized his armor, and the many varieties that were worn on the American frontier were a matter of personal preference. No matter to what extent one sheathed his body in steel, the helmet was an absolute must. Generally, the foot soldiers opted for the morion and cabasset. The chapel de fer had been more popular in the two preceeding centuries, but still found favor among the pikemen. The barbute offered more protection for the face and neck. While most were open in front, others covered much of the face. Traditionally, the barbute was worn by archers. The burgonet was popular with the horsemen, who often combined such headgear with a full suit of armor.

MORION

CABASSET

CHAPEL DE FER

BARBUTE

LIGHT AND COOLER
MODIFIED BARBUTE

BURGONET

The morion helmet tradition is carried on today by the Vatican Swiss Guard.
By all odds, the chain-link coat was favored for bodily protection. Made in the old Viking way, the rings of heavy wire were flattened at the forge and riveted to companion links. In the hot and steamy jungles of South America and the baked plains to the west, the covering gave more ventilation, chafed the skin less, and was not as weighty as the plated armor. It added between fifteen and thirty pounds to any other metal works.

The chain-link coat did have its problems. As one observer recorded on the de Soto march. "An [Indian] arrow where it findeth no armour, pierceth as deeply as a crossebow. Their bows are very strong, and their arrowes are made of certain cane like reedes, very heavy & so strong that a sharp cane passeth thorow a Target . . . For the most part when they light upon an armour, they breake at the place where they are bound together. Those of cane do split and pierce a coate of maile, and are more hurtful than the other."

The horseman, perched high on his mount, made an inviting target. His outer metal skin would usually include a closed helmet with a visor that could be raised on the march and lowered in battle. Breast and back plates had shingled, movable plates below the waist. Steel cylinders enclosed the upper arms, and strapped-on plates covered the front and outer parts of the thighs. Each lower arm and leg was protected by two hinged pieces. Overlapping strips of steel were loosely riveted to give free joint movement, much like a lobster's tail.

FOOT SOLDIER WEARING CABASSET, GORGET, CHAIN MAIL COAT, AND ARM AND LEG ARMOR.

All of this metalwork would seem impossibly awkward and burdonsome. Actually, the suit of armor averaged about sixty pounds—light enough for any horseman to mount his horse without help or regain the saddle if he was thrown to the ground. That is not to say that these steel encasements were in any way comfortable, and the oven effect from the southern sun without ventilation can only be imagined.

The American Indian was filled with wonder and fear when the first conquistadors leveled their "firesticks." They were the matchlocks, then known as arquebuses, and were as a slightly later English playwright might have said, "full of sound and fury, signifying nothing." They were so heavy and cumbersome that a forked rest was needed.

HORSEMAN WITH BURGONET AND HALF ARMOR

71

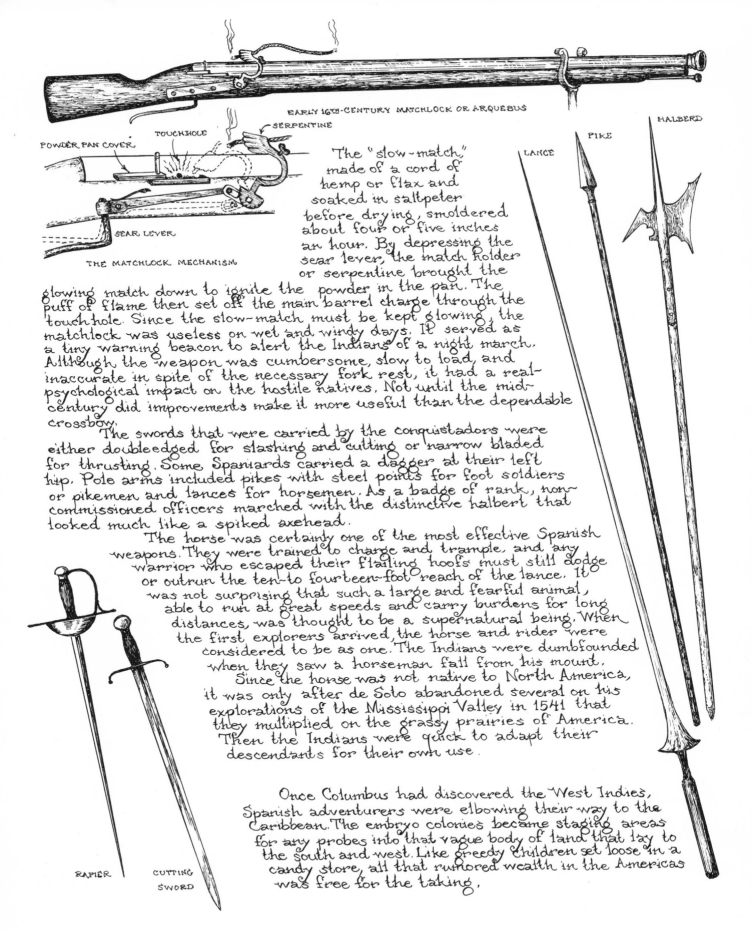

EARLY 16TH-CENTURY MATCHLOCK OR ARQUEBUS

POWDER PAN COVER

TOUCHHOLE

SERPENTINE

SEAR LEVER

THE MATCHLOCK MECHANISM

LANCE

PIKE

HALBERD

The "slow-match" made of a cord of hemp or flax and soaked in saltpeter before drying, smoldered about four or five inches an hour. By depressing the sear lever, the match holder or serpentine brought the glowing match down to ignite the powder in the pan. The puff of flame then set off the main barrel charge through the touchhole. Since the slow-match must be kept glowing, the matchlock was useless on wet and windy days. It served as a tiny warning beacon to alert the Indians of a night march. Although the weapon was cumbersome, slow to load, and inaccurate in spite of the necessary fork rest, it had a real psychological impact on the hostile natives. Not until the mid-century did improvements make it more useful than the dependable crossbow.

The swords that were carried by the conquistadors were either doubleedged for slashing and cutting or narrow bladed for thrusting. Some Spaniards carried a dagger at their left hip. Pole arms included pikes with steel points for foot soldiers or pikemen and lances for horsemen. As a badge of rank, non-commissioned officers marched with the distinctive halbert that looked much like a spiked axehead.

The horse was certainly one of the most effective Spanish weapons. They were trained to charge and trample, and any warrior who escaped their flailing hoofs must still dodge or outrun the ten-to fourteen-foot reach of the lance. It was not surprising that such a large and fearful animal, able to run at great speeds and carry burdens for long distances, was thought to be a supernatural being. When the first explorers arrived, the horse and rider were considered to be as one. The Indians were dumbfounded when they saw a horseman fall from his mount.

Since the horse was not native to North America, it was only after de Soto abandoned several on his explorations of the Mississippi Valley in 1541 that they multiplied on the grassy prairies of America. Then the Indians were quick to adapt their descendants for their own use.

Once Columbus had discovered the West Indies, Spanish adventurers were elbowing their way to the Caribbean. The embryo colonies became staging areas for any probes into that vague body of land that lay to the south and west. Like greedy children set loose in a candy store, all that rumored wealth in the Americas was free for the taking.

RAPIER

CUTTING SWORD

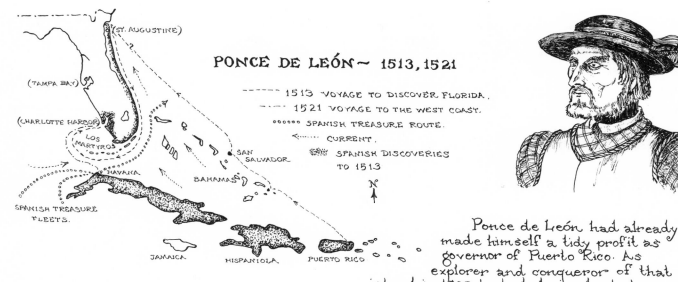

PONCE DE LEÓN ~ 1513, 1521

- - - - - - 1513 VOYAGE TO DISCOVER FLORIDA.
- · - · - 1521 VOYAGE TO THE WEST COAST.
°°°°°°° SPANISH TREASURE ROUTE.
←- - - - CURRENT.
⚓ SPANISH DISCOVERIES
TO 1513

N
↑

Ponce de León had already made himself a tidy profit as governor of Puerto Rico. As explorer and conqueror of that island in 1508, he had drained whatever wealth he could from the Carib Indians. Ambitious and restless, he had become intrigued by an Indian tale of a land to the north called Bimini. Gold was said to be there in plenty, and even more appealing was a fountain or river that restored one's youth, vitality, and health. Since the governor was getting along in years, becoming young again with plenty of jingle in his pockets was an appeal that he couldn't ignore. After suppressing a general native uprising that came from his heavy-handed rule, he sank what monies he had into outfitting and manning three vessels. In March 1513, he set sail with high expectations for the northwest.

Ponce de León may have recalled the stories of St. Brendan and his Irish monks exploring the "Coral Sea" some nine centuries earlier. He had sailed with Columbus on his second voyage in 1493 and no doubt was familiar with Toscanelli's 1474 world map that was carried aboard. St. Brendan's Island had been clearly outlined and might be the Bimini he sought. The contemporary historian Peter Martyr had also indicated a similar "isle of Beimeni" to the north of Cuba on his 1511 map. He noted that the Spanish court was excited over the prospect of such "marvellous countries."

Exploration of a Bahama landfall and then San Salvador yielded neither gold nor the Fountain of Youth. Continuing on, the lookout spotted a shoreline on the horizon. Somewhere between St. Augustine and Jacksonville, the party landed to find the country alive with fresh green foliage and flowers. Since it was Easter Sunday, Ponce de León called the land Pascua Florida ("Flowery Easter"). There were no discoveries of note.

Coasting southward, the ships could make little headway in spite of a favorable wind. Even when the anchors were down, the ships were in danger of being carried northward by a powerful current. They had found the Gulf Stream. Ashore, the explorers saw their first Indian settlement. The natives seemed friendly enough and beckoned to them to land. When they had done so, the members of the Calusa tribe became bold enough to begin carrying away

"SATURIOUA, KING OF FLORIDA IN NORTH AMERICA, IN THE ACT OF GOING TO WAR." JACQUES LE MOYNE, 1564.

whatever gear, oars and even whatever landing boats they could lay their hands upon. Surprised and outnumbered, the Spaniards made little objection until a warrior struck and nearly killed one of the party. Since the Indians had usually regarded the strangers as gods to be worshipped and showered with gifts, the sudden hostility was quite unexpected. In the pitched battle that followed, two of the Spaniards were wounded. Not until nightfall could the landing party return to the safety of their vessels, still pondering the reception by the new and unwilling subjects of the Spanish crown. Possibly, the Florida natives had heard of Ponce de León's subjugation of the Puerto Ricans and had no wish to be part of such misery.

Again under sail and still bucking the Gulf Stream, the ships passed by a string of islands and rocky projections at the southern tip of Florida. The sailors likened their profiles to men fixed on stakes "like men who are suffering." They were thereafter called Los Martyros ("the Martyrs"). The name was prophetic. Many a treasure-ladened galleon, sailing from Mexico, Panama, and South America to Havana and then homeward, was driven on the reefs. Their wooden skeletons, occasionally uncovered by the shifting ocean sands, serve as grave markers for those who "suffered" there.

After rounding the Florida Keys, Ponce de León's people came upon a deep inlet on the western coast ~ likely Charlotte Harbor or Tampa Bay. The explorers believed they had come to the northern border of Florida "Island." Again they were set upon by Calusa warriors, not only on landing but also by several canoe raids upon the ships. Enough was enough, and the course was set for the kinder hospitality of Puerto Rico.

QUARTER DOUBLOON, STRUCK IN MEXICO FROM MINED GOLD. FROM SHIPWRECK OFF THE YUCATAN COAST, 1741

Ponce de León's explorations did have their compensations. The Spanish king awarded him the governorship of the Bahamas and Florida in addition to his Puerto Rican authority. Colonization would logically follow, but for some reason any such effort was delayed for eight years. His expedition had made him poorer, he certainly had grown older, and perhaps a bit wiser after those Indian attacks. Some said that his old fire and enthusiasm ~ and jealousy ~ were rekindled after hearing of Hernando Cortés' swashbuckling march in 1519 through the rich Aztec lands in Mexico. The thirty-four-year-old Cortés seemed the ideal conquistador. He was young and good looking, a lady's man (at the age of seventeen he had fallen from the balcony of a lady with whom he was having a love intrigue), courageous, resourceful, and never one to let scruples, honoring his word, compassion, or murder stand in his way. In short, his end was justified by any means available. And so the governor, flushed with envy, may have stirred his bones for another go at New World fortunes and that illusive Fountain of Youth.

In February of 1521, he sailed off to populate his piece of America. With two hundred colonists, fifty horses, and all manner of livestock, the course was set for the Bay of Carlos ~ probably Charlotte Harbor. The settlement lasted for but five months, for the Indians had launched a fierce attack. Among the casualties lay Ponce de León, severely wounded by an arrow. Discouraged, the colonists collected their belongings and returned to Havana with their dying governor. Several days later the discoverer of Florida was laid to rest, along with his dreams of conquest.

GOLDEN ORNAMENT FROM PANAMA.
(HEYE MUSEUM OF THE AMERICAN INDIAN)

THIS AZTEC WOMAN, WITH HER FEATHERED CAPE, WAS BROUGHT TO THE COURT OF CHARLES I BY CORTES. SHE IS AS SEEN BY ARTIST CHRISTOPHER WEIDITZ IN 1529.

74

RECORDING THE FLORIDA INDIANS

"We Spaniards," as conquistador Hernando Cortés had said, "suffer from a disease that only gold will cure." Any such illness was making a rapid recovery as the galleon shuttle service siphoned off the riches of the Aztec and Inca empires. Perhaps there was more of the glitter in the unexplored vastness of North America, and Florida would make an admirable entrance to the interior. But first must come the subjugation of the less-than-friendly Indians and then the Spanish settlements that would replace their villages.

The Spanish successes were not lost on the competing nations, and despite the claim that "Florida" included all the coastline to the north, France and England would soon have their own exploring parties searching out the lands between the St. Lawrence River and Florida.

Back home, the heads of states and their subjects were eager to read about the latest accounts of those new lands. And read they could, for the old medieval days were long gone when only the most learned could make sense of the few hand-printed books in Latin that were available. With the Renaissance had come education, and the European middle class followed the most recent exploits across the Atlantic. Since the printing press was no longer a novelty, popular books in the language of the people were describing the unpredictable American Indian, his primitive existence and curious beliefs, as well as such natural resources as mineral deposits, the forests of great mast trees, strange plants and animals, fisheries, waterpower sources, and the rich soil that yielded tobacco and edibles.

Soon after such authors as Harriot and Hakluyt were turning out their glowing reports later in the sixteenth century, the Flemish engraver Theodore De Bry added a new dimension to New World understanding. He obtained the original paintings of artist Jacques Le Moyne de Morgues, who had been sent to Florida by France in 1564 to record the natives, their habits, and their surroundings. In 1591, his copper-engraved impressions, along with Le Moyne's comments were published in a series of books that were instant successes.

The printed word and the early engravings, although not without a hint of prejudice and propaganda, have given a reasonably accurate insight into what pre-colonial America was like. They must replace the ancient mythical Indian legends as a more reliable source of history. Several of De Bry's engravings of the Florida natives follow and are of as much interest to us as they were to the readers of four centuries ago.

"THE INDIANS BUILD THEIR FORTIFIED VILLAGES IN THIS WAY. THEY CHOOSE A SITE NEAR THE CHANNEL OF A SWIFT STREAM, WHICH THEY LEVEL AS EVENLY AS POSSIBLE. THEY DIG A CIRCULAR DITCH AROUND IT, INTO WHICH THEY DRIVE THICK, ROUND PALINGS, PLACED CLOSE TOGETHER, TO A HEIGHT TWICE THAT OF A MAN. THIS FENCING IS CARRIED TO A POINT BEYOND ITS BEGINNING, SPIRALWISE, MAKING A NARROW ENTRANCE AND ADMITTING NOT MORE THAN TWO PERSONS AT A TIME. THE COURSE OF THE STREAM IS DIVERTED TOWARDS THIS ENTRANCE, AND AT EACH END OF IT A SMALL GUARDHOUSE IS BUILT.

"THE CHIEF'S HOUSE STANDS IN THE CENTER OF THE ENCLOSURE AND IS SOMEWHAT SUNKEN INTO THE GROUND TO AVOID THE HEAT OF THE SUN. IT IS SURROUNDED BY THOSE OF THE PRINCIPAL MEN. THE ROOFS OF THESE HUTS ARE ONLY LIGHTLY

THATCHED WITH PALM BRANCHES, SINCE THEY ARE OCCUPIED FOR NOT MORE THAN NINE MONTHS IN THE YEAR. THE OTHER THREE WINTER MONTHS ... BEING SPENT IN THE FORESTS, WHEN THEY RETURN FROM THE WOODS, THEY GO BACK TO THEIR OLD HOMES ~ IF THE ENEMY HAS NOT BURNED THEM DOWN WHILE THEY WERE AWAY."

"THE YOUNG MEN ARE TRAINED TO RUN RACES, AND A PRIZE IS GIVEN TO THE ONE WHO SHOWS THE GREATEST ENDURANCE IN THE CONTEST. THEY ALSO PRACTICE A GREAT DEAL WITH BOW AND ARROW.

"THEY PLAY A GAME IN WHICH THEY CAST A BALL AT A SQUARE TARGET PLACED ON TOP OF A HIGH TREE, AND THEY TAKE GREAT PLEASURE IN HUNTING AND FISHING."

"THE INDIANS HUNT DEER IN A WAY WE HAVE NEVER SEEN BEFORE. THEY HIDE THEMSELVES IN THE SKIN OF A VERY LARGE DEER WHICH THEY HAVE KILLED SOME TIME BEFORE. THEY PLACE THE ANIMAL'S HEAD UPON THEIR OWN HEAD, LOOKING THROUGH THE EYEHOLES AS THROUGH A MASK. IN THIS DISGUISE THEY APPROACH THE DEER WITHOUT FRIGHTENING THEM. THEY CHOOSE THE TIME WHEN THE ANIMALS COME TO DRINK AT THE RIVER, SHOOTING THEM EASILY WITH BOW AND ARROW.

"TO PROTECT THEIR LEFT FOREARM FROM THE BOWSTRING, THEY USUALLY WEAR A STRIP OF BARK, AND THEY

PREPARE THE DEERSKINS WITHOUT ANY IRON INSTRUMENTS, USING ONLY SHELLS, IN A SURPRISINGLY EXPERT WAY. I DO NOT BELIEVE ANY EUROPEAN COULD DO THIS BETTER."

"HOW THEY TREAT THEIR SICK. THEY BUILD A BENCH LONG AND WIDE ENOUGH FOR THE SICK PERSON, AND IS LAID UPON IT EITHER ON HIS BACK OR HIS STOMACH. THIS DEPENDS ON THE NATURE OF HIS ILLNESS. THEN, CUTTING THE SKIN OF HIS FOREHEAD WITH A SHARP SHELL, THEY SUCK THE BLOOD WITH THEIR OWN MOUTHS, SPITTING IT OUT INTO AN EARTHEN JAR OR A GOURD. WOMEN WHO ARE NURSING OR ARE PREGNANT COME AND DRINK THIS BLOOD, ESPECIALLY IF IT IS THAT OF A STRONG YOUNG MAN. THEY BELIEVE THAT DRINKING IT MAKES THEIR MILK BETTER AND THEIR CHILDREN HEALTHIER, AND MORE ACTIVE.

"FOR THE SICK, WHOM THEY LAY FACE DOWNWARD, A FIRE OF HOT COALS IS PREPARED, ONTO WHICH SEEDS ARE THROWN. THE SICK MAN INHALES THE SMOKE THROUGH HIS NOSE AND MOUTH;

THIS ACTS AS A PURGE, EXPELLING THE POISON FROM THE BODY AND THUS CURING THE DISEASE.

"THEY ALSO HAVE A PLANT WHICH THE BRAZILIANS CALL 'petum' AND THE SPANIARDS 'tapaco'. AFTER CAREFULLY DRYING ITS LEAVES, THEY PUT THEM IN THE BOWL OF A PIPE. THEY LIGHT THE PIPE, AND HOLDING ITS OTHER END IN THEIR MOUTHS, THEY INHALE THE SMOKE SO DEEPLY THAT IT COMES OUT THROUGH THEIR MOUTHS AND NOSES; BY THIS MEANS THEY OFTEN CURE INFECTIONS.

"VENEREAL DISEASE IS COMMON AMONG THEM, AND THEY HAVE SEVERAL NATURAL REMEDIES FOR IT."

"THERE IS A TIME OF THE YEAR WHEN THE NATIVES FEAST EACH OTHER. FOR THIS PURPOSE THEY CHOOSE SPECIAL COOKS. THESE COOKS TAKE A GREAT ROUND EARTHENWARE POT (WHICH THEY BAKE SO WELL THAT WATER CAN BE BOILED THEREIN AS EASILY AS IN OUR OWN KETTLES) AND PUT IT OVER A LARGE WOOD FIRE. THE PLACE WHERE THE COOKING IS DONE SWARMS WITH ACTIVITY. THE HEAD COOK EMPTIES THE RAW FOOD INTO A HOLE IN THE GROUND; WOMEN BRING WATER IN LARGE VESSELS; HERBS TO BE USED FOR SEASONING ARE GROUND ON A STONE.

"ALTHOUGH THEY GIVE BIG FEASTS, THEY NEVER OVEREAT, AND THEREFORE USUALLY LIVE TO A GREAT AGE. ONE OF THEIR CHIEFS SWORE THAT HE WAS THREE HUNDRED YEARS

OLD AND THAT HIS FATHER, WHOM HE POINTED OUT TO ME, WAS FIFTY YEARS OLDER THAN HIMSELF — AND INDEED HE LOOKED TO BE NOTHING BUT SKIN AND BONES. SUCH FACTS MIGHT WELL MAKE US CHRISTIANS ASHAMED, FOR WE ARE SO IMMODERATE IN BOTH OUR EATING AND OUR DRINKING HABITS THAT WE SHORTEN OUR LIVES. THEREBY, WE MIGHT EASILY LEARN SOBRIETY AND WISDOM FROM THESE MEN WHOM WE CONSIDER ONLY AS SAVAGES AND BEASTS.

"THE SACRIFICE OF FIRST-BORN CHILDREN.
THEY OFFER THEIR FIRST-BORN SON TO THE
CHIEF ON THE DAY OF SACRIFICE. THE CHIEF
GOES TO THE PLACE DEDICATED TO THAT
PURPOSE. THERE HE TAKES HIS SEAT ON A
BENCH. NOT FAR OFF IS A TREE STUMP
ABOUT TWO FEET HIGH AND AS MANY THICK,
IN FRONT OF WHICH THE MOTHER OF THE
FIRST-BORN SON SQUATS ON HER HEELS, HER
FACE COVERED WITH HER HANDS IN SORROW.
ONE OF HER WOMEN FRIENDS OR
RELATIVES THEN OFFERS THE CHILD TO
THE CHIEF IN WORSHIP. AFTER THE OFFERING
IS MADE THE WOMEN WHO HAVE ACCOMPANIED
THE MOTHER DANCE IN A CIRCLE AROUND
THE STUMP WITH GREAT DEMONSTRATIONS
OF JOY. IN THEIR MIDST, SINGING
THE CHIEF'S PRAISES, DANCES THE
WOMAN WHO HOLDS THE CHILD.
  "NEAR BY STANDS A GROUP OF
SIX INDIANS. THEY SURROUND A

MAGNIFICENTLY DECORATED MAN HOLDING A CLUB. IT IS HE WHO WILL PERFORM THE SACRIFICE. WHEN THE
DANCE ENDS, HE TAKES THE INFANT AND KILLS IT ON THE WOODEN STUMP IN HONOR OF THE CHIEF. I SAW THIS
RITUAL PERFORMED ONCE WHILE I WAS THERE."

  "FLORIDIANS CROSSING OVER TO AN ISLAND ON A PLEASURE TRIP. THE COUNTRY HAS MANY DELIGHTFUL ISLANDS,
LYING IN SHALLOW WATERS OF CLEAR, PURE WATER, RUNNING NO MORE THAN BREAST HIGH. WHEN THE NATIVES WISH
TO GO TO ONE OF THE ISLANDS TO ENJOY THEMSELVES, THEY SWIM SKILLFULLY ACROSS THE RIVERS, OR, IF THEY
HAVE THEIR YOUNG CHILDREN WITH THEM, THEY WADE. THE MOTHER TAKES WITH HER THREE OF HER CHILDREN, THE
SMALLEST ONE ON HER SHOULDER, WHILE THE TWO OTHERS CLING TO HER ARMS. SHE ALSO CARRIES FRUIT AND
PROVISIONS FOR THE TRIP IN A BASKET.
  "WHEN THERE IS DANGER OF MEETING AN ENEMY, THE MEN TAKE THEIR BOWS AND ARROWS ON THE TRIP. TO
KEEP THE WEAPONS FROM GETTING WET, THEY ATTACH THE QUIVER TO THEIR HAIR, AND THEY HOLD THE BOW AND
ONE ARROW ABOVE THE WATER, READY FOR USE."

THE SPANISH PUSH INLAND

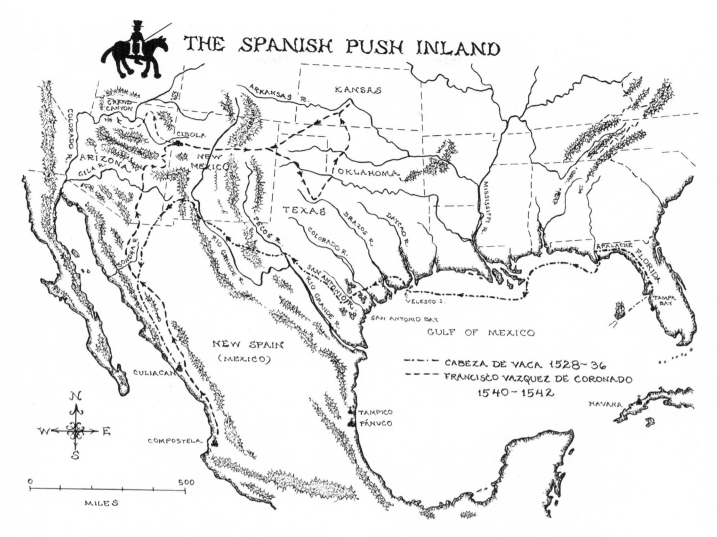

CABEZA DE VACA ~ LOST IN THE SOUTHWEST 1528~36

Panfilo de Narváez entered history as the wrong man at the right time. In 1520 he had been commissioned by the governor of Cuba to take over the command of the Cortés expedition. It seemed that the conquerer of Mexico was an independent spirit who ransacked the Aztec nation as he saw fit. This was not to the governor's liking. Narváez, by contrast, could only offer incompetence in place of Cortés' perseverance and ruthlessness. When Cortés learned of his demotion, he quickly mustered seventy soldiers for a forced march to the coast where Narváez' fleet lay anchored. After a disarming bit of negotiation with his would-be successor, he attacked one dark and stormy night. Narváez was caught unprepared and was handily defeated. He limped back to Cuba, minus one eye lost in the battle and with most of his command who had deserted to become soldiers of fortune.

As for Narváez, opportunity knocked twice. Seven years later he was authorized to take over Ponce de León's discovered "island" of Florida and "to conquor and governe the Provinces which lye from the River of Palms [the Rio Grande] into the cape of Florida." This indefinite piece of real estate extended to the southwest, almost to the Spanish outpost of Pánuco. There he planned to out-plunder his old enemy Cortés.

His large invasion force sailed from Cuba in 1527 and into the teeth of

79

a hurricane. Two ships and sixty men were lost. The battered fleet put in to San Domingo, where some three hundred soldiers deserted~ bad omens for success. Finally, one year later, the remaining three hundred men made their landing on the west coast of Florida near Tampa Bay. One of their number was Alvar Nuñez Cabeza de Vaca, who represented the Crown as treasurer. He was to see that the king received his due share of the wealth that surely must be found in the interior. It was he who later wrote the detailed adventures of what lay beyond.

The godlike status that the Spaniards enjoyed to the south was shrugged off by the Florida Indians. More than that, they were openly hostile, "made many signs and menaces, and appeared to say we must go away from the country." This good advice was soon forgotten by the governor when he learned from four captured natives that the Apalachee tribe to the north had "much gold" and "any thing that we at all cared for." Time and again, this old Indian trick would be used to wave unwanted intruders into the interior wilderness and away from their tribal lands. The glitter of gold was in Narváez's eyes when he ordered the fleet to cast off and await his land expedition at the Pánuco settlement. It was assumed that a few days march was enough to bring the troops to that Mexican anchorage.

It was a hellish northwestward march through swamps, tangled woods and fallen trees, blistering heat, and clouds of mosquitoes. When the exhausted troops finally arrived at the Apalachee village, they found no city of gold~ only forty or so poor huts. The vain and arrogant Narváez ordered the capture of the Indian chief, an act that in no way endeared him to the displaced villagers. With morning came the start of constant attacks by the warriors. De Vaca worried that the Spanish armor gave scant protection from the arrows, and "there were those that day who swore they had seen two oaks, each the thickness of the lower part of the leg, pierced through from side to side by arrows." The Indians had an unexpected ally, for illness swept through the Spanish camp, laying low more than a third of the expedition. Hunger stalked their ranks, for the inept governor had issued but a pound of biscuit and another of bacon to each man. It was thought that supplemental produce could be had from the villagers. Dissension grew to a near rebellion, although cooler heads argued against abandoning the sick~ and the governor himself~ to their fate.

DE VACA WROTE THAT AFTER THE "DETENTION" OF THE CHIEF, THERE WAS GREAT EXCITEMENT AMONG THE INDIANS, "IN CONSEQUENCE OF WHICH THEY RETURNED FOR BATTLE EARLY THE NEXT DAY, AND ATTACKED US WITH SUCH PROMPTNESS AND ALACRITY THAT THEY SUC~ CEEDED IN SETTING FIRE TO THE HOUSES IN WHICH WE WERE."

APALACHEE, FLORIDA
JUNE 25, 1528.

(FROM LE MOYNE, ENGRAVING BY DE BRY, AMERICA, 1591)

80

Nearly three and a half months had passed in this "miserable country." It was high time to seek out the seacoast and the safety of the fleet. After running a gauntlet of Indian ambushes, the expedition reached St. Marks Bay. This was in no way Pánuco, and they had no idea that their haven was still a thousand miles away across the gulf. With an empty sea ahead and a wilderness trap behind, the only solution seemed to be to build their own escape vessels. For gentlemen conquistadors, more practiced at swinging swords than axes, the idea seemed impossible. More than that, they had no tools and even less nautical know-how, yet one of the company was able to fashion a pair of bellows from slabs of wood and deerskins. Any thing iron~ armor, stirrups, spurs, and crossbows~ were wrought into crude saws, axes, and nails. Twisted palmetto husks and pine pitch were collected for caulking. The same husks, along with the tails and manes of the horses that had also served as food, were fashioned into ropes and rigging. Off the backs of the

SHIPBUILDING IN THE NEW WORLD (DE BRY, 1594)

soldiers came their shirts for makeshift sails. Oars were chopped from evergreen trees. The intact skin from the horses' legs served as water bottles. In a scant seventeen days, as the sickness and Indian attacks increased, five boats were ready for the launching.

Such was the will to survive. Forty men had been lost at the seashore from illness and arrows. Those remaining crowded aboard~ just under fifty in each of the wooden shells that were no longer than thirty to forty feet. With the gunwales but nine inches above the surface of the water, the clumsy crafts headed along the southwest coast for the Pánuco outpost. As the days passed, the water bottles rotted and several died from drinking sea water. Others were lost in skirmishes when landings were attempted.

Off the mouth of the Mississippi River, the strength of the current swept the boats seaward, then were scattered by a storm. De Vaca's boat, with his crew too weak to man the oars, finally drifted within hailing distance of the governor's. Narváez, who had selected the fittest men for his boat, refused to pass a towline. For some, a crisis brings out the best. On the other hand, there was the expedition's leader, thinking only of self-preservation and above the good of his followers. Abandoned and alone, de Vaca and another paddled as best they could until breakers were seen in the distance. After riding out another storm, a great afterwave shot the boat ashore. More dead than alive, the survivors were met by curious Indians who provided enough fish, roots, and water to make an attempt to refloat the boat. The surf would have it other-wise, for the boat capsized. Now reduced to skeletons and naked as jaybirds, they threw themselves on the mercy of the natives.

Their new home was probably Velasso Island, next south to the larger Galveston Island, and appropriately dubbed Malhado or "Isle of Misfortune." A bit up the coast, a second boat had turned turtle. Among their number were Andrés Dorantes de Carrança, a captain in the infantry, Captain Alonzo del Castillo Maldonado, and Estevan a black from Morocco and a slave of Dorantes.

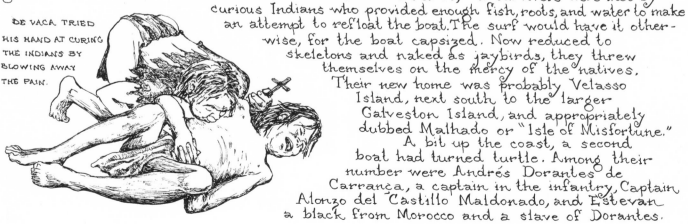

DE VACA TRIED HIS HAND AT CURING THE INDIANS BY BLOWING AWAY THE PAIN.

Although their arrival was at that time unknown to de Vaca, he and the three would be the only members of the expedition to ever see civilization again. Meanwhile, the full fury of winter was upon the island, and the blustery weather prevented the befrienders of de Vaca from digging roots or catching fish in their weirs. It was later learned by the Indians that five starving Spaniards, isolated on the coast, had subsisted on the dead. So horrified were they that if it was known at the time, all of the strangers would have been put to death.

Hunger was compounded by an "illness of the bowels" that swept through the Indian camp. Half their number perished. In their desperation, they prevailed upon de Vaca to act as a medicine man. The usual native treatment was to cure by blowing on the ill and rubbing out the demons by passing a stone over the abdomen. Going one step better, the practitioner would make a series of cuts over the painful site and suck out the wound. De Vaca could do little more than bless the sick, breathe upon them, recite the Paternoster and an Ave Maria while making the sign of the cross. Either the disease had run its course or de Vaca was due for a few miracles, for the ill seemed to respond and be on the mend. His reputation as a healer was assured. Exalted or not, he was still expected to seek out food and firewood. After a year, he made good an attempt to reach the mainland and leave the island poverty behind.

There, our innovative treasurer learned that beads made of sea snails, conch shells, and cones, as well as a special bean used in dances and festivities, were highly prized by the inland tribes. Because of the continual tribal wars, these people could not travel in safety to the coast for such finery. As a white man, and the purveyor of such wants, he could safely pass through the country without being molested. In turn, he would bring back hides, ochre for face painting, deer-hair tassels dyed red, sturdy arrow shafts, flint for arrow-heads, and pitch and sinews for securing the stone points to the shafts. For nearly six years, de Vaca made a happier existence for himself.

It was not so with the other casta-ways, for Dorantes, Castillo, and Estévan had been carried away as slaves to the western mainland by the coastal Indians. The cruelty that they and their party endured can hardly be imagined. Their beards were pulled out for amusement, and they became the targets for mud balls and frequent beatings. Two of their group had been killed by the superstitious natives because of a dream. Three others were put to death because they left one hut for another. De Vaca had learned that Castillo and Estevan, then with new masters, would be brought down from their San Antonio River village at walnut gathering time. Dorantes had been kept by the coastal

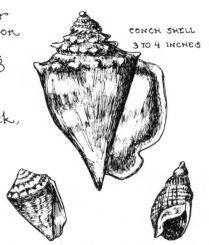

SOME OF THE TRADE GOODS
CARRIED INLAND BY DE VACA

CONCH SHELL
3 TO 4 INCHES

CONE SHELL, 1⁺INCHES   MUD SNAIL, 1 INCH

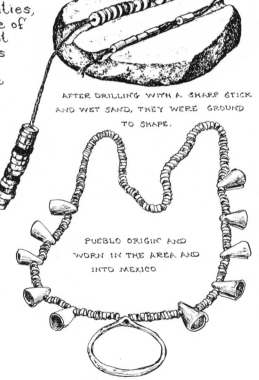

AFTER DRILLING WITH A SHARP STICK
AND WET SAND, THEY WERE GROUND
TO SHAPE.

PUEBLO ORIGIN AND
WORN IN THE AREA AND
INTO MEXICO

NECKLACE OF CONE SHELLS AND SHELL
DISKS WITH A BONE PENDANT, NORTHERN
MEXICO   (MUSEUM OF NEW MEXICO)

Indians. When the tribes gathered, he sought out his old friends. After a joyful reunion, he learned of the fate of two of the other boats. One had capsized, spilling her crew onto dry land at the Mississippi delta. The other was the governor's vessel, and had landed nearby. Narváez opted to stay aboard while his crew sought out the others. During the night, a north wind blew the flimsy craft to sea, and he was never seen again. Probably there were no moist eyes among the landing party. Faced with extreme hunger, one after the other died and were eaten by those still alive. A single survivor became a slave to a nearby tribe and was able to pass along the news. Shortly after, he attempted an escape and was hunted down.

De Vaca and his newly found companions hoped to be more successful in a planned getaway. In six months, the tribes would gather for the prickly pear season. With any sort of luck, they could steal off to the west during the feasting. For the while, de Vaca became the slave of the same Indian who owned Dorantes. Castillo and Estevan returned inland with their masters. When the tribes finally came together, their masters fought over a woman. In anger, they returned to their own lands with their captives in tow.

A year~a very long one~ passed before the four could come together again. There was further news. The fifth and last boat had made shore, only to be attacked by warriors from the northeast. The men were so weak from hunger that no resistance could be given. They were slain to a man.

THE PRICKLY PEAR CACTUS. THE PRICKLES WERE REMOVED BY SINGEING.

While their captors were otherwise diverted by the ripe prickly pears, the Spaniards stole away to the north. An inland route, while hardly in the direction of Pánuco, would give more distance from the cruel coastal tribes. Nightfall found the wanderers among the friendly Avavares Indians~and regarded as celebrities of sorts. They were aware of the miraculous cures by de Vaca, and soon the ill and disabled thereabouts were heading for his healing hand. Each brought gifts of furs, nuts, flint knives, prickly pears, or whatever was considered of great value. After eight months of good living, they began to follow the sunset toward a ragged country that was beset with thorns and arid deserts.

Because distances and directions in de Vaca's narrative have been difficult to interpret, the route taken is speculative. Most likely, however, their search for civilization had taken them from the prickly pear fields, about ninety miles inland from San Antonio Bay, to the Colorado River in Texas. This was the Avavares country from which they were now leaving. The trek brought them westward across the lower Pecos River to the Rio Grande, just above the junction of the Conchos River. From there they traveled in a rather straight line across Chihuahua and Sonora in Mexico to the Rio Sonora. There the four companions would happen upon the first countrymen they had seen since the start of the nine-year survival march.

The Indian tribes are also difficult to place. But de Vaca does go into some detail about the native customs that he observed throughout Texas. For example, husbands did not sleep with their pregnant wives until two years after giving birth. A barren wife was reason enough to search out a more productive partner. In this land of poverty, no food may be found for three or four days. Therefore, a child would be breast~fed until the age of twelve.

Intertribal wars were no novelty among the Texas Indians. When close to enemy territory, it was usual to hide their dwellings at the edge of a wood~land, amidst the thickest tangle of brush available. Inside, campfires were lit at dusk while the women and children were secreted deep in the woods. Near the lodges, trenches were dug and then covered with brush and sticks, leaving spaces for aiming arrows. There the warriors slept, ready to strike out against the unsuspecting raiders. If such a visit seemed at all likely, each warrior remained awake throughout the night with his strung bow and a dozen arrows by his side.

When in combat, they would crouch close to the ground or race from one place to another to dodge the enemy arrows. As for the Spanish crossbow or arquebus, the Indians were so fleet that they had no fear of such cumbersome weapons. Throughout the battle, the warriors would show no sign of fear or timidity, lest their opponents gain strength from any weakness. Revenging a wrong was a point of honor among those Indians as it was elsewhere.

Meanwhile, the four wanderers were met by kindness and rejoicing wherever they came upon another village. Word of the extraordinary medicine man had preceeded them, and gifts were plentiful. After leaving the large village by the Rio Sonora, they were distressed to find torched lodges, the rich garden soil abandoned and covered with brush, and the people fleeing to the safety of the mountains. Spanish slavers had cut a swath of destruction through the countryside, taking away the men in chains and laying waste to the tribal lands. When, at last, DeVaca and his fellows met up with four mounted Spanish slavers, there was no happy reunion. The slavers shrugged off the tongue lashing, and rode off to continue the hunt. Still fuming, the four survivors finally reached Culiacan and were given a warm welcome and a sympathetic ear by the mayor.

A pagan Indian, to the Spanish mind, was nothing more than a savage animal, but he who had been converted to the Catholic faith was in no danger of slavery. Therefore the mayor suggested that his guests spread the word that Christians would be considered as brothers. They could then return to their homes in safety and live in peace and friendship. Convinced by the messengers sent out by de Vaca, the villagers did indeed return to their lands, built churches, and lived without fear under the Spanish cross. The survivors of the Narváez expedition thereby repaid the people who had treated them with kindness and trust.

FRANCISCO VASQUEZ DE CORONADO
1537~42

The news swept New Spain like a tidal wave. It was nothing short of a miracle that four survivors of the disastrous Narváez expedition had made their way out of that northern wilderness and back to civilization. De Vaca, still in his scant Indian clothing, had told of their nine years of starvation and the all too frequent brushes with death. His honest, no-nonsense account carried no sensational tales of golden cities, although he had heard of populous towns and very large houses "of four to five stories" that reached to the sky. The idled conquistadors were quick to remember Indian rumors of seven large cities, resplendent with turquoise, in the north country. Many believed that they must be the long-sought Seven Cities of Antilia, earlier shown on Scandelli's world map and described by such writers as John Day.

Now that the Mexican Aztecs had been largely relieved of their treasures and Pizarro had drained off much of the wealth of Peru in the 1530s, perhaps the interior of North America was ripe for the plucking. The Viceroy of the Spanish colonies thought so, and chose his good friend Francisco Vasquez de Coronado to organize an

THE CORONADO EXPEDITION.

expedition of discovery. Coronado had just become governor of Mexico in 1539, and was eager to lead such a march to further his fame and fortune. But before the troops could be mustered, there must be an advance party to scout the best route through the mountains and deserts to the objective~the wealth of the Seven Cities.

De Vaca, Dorantes, and Castillo knew much of the north country and were revered by the tribespeople. One or all could bring back just the information needed for the invasion. All declined~understandably. Dorantes' slave, Estevan was the only remaining choice, and he was purchased by the viceroy. Since he had little to say in the matter he would act only as a guide. With his reliability uncertain, three Franciscan friars would make any observations and decisions. Friar Marcos of Nice would head the quartet by virtue of his part in the conquest of Peru and his knowledge of celestial navigation. Unfortunately, he was also adept at turning fact into fantasy. His reports, such as they were, would help decide if a full-scale expedition was justified.

There was no time for frittering. At that moment de Soto, the newly proclaimed governor of Cuba and Florida, was completing his own plans for a westward march from Tampa Bay. Here was a man to be reckoned with, for he was as determined and courageous a leader as he was ruthless and cruel. He had a mind set on reaching those seven gilded cities somewhere in the interior of North America, and so the race for new treasure troves was off and running.

By March of 1539, the three friars, Estevan, and a party of friendly Indians left Culiacan. They soon learned that Estevan was much more of a celebrity than a slave. Recognized as one of the sun gods who had passed that way with de Vaca, the black was in his glory. From his belt hung the sacred medicine rattle that had been given to him by more easterly tribesmen during the survival march. As befitting his godlike status, he had decorated his waist and ankles with dyed feathers and tinkling bells. Village admirers gave him a bevy of beautiful maidens and quantities of turquoise. The friars, however, took a dim view of their guide's growing harem. After sharp words, they sent him on ahead and out of their sight.

The plan was for the friars to linger a bit and learn what they could of what lay to the north. Estevan was to send back a cross one span long (the length of a fully extended hand, from the tip of the thumb to the tip of the small finger, or about nine inches), if he should hear of "a rich country, some-thing really important." If he learned of something even more important, the cross would be two spans. "And if it were something greater and better than New Spain, he would send me a large cross."

Four days after Estevan had taken his leave, a runner arrived with a cross taller than a man! Somewhere ahead were riches beyond those of the Aztecs, and Friar Marcos and his companion (one of the three became ill and returned to Mexico) made all haste to follow. There were other great crosses that they found erected along the trail. From other messengers they learned more of their goal~the Seven Cities of Cíbola (Cibolo was the Spanish word for buffalo). Beyond them were two other rich lands, each with their own seven cities.

Up ahead, Estevan had managed to cross some two hundred and fifty miles of difficult desert. At last he and his throng of followers~he had demanded and received many more young women~looked down on the first of six Zuni pueblo towns. Like a great apartment complex, its stone and adobe walls did indeed reach the level of four or five stories. While his admirers looked on in awe, Estevan sent his badge of office, the medicine rattle, ahead to notify the elders of his presence. And of course, he demanded more women and more of the bluish green gemstones.

This was to be no triumphal entry. The wise men of the Zunis immediately recognized the rattle as the medicine from their old eastern enemies. He and his escort were ordered away from their city of Háwikuh. Since a god was not to be commanded by mortals, he strode into the city~almost. The would-be medicine man was placed under guard in a small hut on the city's outskirts.

Estevan had overplayed his hand.
For three days the Zuni council grilled
their prisoner. "The account which
the negro gave them of two white
men who were following him, sent
by a great lord, who knew about
the things in the sky, and how these
were coming to instruct them in divine
matters, made them think that he
must be a spy or a guide from some
nations who wished to come and
conquer them, because it seemed
to them unreasonable to say that
the people were white in the
country from which he came
and that he was sent by them,
he being black. Besides these
and other reasons, they thought
it was hard of him to ask for
turquoises and women, and so
they decided to kill him. They
did this, but they did not kill
any of those who went with him,
although they kept some young
fellows and let the others, about
sixty persons, return freely to
their own country. As these, who
were badly scared, were returning

HÁWIKUH, THE FIRST OF THE
ZUNI "SEVEN CITIES" PUEBLOS,
WAS DISCOVERED BY ESTEVAN
AND HIS FOLLOWERS.

in flight, they happened to come on the friars in the desert sixty leagues from
Cibola, and told them the sad news, which frightened them so much that they
would not even trust these folks who had been with the negro, but opened the packs
they were carrying and gave away every thing they had except the holy vestments
for saying mass. They returned from here by double marches, prepared for anything,
without seeing any more of the country except what the Indians told them."

Once back in the safety of Spanish Culiacan, Friar Marcos basked in his
moment of glory. By June he held the viceroy and Coronado spellbound with his fiction-
is-stranger-than-truth telling of his "observations." After learning of Estevan's death,
he fearlessly faced the dangers of the desert to see for himself Cibola from a hilltop.
Its fabulous walled stories and terraces glittered in the sunset, all "bigger than
the city of Mexico." No need for such a hero to recall his return in panic "with
his gown gathered up to his waist."

Now an expedition was a certainty. From all corners of New Spain (Mexico)
came idled adventurers, eager to have their own piece of the North American
treasure. By April 1540, "the most brilliant company ever collected in the Indies to go
in search of new lands" was ready to march from Campostéla. Two hundred mounted
caballeros, resplendent in their armor, leather cuirras or coats of mail, formed the
heart of the army. There were sixty-two foot soldiers, nearly a thousand friendly
Indians, five friars with a host of assistants, a military guard and their private
Indian servants. At least fifteen hundred horses, mules, and beef cattle were
in that grand parade. At the head of this mighty column, the pride of New Spain,
was Coronado, outstanding in his guilded armor and the plumes that waved
atop his helmet. Martial music made the departure all the more festive.

Before joining the ranks for the northward march, do consider the following
quotes of Pedro de Castaneda. This Culiacan settler-turned soldier wrote these
first eyewitness impressions of the Southwest Indians, their towns, and their
customs and serve to acquaint us with the lands that Coronado would be
discovering.

86

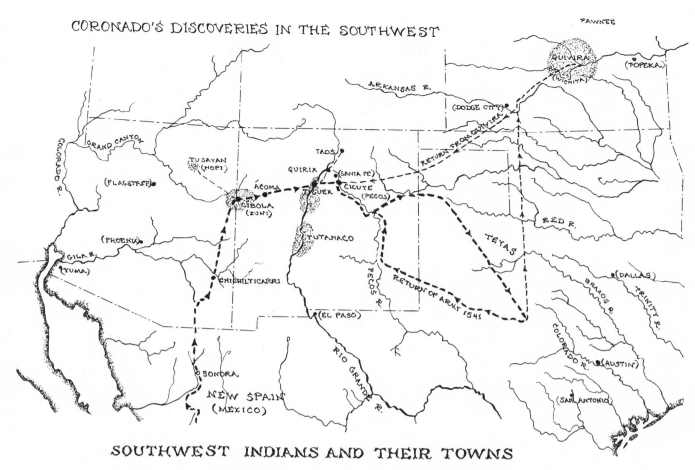

SOUTHWEST INDIANS AND THEIR TOWNS

SONORA~ PIMA TRIBE. "Soñora is a river and valley thickly settled by able-bodied people. The women paint their chins and eyes··· and wear petticoats of tanned deerskin, and little san benitos [square cloth with a hole for the head] reaching half way down the body··· They are great sodomites··· The chiefs of the villages go up on some little heights they have made for the purpose, like public criers, and there make lamentations for the space of an hour, regulating those things they have to attend to.

They have some little huts for shrines, all over the outside of which they stick many arrows, like a hedgehog. They do this when they are eager for war··· They drink wine made of the pitahaya, which is the fruit of a great thistle which opens like a pomegranate. The wine makes them stupid···They make bread of the mesquite like cheese, which keeps good for a whole year. There are native melons in this country so large that a person can only carry one of them. They cut these into slices and dry them in the sun. They are good to eat, and taste like figs, and are better than dried meat.

"In this country there were also tame eagles, which the chiefs esteemed to be something fine."

FROM DE BRY'S ENGRAVING OF FLORIDA INDIANS DECLARING WAR, 1591.

CÍBOLA ~ THE ZUNI TRIBE. "Cíbola is seven villages. The houses are ordinarily three or four stories" occasionally rising to seven stories. "These people are very intelligent. They cover their privy parts and all the immodest parts with cloths made like a sort of table napkin, with fringed edges and a tassel at each corner, which they tie over their hips. They wear long robes of feathers or the skins of hares, and cotton blankets. The women wear blankets, which they tie or knot over the left shoulder, leaving the right arm out [as did the warriors to keep their bow arm free]... They wear a neat well~shaped outer garment of skin. They gather their hair over the two ears, making a frame which looks like an old fashioned headdress.

BREECHCLOTH (OR BREECH-CLOUT) FOR MODESTY

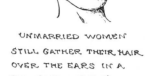

UNMARRIED WOMEN STILL GATHER THEIR HAIR OVER THE EARS IN A BUTTERFLY STYLE.

"The country is a valley between ridges resembling rocky mountains. They plant in holes. Maize does not grow high; ears from a stalk three or four to each cane, thick and large, of eight hundred grains... There are a large number of bears in this province, and lions [mountain lions], wildcats, deer and otter. There are very fine turquoises, although not so many as reported. They collect the pine nuts [the edible, nutlike seeds of the <u>Pinus edulis</u>] each year, and store them up in advance. A man does not have more than one wife.

"They do not have chiefs as in New Spain, but are ruled by a council of the oldest men. They have priests who preach to them, whom they call papas. These are the elders. They go up on the highest roof of the village and preach to the village from there, like public criers, in the morning while the sun is rising, the whole village being silent and sitting in the galleries to listen. They tell them how they are to live, and I believe that they give certain commandments for them to keep, for there is no drunkenness among them, nor sodomy nor sacrifices, neither do they eat human flesh nor steal, but they are usually at work... They make the cross as a sign of peace [many friars believed the Indians were converted to Christianity when they saw this sign of the cross!] They burn their dead, and throw the implements used in their work into the fire with the bodies [for use in the spirit world]."

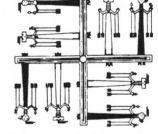

THE INDIAN SWASTIKA, WITH THE GODS OF RIVERS, MOUNTAINS AND RAINS. THE NAZI SYMBOL WAS NOT ADOPTED UNTIL 1935 AND CERTAINLY DID NOT HAVE THE INDIAN MEANING OF GOOD LUCK AND PEACE!

TUSAYAN ~ HOPI TRIBE. "Its seven villages to the north-west of Cíbola, had the same customs, dress and traditions."

ÁCOMA (ACUCO) was fifty miles east of Cíbola and perched on a mountain plateau "as high as a musket shot." The only entrance was a "stairway" of two hundred chipped grooves with one hundred narrower steps. With its stone wall at the top, the town was impregnable. Crops were grown on its top, and cisterns collected snow and rainwater (as they still do, for Ácoma is still occupied).

TIGUEX ~ PECOS TRIBE. "Tiguex is a province with twelve villages on the banks of a large, mighty river [Rio Grande]; some villages on one side and some on the other. It is a spacious valley two leagues wide, and a very high, rough, snow~covered mountain chain lies east of it [the Sandia Mountains]. There are seven villages in the ridges at the foot of this... There are seven villages seven leagues to the north, at Quirix, and seven villages of the province of Hemes are forty leagues northeast [northwest]. In general, the villages

BLACK SILVER GLAZE ON WHITE POTTERY LADLE. MESA VERDE, COLORADO (AM. MUSEUM. NATURAL HISTORY)

all have the same habits and customs… They are governed by the opinions of the elders. They all work together to build the villages, the women being engaged in making the mixture and the walls, while the men bring the wood and put it in place. They have no lime, but they make a mixture of ashes, coals, and dirt which is almost as good as mortar, for when the house is to have four stories, they do not make the walls more than half a yard thick. They make round balls of this, which they use instead of stones after they are dry, fixing them with the same mixture, which comes to be stiff clay…

"When a man wishes to marry, it has to be arranged by those who govern. The man has to spin and weave a blanket and place it before the woman, who covers herself with it and becomes his wife. The men spin and weave. The women bring up the children and prepare the food. The country is so fertile that they do not have to break up the ground the year round, but only have to sow the seed… In one year they gather enough for seven.

The villages are free from nuisances, because they go outside to excrete, and they pass their water into clay vessels, which they empty at some distance from the village. They keep separate houses where they prepare the food for eating and where they grind the meal, very clean… They take off their shoes, do up their hair, shake their clothes and cover their heads before they enter the door. A man sits at the door playing a fife as they grind, moving the stones to the music and singing together. They grind a large quantity at one time, because they make all their bread of meal soaked in warm water, like wafers… They have their preachers. Sodomy is not found among them. They do not eat human flesh nor make sacrifices of it. The people are not cruel…" Castañeda asked "the reason why the young women in that province went entirely naked, however cold it might be, and he told me that the virgins had to go around this way until they took a husband, and that they covered themselves after they had known man. The men wear little shirts of tanned deerskin, and their long robes over this. In all the provinces they have earthenware glazed with antimony [silver] and jars of extraordinary labor and workmanship, which are worth seeing."

CICUYE ~ PECOS PUEBLO, TANOAN TRIBE. "We have already said that the people of Tiguex and all the provinces on the banks are all alike, having the same ways of living and the same customs… Cicuye is a village of nearly five hundred warriors, who are feared throughout that country. It is square, situated on a rock, with a large court or yard in the middle… The houses are all alike, four stories high. One can go over the top of the whole village without there being a street to hinder. There are corridors going all around it at the first two stories, by which one can go around the whole village. These are like outside balconies, and they are able to protect themselves under these. The houses do not have doors below, but they use ladders, which can be lifted

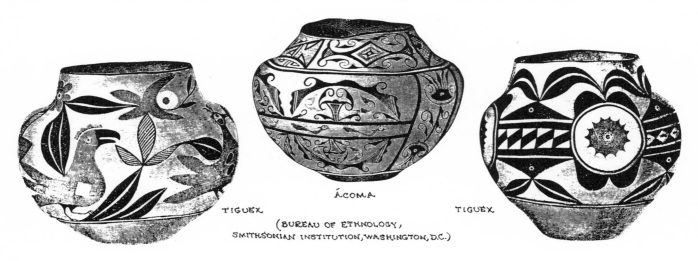

TIGUEX

ÁCOMA

TIGUEX

(BUREAU OF ETHNOLOGY,
SMITHSONIAN INSTITUTION, WASHINGTON, D.C.)

89

up like a drawbridge, and so go up to the corridors which are on the inside of the village. As the doors of the houses open on the corridor of that story, the corridor serves as a street. The village is enclosed by a low wall of stone. There is a spring of water inside, which they are able to divert. The people of this village boast that no one has been able to conquor them and that they conquor whatever villages they wish."

THE GREAT PLAINS ~ QUERECHOS AND TEYAS TRIBES. Castañeda found no villages beyond the mountains east of Cicuye. The land was flat with short grasses. The people were nomadic, and on the move hunting buffalo. "They have better figures, are better warriors, and are more feared. They travel like Arabs, with their tents and troops of dogs loaded with poles and having moorish pack- saddles with girths ··· They are kind people and not cruel. They are faith~ ful friends. They are able to make themselves very well understood by means of signs. They

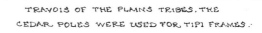

TRAVOIS OF THE PLAINS TRIBES. THE CEDAR POLES WERE USED FOR TIPI FRAMES.

dry the flesh in the sun, cutting it as thin like a leaf [the later "jerked beef" of the settlers], and when dry they grind it like meal to keep it [pemmican] and make a sort of sea-soup of it to eat. A handful thrown in a pot swells up so as to increase very much."

QUIVIRA ~ WICHITA TRIBE OF KANSAS. Coronado believed he would find the illusive treasure hoards of North America at this place. He would be nearing his goal when he saw the distinctive houses that "are round, without a wall and they have one story like a loft, under the roof, where they sleep and keep their belongings. The roofs are of straw." They would be in the prairie lands of tall grass and islets of woods, and the Indians were of the same appearance and customs as the plains people to the south.

Such were the unknown lands and the tribes that were to be discovered along Coronado's line of march. We rejoin that mighty army column as it moved northward in Mexico. Of course, Friar Marcos was along to live out his fantasies. It would be an easy trek to Cíbola, for he had said that the roads were smooth and level, and there was food and forage aplenty along the way. It was so until they came to the fertile river valley of Sonora, where the Lower Pima Indians welcomed the troops as they had Cabeza de Vaca, and more recently, Friar Marcos.

Thereafter, it was literally up hill. Beyond the Gila River was a desolate mountain country that defied entry. There were few Indians and no food to requisition, and rations were meager. Water became a luxury. The tortuous trails over the steep slopes were more than many of the horses could manage. The going was so painfully slow that Coronado went ahead with an advanced column of about one hundred mounted men. Beyond, there would be the one hundred and fifty miles of barren desert wastes that must be crossed. It was no Sunday stroll.

Finally, on July 7th, the hot and haggard horsemen had their first glimpse of Háwikuh. This was the first of the Seven Cities of Cíbola, and the pueblo where Estevan had made his last demand. They had arrived none too soon ~ there were but two bushels of corn remaining in their rations. This was no glittering city, and "such were the curses that some hurled at Friar Marcos that I pray God may protect him from them. It was a crowded village, looking as if it had been crumpled all up together." Indeed, the pueblo was a sort of adobe apartment house, one dwelling stacked on the

THIS SORRY-LOOKING BUFFALO WAS THE EARLY EUROPEAN IMPRESSION OF THE SOUTHWESTERN "COWS."

with the roof of one tier forming a porch for the dwelling above it.

The advance column rode down into the valley and drew up in divisions before the walls. When peace was offered for submission to the Spanish king and Christian conversion, the two hundred Zuñi villagers seemed unimpressed~ even defiant. The frustrated troopers yelled "Santiago!"~ the centuries~old Spanish war cry given when attacking infidels~ and galloped forward with lances aslant. After forcing the narrow, crooked corridors, the town was theirs within the hour. It was not before several conquistadors had been wounded and Coronado was knocked flat with a stone dropped from the rooftop.

Meanwhile, the main army had returned to the more hospitable surroundings of Sonora to await further orders. By the middle of October, dispatches were received to strike camp and march for Cibola. The messenger was to continue south- ward with his report to the viceroy. "Friar Marcos was going back with him, because he did not think it was safe to stay in Cibola, seeing that his report had turned out entirely false, because the kingdoms he had told about had not been found, nor the populous cities, nor the wealth of gold, nor the precious stones which he had reported, nor the fine clothes, nor the things he proclaimed from the pulpits."

Although Háwikuh had been a shock to the treasure seekers, it was but one of many in that unknown land. While waiting for the main army, Coronado planned a more peaceful conquest of the Southwest by sending Zuñi runners to their neighbors with word that the Spanish had come as friends. Once the Indians had been softened by his goodwill message, he would send out his restless men to scout the country.

One such probe reached to Tusáyan, the center of the Hopi culture. Another discovered the valley of the Colorado River and brought back reports of the breathtaking Grand Canyon. Still another came upon Ácoma, a large pueblo on the plateau of a steeply sloped mesa. This party then pushed eastward to Tiguex, where twelve pueblo towns rimmed the Río Grande. Leaving this center of Pueblo culture they pushed on to the Pecos River and the town of Cicuye. There, the glint of gold once again lit the eyes of the Spaniards, for it was there they first met "the Turk." This captive Pawnee was so named because he happened to look like one. Turk was smart enough to know these white soldiers were on no sight-seeing trip. If he played his hand well, he could lead away these treasure hunters with some convincing yarn and, at the same time, gain his freedom from the grateful villagers of Cicuye.

THE "SKY CITY" OF ÁCOMA ATOP ITS MESA FORTRESS

Turk, with an imagination that rivaled Friar Marcos, described the wondrous land of Quivira to the north. By sign language he said "that in his country there was a river in the level country, which was two leagues wide, in which there were fishes as big as horses, and large numbers of very big canoes with more than twenty rowers on a side, and that they all carried sails, and that their lord sat in the poop under awnings, and on the prow they had a great golden eagle. He also said that the lord of that country took his afternoon nap under a great tree on which were hung a great number of little gold bells, which put him to sleep as they swung in the air. He also said that every one had their ordinary dishes made of wrought plate, and the jugs and bowls were of gold."

When the story was mentioned to Coronado back in Cibola, he could hardly believe this happy turn of events~ and shouldn't have! The many pueblos of Tiguex would make ideal winter quarters for the main army that would be arriving, and those towns were on the way to Quivira, the long~sought land of gold and jewels. The general left word for the main body of troops to join him at

Tiguex, then hurried off to personally quiz the Turk about his new objective. The captive Indian was somewhat on the spot when asked for proof of his story, but the wily Turk had an answer ~ his gold bracelets had been taken from him by his captors back in Cicuye.

Up to this point, the conquest of the Southwest Indians had gone peacefully enough. But when Coronado sent soldiers to Cicuye to demand the golden bracelets, they were told that the Turk had spoken falsely! When two of the tribal leaders were put in chains for their denial, the villagers came out fighting. Clearly, the Spanish "had no respect for peace and friendship." The two were removed to Tiguex, where the people were most upset to see the neighboring elders shackled like criminals. All of the general's talk of good fellowship must have been spoken with a forked tongue. They were all the more concerned when their people were ordered out of several of the larger pueblo towns to make room for the coming army. Then, with the arrival of the snow-chilled troops in December, the Tiguex people were ordered to give up over three hundred of their blankets and cloaks. Without consulting the elders of the twelve pueblos, the Spanish went among the people removing any clothing that struck their fancy. No doubt about it ~ the conquistadors had a knack for making enemies.

The tolerance of the Indians reached a breaking point when one of the troopers spotted a comely woman in one of the pueblos. Calling out her husband to hold his horse, he went inside and attacked her. The elders were quick to bring the outrage to the attention of the general, but when the husband could only identify the horse and not its rider (perhaps because of a change of clothes), no judgment was made. The next day, the Indians of that pueblo sought revenge by driving off many of the army's horses. A brisk fight followed, and, when the villagers laid down their bows in exchange for pardon, almost one hundred warriors were taken prisoner. Thirty were burned alive at the stake, and, when the remainder made a break for freedom, they were hunted down and killed to a man. And so the Indians learned another hard lesson, and in no way could these white intruders be trusted.

December brought the main force to an uneasy Tiguex, where the growing Indian hostilities added to the harshness of winter. Many lives on both sides would be lost before the army took leave of their unwilling Tiguex hosts in April. Turk had been made chief guide and had

EXECUTION FRAME. DRAWN BY DU PRATZ, 1758 ACCOUNT OF THE NATCHEZ.

become a past master at dangling his golden carrot before the eager Spanish. He alone led the column of fifteen hundred men ~ conquistadors and Indians auxiliaries ~ on to the headwaters of the Colorado River in Texas. There they found Indians who had seen de Vaca, "incredible" numbers of buffalo, but no gold. Provisions were running low, for the Turk had cautioned not to load the horses too heavily. They might tire and be unable to carry off the great quantities of gold and silver from Quivira. But with that goal still far to the north, the general ordered most of his army to return to the Pecos River and back to Tiguex. With thirty horsemen and a few foot soldiers, he continued over the flat and featureless plains, bearing northward. They knew they were nearing Quivira when they came to the grassy vastness of the Kansas prairies. Yet there were no grand stone houses, only humble straw dwellings. The Wichita tribe, clustered near the confluence of the Arkansas and the Kansas rivers, knew nothing of any riches, there or elsewhere. The only "treasure" was a copper plate that the Wichita chief proudly wore around his neck.

By then, the Turk was in chains and in trouble. A little persuasion brought

92

the confession. In exchange for his freedom, the Turk was to lead the army of New Spain out into the plains and lose them in the nothingness. With that, the guide for the wild goose chase of the century was strangled to death.

Friendly Wichitas guided the dispirited reconnaissance party back to the Arkansas River and then along an ancient Indian trail that would be known as the Santa Fe Trail in a later day. By September, Coronado had rejoined his army at the Tiguex camp. The chilled winds of winter ended further exploration. A blow from a horse's hoof had bedded the general for several of the months that followed, and it was learned that the supply camp above Sonora had been wiped out by vengeful warriors. Further probes were out of the question. By April 1542, the dejected army returned by retracing their steps to Mexico.

SOUTHWESTERN INDIAN PETROGLYPH
OF A SPANISH HORSEMAN INVADER

Since gold was the Spanish measure of success for any such venture, Coronado was at first considered an incompetent commander. He lost his governorship and was charged with mistreatment of the Indians. He was found innocent of any wrongdoing, but the officer who had ordered the burning and massacre of the Tiguex warriors was convicted of cruelty. Before many years had passed, Coronado's reputation had rebounded. It was realized that he was a most capable military leader, able to lead a great army into the wilderness, over great distances with few casualties. His expedition proved to be the most successful exploration of North America during that century, and one day colonists would settle the southwestern lands that he had discovered.

INDIAN DRESS AND DWELLINGS SEEN ON CORONADO'S MARCH

PIMA TRIBE ~ FROM SONORA, MEXICO, TO
ARIZONA AND EASTERN CALIFORNIA.

PUEBLO INDIANS ~ NEW MEXICO AND ARIZONA.

WOMEN ① CAPE AND SHORT SKIRT OF WOVEN
WILLOW BARK ② DEERSKIN PETTICOAT.
MEN ~ BREECHCLOUT AND SANDALS.
LODGE ~ EARTH WITH FLAT TOP AND
NO SMOKE HOLE

RAWHIDE
SOLE SANDAL

WOMAN'S SHOE ~ WHITE
WITH STRIP WOUND TO KNEE

MEN'S

WOMEN ~ WOVEN COTTON BLANKET
RECTANGLE, PINNED OVER LEFT
SHOULDER. MEN ~ BREECHCLOUT
OR KILT WITH SASH.
DWELLINGS ~ PUEBLOS OF
STONE OR MUD. BOTH
MEN AND WOMEN WORE
WOVEN COTTON, RABBIT
STRIPS, AND FEATHER ROBES.

PLAINS INDIANS ~ TEXAS, OKLAHOMA, AND NORTHWARD

PRAIRIE ~ KANSAS

DRESS WAS SIMILAR ON PLAIN OR PRAIRIE

DRESS OF 2 SKINS, OPEN SIDES

MEN'S 2-SKIN SHIRT, OPEN SIDES   LEGGING

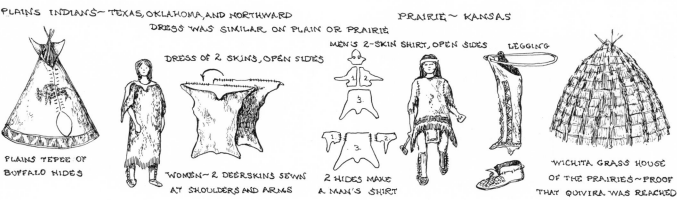

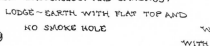

PLAINS TEPEE OF
BUFFALO HIDES

WOMEN ~ 2 DEERSKINS SEWN
AT SHOULDERS AND ARMS

2 HIDES MAKE
A MAN'S SHIRT

WICHITA GRASS HOUSE
OF THE PRAIRIES ~ PROOF
THAT QUIVIRA WAS REACHED

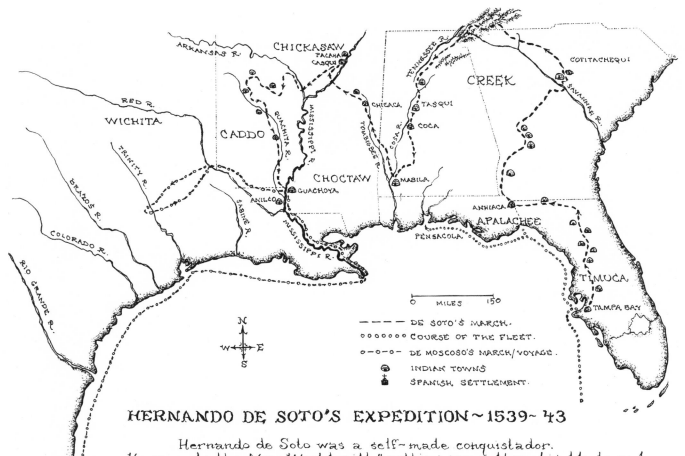

HERNANDO DE SOTO'S EXPEDITION ~ 1539 ~ 43

Hernando de Soto was a self-made conquistador.

He came to the New World with "nothing more than his blade and buckler [shield]" and captained a troop of horsemen during the subjugation of Peru in 1531. Returning to Spain a well-heeled hero, he was granted the governorship of both Cuba and Florida six years later.

All lands north of the Mexican border were his to exploit, and ambitious de Soto meant to find the storied treasures of North America that would out-glitter those of the Pizarro and Cortez expeditions. He had met with Cabeza de Vaca, the one man who knew something of the interior of the new continent, and had mulled over the Indian rumors of their seven fabulously rich cities. Certainly de Vaca would have made an ideal guide, but all inducements were declined.

No matter ~ for once de Soto had locked in on an objective, neither hell nor high water could stand in his way. He handpicked his army of eager treasure hunters and, with all the pomp and circumstance befitting his new station in life, landed at Tampa Bay on May 25, 1539. The army was impressive by any standards ~ six hundred soldiers encased in their armor and carrying the latest weapons,* over one hundred servants and slaves, two hundred horses, and even three hundred pigs for meat on the hoof. All that was lacking was a knowledge-able wilderness guide, and the local Indians had seen to that by making them-selves scarce. Unexpectedly, fortune smiled on the invaders in the person of one Juan Ortiz. Sunburned and with native tatoos on his arms, he looked every inch an Indian and was very nearly run through with a horseman's lance. As a survivor of the ill-fated Narváez expedition, he had spent twelve years as a slave to the Timuca Indians. The reclaimed Spaniard knew the language, the customs, and the country. The army had its translator and guide.

The general plan was to march north and westward in search of Indian

* ONE WAS "THE GENTLEMAN OF ELVAS," AND WE ARE INDEBTED TO HIM FOR HIS EYEWITNESS ACCOUNTS.

"PUBLIC GRANARY" OF THE FLORIDA INDIANS. FROM JACQUES LE MOYNE, 1564.

plunder. The corn-rich Apalachee region seemed the best suited for a base camp, and, on August 1st, the long and mighty column started northward. The going was painfully slow, for the country was "low, very wet, pondy, and thickly covered with trees." For a month and a half the troops struggled and grumbled their way, building many bridges and swatting mosquitoes.

The main town of Anhiara, at the present site of Tallahassee, was taken without difficulty. De Soto had planned a formula of conquest that could manipulate the natives at will. First, he would seize the local chieftain as a hostage, force him to turn over any housing and provisions that the army might need, and to deliver up women as prostitutes and men as burden carriers for the trek to the next village. Any who dared take up arms against the Spanish or attempt an escape would be hunted down and either killed or clapped in chains as slaves. To prevent too cumbersome a march, the chief, his baggage carriers, and women were usually released when the next town was at hand.

Cold weather was approaching, and the army became the unwelcomed guests of Anhiara for the winter. They dined on the plentiful Indian stores of corn, beans, pumpkins, and dried persimmons. The commander sent out a mounted party to search out a decent harbor to the south ~ one with enough depth for his ships to anchor. Pensacola Bay was chosen and dispatches sent back to Tampa Bay. The fleet was to bring supplies from Cuba for the coming spring offensive. Meanwhile, Ortiz had learned from the Indians that a very wealthy Creek tribe to the north was ruled by a queen. Probably there they would find the gold that they valued so highly. The goal seemed reasonable, particularly since the displaced villagers were becoming worrisome with attacks and ambushes. One warrior managed to set fire to much of the town in the dead of winter, much to the soldiers' distress.

The Spaniards took their leave in March 1540 to begin the treasure hunt to the north. Because most of the captured slaves had died in their chains during the harsh winter, the foot and mounted troops were ladened with the load of provisions until Indian carriers could be taken along the way. Still, the going was easier in this pleasant country of low lands, ponds, and pine trees. An Indian boy, a subject of the Creek Indian queen, was captured. When the distance to her town was farther than he had indicated, food supplies became a problem. Had he not been useful for translating his tribal language, he surely would have been thrown to the dogs (perhaps the New World version of a Spanish bull fight). At last they were in view of the village

FROM AN ENGRAVING BY DE BRY AFTER LE MOYNE, LE CHALLEUX'S NARRATIVE OF 1591.

of Cofitachequi across the Savannah River. The greetings from the queen were warm and friendly. "She came out of the town, seated in a chair, which the principal men having born to the bank, she entered a canoe. Over the stern was spread an awning, and in the bottom lay extended a mat where were two cushions, one above the other, upon which she sate, and she was accompanied by her chief men, in other canoes, with Indians."

Approaching the opposite bank, she removed a heavy string of pearls and placed them about de Soto's neck with "many gracious words of friendship and courtesy." There was no mistaking the ripple of excitement that ran through the treasure-hungry ranks. Noting this, the queen told the "son of the Sun" god of a nearby village that had been ravaged by illness. There the newcomers would find many such decorations. After being ferried across the river in canoes and after feasting on a banquet of turkey, the Spanish searched out the cache of pearls. There they found three hundred and fifty pounds of the glossy spheres that included "figures of babies and birds made of them."

As gods, the Spanish were entertained royally, and their wishes were made known by the captive boy translator and Ortiz. Perhaps the young Indian was so impressed by his status that he asked to be baptized into the religion of these exalted newcomers. It "was done, he receiving the name Pedro, and the Governor commanded the chain to be struck off that he had carried until then."

This country of the Creeks was so likable that many in the ranks wished to remain and establish a Spanish colony at Cofitachequi. Single-minded de Soto would entertain no such dallying. On May 3rd, the troops were again in the saddle and off for even greener - or golden - fields beyond. In spite of the queen's kindnesses and "outrages committed on the inhabitants," she was taken along on foot as a hostage. She had been forced to provide Indian baggage carriers, but had been permitted to have her women servants carry along her box of unbored pearls. (The Indian craftsmen heated pearls for easier boring and stringing, thereby destroying much of their luster and value to the Spaniards.) In due course, de Soto planned to relieve the queen of her burden - his first really worthwhile American treasure.

The long column followed the rumors of gold into a sorry country with a desert and then the Appalachean Mountain barrier to cross. It was in that rugged terrain that the captive queen excused herself for the moment and, with her women and the box of pearls, disappeared into a thicket. That was the last that was seen of her and the considerable treasure. Empty-handed, de Soto turned southwestward and out of the mountains.

At each village in their path, the same scenario took place. The welcoming chief became a hostage, the fearsome charge of the horsemen snuffed out any resistance, and the army appropriated food and clothing as well as a new line of chained slaves to shoulder the army's baggage.

Marching by the banks of the Cosa River, they reached Tastaluca - and a change in fortunes. There, ruled a chief who did not take kindly to invaders, be one the "son of the Sun" god or whoever. He was "tall of person, muscular, lean, and symmetrical." As with the previous chieftains, he

DE SOTO'S ARMY ON THE MARCH IN SEARCH OF NORTH AMERICAN RICHES LOOKED MUCH LIKE THAT OF THIS 16th-CENTURY INDIAN PAINTING OF CORTEZ. (BIBLIOTHÈQUE NATIONALE.)

welcomed de Soto, but added that "you shall learn how strong and positive is my will, and how disinterested my inclination to serve you." Still, de Soto had the might of a great army of men and horses to make his own will absolute. The chief was, of course, taken hostage and marched through his considerable territory to his town of Mabila (Mobile, Alabama). On the pretext that he wished to have all in readiness for the coming of the invaders, he sent a message that all the warriors should gather at that place to do battle.

SPANISH CAVALRY CHARGE, FROM A SECTION
OF A DE BRYS ENGRAVING.

On October 18, 1540, an advance guard reported that Mabila seemed to be heavily occupied, with many under arms and the stockade recently strengthened. Shortly after, de Soto rode into the fortified village with the captured chief surrounded by seven or eight guards and forty cavalry. During the council, the chief rose and disappeared into one of the houses where some of his warriors waited. At a signal, the general and his escort became targets for the Indian arrows. All were wounded and five were killed outright. Somehow the survivors managed to escape the stockade, but the villagers were hard on their heels. The burden carriers, waiting with packs just outside the enclosure, were freed of their chains and given bows and arrows. The bulk of the army's supplies were brought within the stockade before the main body of troops could come up for the attack.

The outcome of the battle was very much in doubt until the Spanish were able to set the entire town afire. Although the chief escaped, it was reported that two thousand five hundred of his people perished that day from flame and sword. Eighteen soldiers also died and one hundred and fifty were badly wounded. All of their spare provisions, clothing, and weapons had been lost to their own torches.

If ever there was a time to call the treasure hunt a failure and lick their wounds in the safety of Cuba, this was it. Indian runners had just reached Juan Ortiz with word that the fleet was waiting for them just six days away at Pensacola Bay. The word never reached the dispirited troops. De Soto had sworn his translator to secrecy. In no way would he consider returning home a failure, a penniless has-been with his reputation lost in the North American wilderness.

Since the general's military might had landed at Florida, one hundred and two soldiers had been lost to Indian arrows and sickness. After a month of recuperation, the column was once again on the move to the north between the Tombigbee and the Alabama rivers near modern Montgomery. Although the army's imposing array of arms and armor was rusting, and the men were making do with makeshift Indian clothing, they were no less of a fighting force. They moved into the lands of the Chickasaws and appropriated the village of Chicaca for the coming winter months of 1540~41. Raids into the countryside brought in food and furs to see the cold weather, and there was the added delicacy of pork from the pigs that had actually multiplied over the past year. The natives, too, were intrigued by the strange porkers. When three tribesmen were caught making off with several, two were shot on the spot, and a third had his hands chopped off as a warning that only the Spanish could steal provisions. This, and a demand for two hundred burden carriers for the spring march, brought on the wrath of the Chickasaw chieftain.

His warriors attacked in strength, torching the houses where the troops slept. When the smoke had cleared some twelve soldiers had met their maker, fifty horses had been slain, and any remaining food and equipment for the spring offensive were lost once again to the flames. A follow-up Indian attack would have ended de Soto's hopes, then and there. Although no candidate for a Humanitarian-of-the-Year award, the general could claim an iron will and a determination to have a successful expedition. In just eight days, he had lances and saddles carved from ash trees, a forge set up to retemper the heat-damaged swords, and for those soldiers who were naked as jaybirds, sortees into the neighborhood for clothing and food. By April 25, 1540, the ragtag army was off on another adventure to the West ~ perhaps those Seven Cities of gold that would make all their troubles worthwhile.

Moving deeper into Chickasaw territory, each village received the "son of the Sun" with tributes ~ the usual food, clothing, women, and pack carriers. Objectors would soon know the speed, power, and slashing hooves of the horses and the chains that began their life of slavery. By the middle of May, the army had reached the banks of the Mississippi River. It took twenty days to build four barges, and after repeated crossings had landed all safely in eastern Arkansas. There they wallowed waist-deep "in the worst trail for swamps and water that they had found in all Florida [North America]." But there were those persistent rumors of gold ahead, and a warm welcome awaited them at the town of Casqui.

Intertribal wars were usual and frequent, and not without the Indians' own brand of torture and death for captives. At that time the town of Pacaha, a day's march away, was at odds with Casqui. De Soto, although he needed no excuse for plundering, raided that village near the mouth of the St. Francis River. He returned with the chief, a good many prisoners, and many skins and shawls that his men could use to make jerkins, shirts, stockings, shoes, and cloaks. Then, in the rare role of peacemaker, he brought the two chiefs together as friends. The Casqui chief expressed his gratitude by giving the general his daughter. Not to be outdone, the Pacaha leader gave up his two sisters. "They were symmetrical, tall and full." One "bore a pleasant expression; in her manners and features appeared the lady; the other was robust."

Still, gold was de Soto's passion, and he meant to return to Spain as a wealthy conqueror. Again moving westward, the troops had their first view of the Great Prairies where the Plains

DE SOTO'S CRUELTIES IN FLORIDA, T. DE BRY, _AMERICA_, PART V, 1595. TO THE SPANISH, "FLORIDA" WAS THAT VAGUE LAND NORTH OF THE GULF OF MEXICO.

PLAINS INDIANS
"SKULL CRACKERS."

Indians were roaming in search of the buffalo. A scouting party penetrated to the Ocalusa region along the Arkansas River ~ probably near Ford, Kansas. They were no farther than three hundred miles from Coronado's Quivira, but there was no hint of treasure thereabouts. De Soto considered a push to the Pacific Ocean that must be somewhere beyond, but it was clear that his expedition was becoming aimless and exhausted in the American wilderness. When interpreter Juan Ortiz died during the winter encampment of 1541-1542, the army lost its voice and hearing.

Although the Mississippi River country around Guachoya had all the food and clothing they could want, the natives were becoming openly hostile. The general, now on his sick bed, decided that a show of force would put to rest any thoughts of Indian revenge. Nilco, a nearby village of six thousand souls, was to be made the example. At dawn the troopers struck the unsuspecting natives, under orders that no man be spared from the lance and sword. One hundred unprepared braves were slaughtered and many more badly wounded ~ living examples that the will of the Spanish was all powerful. The Gentleman of Elvas, usually mildly matter-of-fact when his narrative concerned Spanish atrocities, flared up when he wrote that "some persons were so cruel and butcherlike that they killed all before them, young and old, not one having resisted little nor much." Eighty women and children were taken into slavery that day.

On May 21, 1542, de Soto's reign of terror ended when he succumbed to his illness. Luis de Moscoso assumed command. His was the problem of leading the the remnants of the army back to civilization. A westward march to the Spanish settlements on the Gulf of Mexico proved an exercise in futility. As de Vaca had found years before, the lands beyond the Trinity River were poverty-ridden. Before starvation beset them, the troops doubled back to the Mississippi River. Seven vessels were built on its banks, and, on July 2, 1543, they cast off, leaving six hundred Indian prisoners behind. There was room enough for one hundred others, who would be sold as slaves ~ hardly the great wealth that the conquistadors had expected at the outset. Indian attacks grew in intensity along the waterway, but at last the ships reached the Gulf of Mexico.

For nearly two months, the cranky craft bucked contrary winds and currents. On September 10th, the three hundred and eleven Spanish survivors finally reached the port of Pánuco. Dressed in their black make-do deerskin clothing, "all went directly to church, to pray and return thanks for their miraculous preservation." They were fortunate that the walls of that place of worship did not come tumbling down about their heads, for behind they had left a trail of some four thousand dead North American Indians and had inflicted countless demands, hardships and depravities upon the living.

POCKET SUNDIAL/ COMPASS
FROM TREASURE GALLEON
SANTA MARGARITA. SUNK IN 1622.

The expeditions of Narváez, Coronado, and de Soto were regarded as expensive failures, and any thoughts of another major exploration and colonization effort by the Spanish were placed on the back burner. As for Hernando de Soto, the contemporary historian Oviedo made a comment that would fit nicely on his gravestone. He "was very fond of this sport of killing Indians."

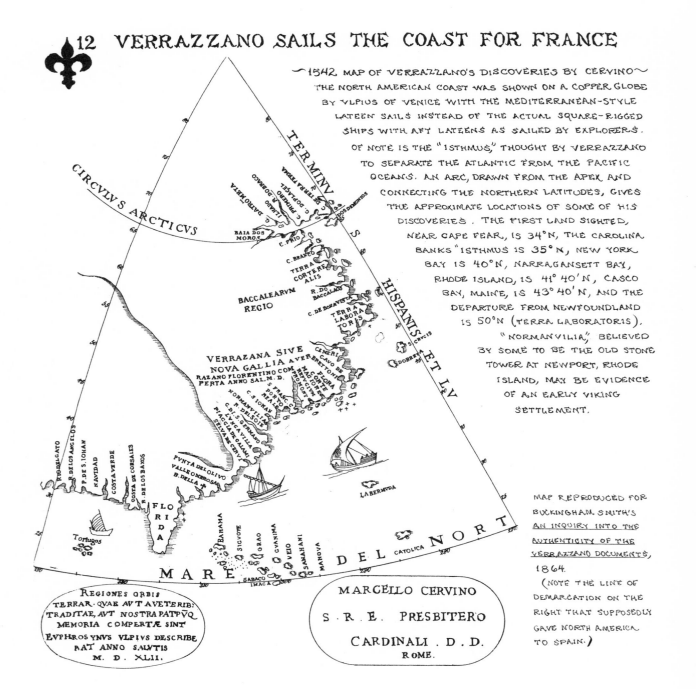

~1542 MAP OF VERRAZZANO'S DISCOVERIES BY CERVINO~ THE NORTH AMERICAN COAST WAS SHOWN ON A COPPER GLOBE BY VLPIUS OF VENICE WITH THE MEDITERRANEAN-STYLE LATEEN SAILS INSTEAD OF THE ACTUAL SQUARE-RIGGED SHIPS WITH AFT LATEENS AS SAILED BY EXPLORERS. OF NOTE IS THE "ISTHMUS," THOUGHT BY VERRAZZANO TO SEPARATE THE ATLANTIC FROM THE PACIFIC OCEANS. AN ARC, DRAWN FROM THE APEX AND CONNECTING THE NORTHERN LATITUDES, GIVES THE APPROXIMATE LOCATIONS OF SOME OF HIS DISCOVERIES. THE FIRST LAND SIGHTED, NEAR CAPE FEAR, IS 34°N, THE CAROLINA BANKS "ISTHMUS IS 35°N, NEW YORK BAY IS 40°N, NARRAGANSETT BAY, RHODE ISLAND, IS 41° 40'N, CASCO BAY, MAINE, IS 43° 40'N, AND THE DEPARTURE FROM NEWFOUNDLAND IS 50°N (TERRA LABORATORIS), "NORMANVILIA," BELIEVED BY SOME TO BE THE OLD STONE TOWER AT NEWPORT, RHODE ISLAND, MAY BE EVIDENCE OF AN EARLY VIKING SETTLEMENT.

MAP REPRODUCED FOR BUCKINGHAM SMITH'S AN INQUIRY INTO THE AUTHENTICITY OF THE VERRAZZANO DOCUMENTS, 1864. (NOTE THE LINE OF DEMARCATION ON THE RIGHT THAT SUPPOSEDLY GAVE NORTH AMERICA TO SPAIN.)

From the Italian Renaissance had come the Who's Who of Early Explorers ~ Christopher Columbus for Spain, Amerigo Vespucci for Portugal, and John Cabot sailing for England. There followed another remarkable navigator, Geovanni da Verrazzano, who would set sail under the flag of France. That country, beset by wars with Spain and a dwindling treasury, had been hard-pressed to seek her fortune beyond the Atlantic Ocean. During the years 1521~23, Verrazzano had made a name for himself by capturing several Spanish treasure galleons sailing by way of the Azores. One, homeward bound from Cortes' conquest of Mexico, contained the royalties and jewels of such Indian rulers as Moctezuma and Quauhtemóc. King Francis I liked what he saw. It was time for France to move out of the exploratory backwaters and seek her share of western riches. Verrazzano was the man for the job.

The dream of finding a passage through North America to the Orient was alive and well. Magellan had sailed around the tip of South America but the route proved to be long and hazardous. Spanish explorations had shown no break in the landmass northward to and including Florida. Cabot had found no promising passages around Newfoundland and Nova Scotia. But somewhere between there might be just such a waterway directly to the Far East spices, silks, and jewels for France. As Verrazzano wrote, "My intention was to reach by this navigation to Cathay [China], in the extreme east of Asia expecting to meet with new land such as was found as an obstacle, but I had reason to suppose that it was not hopeless to penetrate to the eastern ocean."

In the summer of 1523, he cast off with four ships and sailed into disaster. An Atlantic storm sent two of the vessels to the bottom. Those still afloat managed to limp back to port at Brittany. But one ship was seaworthy after repairs ~ a caravel of about one hundred tons, the La Dauphine.

By the middle of January 1524, the explorers were coasting the Madeiras, then turned parallel to Columbus' westward route. Driven off course by a hurricane, they made their first landfall at 34°N latitude. A haze of smoke topped the shoreline in the vicinity of Cape Fear, North Carolina. The Indians

GIOVANNI DA VERRAZZANO, DRAWN BY G. ZOCCHI AND ENGRAVED BY F. ALLEGRINI, 1767

were harvesting and smoking the summer catch of fish and shellfish. La Dauphine headed south to about 32°N in search of a harbor, but found none. Beyond was Spanish Florida where Ponce de León had been fatally wounded by an arrow three years earlier. Those waters would be alive with treasure galleons under convoy, and this was no time to be sighted by France's old enemy.

Returning to the first landfall, La Dauphine was anchored offshore. The crew had their first brief glimpse of the friendly Tuscarora natives. In his later letter to King Francis I, Verrazzano described what he saw there as well as later impressions. His was a refreshing view of North America, and his words are filled with wonder and admiration for the Indians he met and the new lands where they lived.

"They go entirely naked, except that about the loins they wear skins of small animals like martens fastened by a girdle of plaited grass, to which they tie, all round the body, the tails of other animals hanging down to the knees; all other parts of the body and the head are naked. Some wear garlands similar to birds' feathers.

"The complexion of these people is black, not much different from that of the Ethiopians; their hair is black and thick, and not very long, it is worn tied back of the head in the form of a little tail. In person they are of good proportions, of middle stature, a little above our own, broad across the breast, strong in the arms, and well formed in the legs and other parts of the body; the only exception to their good looks is that they have

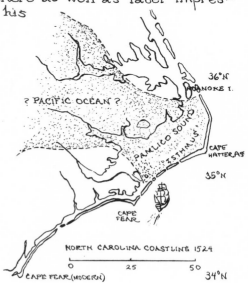

NORTH CAROLINA COASTLINE 1524

0   25   50

CAPE FEAR (MODERN)

36°N
ROANOKE I.
? PACIFIC OCEAN ?
PAMLICO SOUND
ISTHMUS
CAPE HATTERAS
35°N
CAPE FEAR
34°N

broad faces, but not all, however, as we saw many that had sharp ones, with large black eyes and a fixed expression. They are not very strong in body, but acute in mind, active and swift of foot, as far as we could judge by observation."

Sailing northward, the explorers made their first major discovery on March 25th at about 35°N latitude. "We found there an isthmus one mile wide and about two hundred miles long, in which we could see the eastern sea from the ship, half way between west and north. This is, doubtless, the one which goes round the tip of India, China and Cathay." Verrazzano thought he had found a thin sand barrier that separated the Atlantic from the Pacific Ocean. If so, North America would be pinched at its middle with a watery girdle — an isthmus with far less width than found in Panama. Since he didn't wish to chance the safety of his ship and crew by sailing through one of the occasional sand barrier openings, his observations were made from the crow's nest. Since land could not be seen beyond, the assumption had some merit. Sending boats into that sea would have been revealing, for not until Coronado's southwestern probe in 1540 and de Soto's march of 1539 was there any inkling that the land mass was exceedingly broad.

A WARRIOR~ AS SHOWN ON CAPTAIN JOHN SMITH'S "MAP OF VIRGINIA," ENGRAVED BY WILLIAM HOLE IN 1612.

The explorers continued along the Carolina Banks, "about fifteen feet thick, rising in the form of little hills about fifty paces broad" that imprisoned Pamico Sound. This assumed entrance to the Pacific Ocean seemed to end when "an outstretched country appeared at a little distance rising somewhat above the sandy shore in beautiful fields and broad plains, covered with immense forests of trees, more or less dense, too various in colors, and too delightful and charming to be described." Palms, laurels, and cypresses "and other varieties unknown in Europe... sent forth the sweetest fragrance to a great distance." Probably they were sailing by the shoals fronting Roanoke Island. Intrigued by such glowing descriptions, the English would attempt their first settlement there sixty-one years later.

"We sailed from this place, continuing to coast along the shore, which we found stretching out to the west; the inhabitants being numerous, we saw everywhere a multitude of fires. While at anchor on this coast, there being no harbor to enter, we sent the boat on shore with twenty-five men to obtain water, but it was not possible to land without endangering the boat, on account of the immense high surf thrown up by the sea, as it was an open roadstead. Many of the natives came to the beach, indicating that we might trust ourselves on shore. One of their noble deeds of friendship deserves to be known to your Majesty. A young sailor was attempting to swim ashore through the surf to carry them some knick-knack, as little bells, looking-glasses and other like trifles. When he came

A MODEST VIRGINIAN MAIDEN COVERS HER BREASTS.   (WHITE AND DE BRY, 1590)

near three or four of them he tossed the things to them, and turned about to get back to the boat, but he was thrown over by the waves, and so dashed by them that he lay as if he were dead upon the beach. When these people saw him in this situation, they ran and took him up by the head, legs and arms, and carried him to a distance from the surf; the young man, finding himself borne off in this way, uttered very loud shrieks of fear and dismay, while they answered as they could in their language, showing him that he had no cause for fear. Afterwards they laid him down at the foot of a little hill, when they took off his shirt and trousers, and examined him, expressing the greatest astonishment at the whiteness of his skin. Our sailors in the boat, seeing a great fire made up, and their companion placed very near it, full of fear, as is usual in all cases of novelty, imagined that the natives were about to roast him for food. But as soon as he had recovered his strength after a short stay with them, showing by signs that he wished to return aboard, they hugged him with great affection, and accompanied him to the shore, then leaving him that he might feel more secure, they withdrew to a little hill, from which they watched him until he was safe in the boat."

About midway up the Virginia shoreline to New Jersey, the explorers anchored by another land "which appeared very beautiful and full of the largest forests." A landing party of twenty men "found that the people had fled and hid themselves in the woods for fear. By searching around we discovered in the grass a very old woman and a young girl of about eighteen or twenty, who had concealed themselves for the same reason; the old woman carried two infants on her shoulders, and behind her neck a little boy eight years of age; when we came up to them they began to shriek and make signs to the men who had fled to the woods. We gave them part of our provisions, which they accepted with delight, but the girl would not touch any; every thing we offered to her being thrown down in great anger. We took the little boy from the old woman to carry with us to France, and would have taken the girl also, who was very beautiful and very tall, but it was impossible because of the loud shrieks she uttered as we attempted to lead her away; having to pass some woods, and being far from the ship, we determined to leave her and take the boy only. We found them fairer than the others, and wearing a covering made of certain plants, which hung down from the branches of the trees [Spanish moss], tying them together with threads of wild hemp, their heads are without covering and are the same shape as the others."

It has been mentioned that the French explorers often brought back natives as a living example of their discoveries, and that they were generally returned to their tribal grounds. By contrast, any Indian brought aboard a ship flying the Portuguese or Spanish flag could count on a one-way trip into slavery. In this case, it was clear that a woman's screams make an effective first line of defense, and an attempted kidnapping would call for the best of ear splitters.

"In Arcadia," for this was the idealistic name given by Verrazzano for the beautiful countryside and its simple and virtuous inhabitants, "we found a man who came to the shore to see what we were... He was handsome, naked, his

* THE SOUTHEASTERN ALGONQUIN WOMEN WERE ENGRAVED BY DE BRY FROM ARTIST JOHN WHITE'S PAINTINGS IN VIRGINIA, 1585~1587.

103

hair fastened in a knot, and of an olive color." He approached the landing party, holding out "a burning stick, as if to offer us fire." Since the French had never seen a peace pipe in action, they considered this a hostile act and fired a blank musket charge as a warning. The poor fellow "trembled all over with fright" and "remained as if thunderstruck, and, like a friar, pointed a finger at sky, ship and sea as if he were invoking a blessing on us."

As elsewhere along the coast, Verrazzano was very much taken with the scenery. In the Arcadia region there was a profusion of grapes, "sweet and pleasant." The southern Algonquins also thought so, for they removed any competing vegetation for better ripening. "We found also wild roses, violets, lilies, and many sorts of plants and fragrant flowers different from our own." Little wonder the explorers lingered three days despite their lack of a good harbor anchorage. During that time "we saw many of their boats made of one tree twenty feet long and four feet broad, without the aid of stone or iron or other kind of metal. To hollow out their boats they burn out as much of a log as is requisite, and also from the prow any stern to make them float well on the sea." (When the English artist, John White, made sketches of the Indian life around the ill-fated Roanoke Colony sixty-three years later, he was fascinated by the skill needed to level a tree and craft it into a dugout canoe. His illustration may be seen on a later page)

ENLARGED IMPRESSION OF THE SOUTHERN LANDS, ENGRAVED BY DE BRY FROM *AMERICA*, 1591

Although still on his search for a northwest passage, Verrazzano made no mention of two likely candidates ~ the Chesapeake and Delaware bays. He may have been concerned with running aground on the string of sandy shoals that guard the Chesapeake, and then too far at sea to appreciate the broad Delaware Bay entrance. But an easy cruise northward would bring the ship to the second major discovery. At 40°N latitude, the La Dauphine entered the Narrows leading to New York Bay. Perhaps rediscovery would be a better choice of words, for many believe that this was the site of the aborted Viking colony of Hóp, or Tidal Lake, five centuries earlier.

The letter to King Charles I leaves no doubt about the location. "After proceeding one hundred leagues, we found a very pleasant situation among some steep hills, through which a very large river, deep at its mouth, forced its way to the sea; from the sea to the estuary of the river, any ship heavily laden might pass, with the help of the tide, which rises eight feet. But as we were riding at anchor in a good berth, we would not venture up in our vessel, without a knowledge of the mouth; therefore, we took the boat, and entering the river, we found the country on its banks well peopled, the inhabitants not differing much from the others, being dressed out with feathers of birds of various colours. They came toward us with evident delight, raising loud shouts of admiration, and showing us where we could most securely land

VERRAZZANO'S COASTAL DISCOVERIES

NARROWS
NEW YORK
LONG I.
40°N

DELAWARE BAY

38°N

CHESAPEAKE BAY

"ARCADIA"
(NORFOLK)

ROANOKE I.

34°N

0   MILES   200

104

with our boat. We passed up this river, about half a league, when we found it formed the most beautiful lake three leagues in circuit, upon which there were rowing [paddling] thirty or more of their small boats, from one shore to the other, filled with multitudes who came to see us." Little more could be learned about these Algonquin peoples, for a "violent contrary wind blew in from the sea," forcing a return to the ship that was anchored in the Narrows. With regrets for leaving that "commodious and delightful region," La Dauphine made for the safety of the open sea. The course was set for coasting Long Island towards the east.

Beyond was a triangular island that Verrazzano likened to the Island of Rhodes. Roger Williams liked the name well enough to call Aquidneck Island in Narragansett Bay "Rhod~Island in 1644. By 1663, the state's founder had expanded the name to include the entire colony.

At 41° 40' N latitude, the explorers chanced upon their third and most enjoyable discovery. The entrance to Narragansett Bay was inviting, and just off the later city of Newport a safe harbor anchorage was found for the first time during the voyage. They also sailed future historians into an intriguing mystery, for no mention was made in the narrative of just why the Newport area was called "Normanvilia." Yet the contemporary maps all record this descriptive name at the proper celestial sighting for Aquidneck Island.

ALTHOUGH THIS ENGRAVING BY DE BRY WAS TAKEN FROM THE LE MOYNE PAINTING OF THE 1564 FRENCH LANDING IN FLORIDA, THE SHIP AND SMALL-BOAT LANDINGS ARE SIMILAR TO THOSE MADE AT NARRAGANSETT BAY.

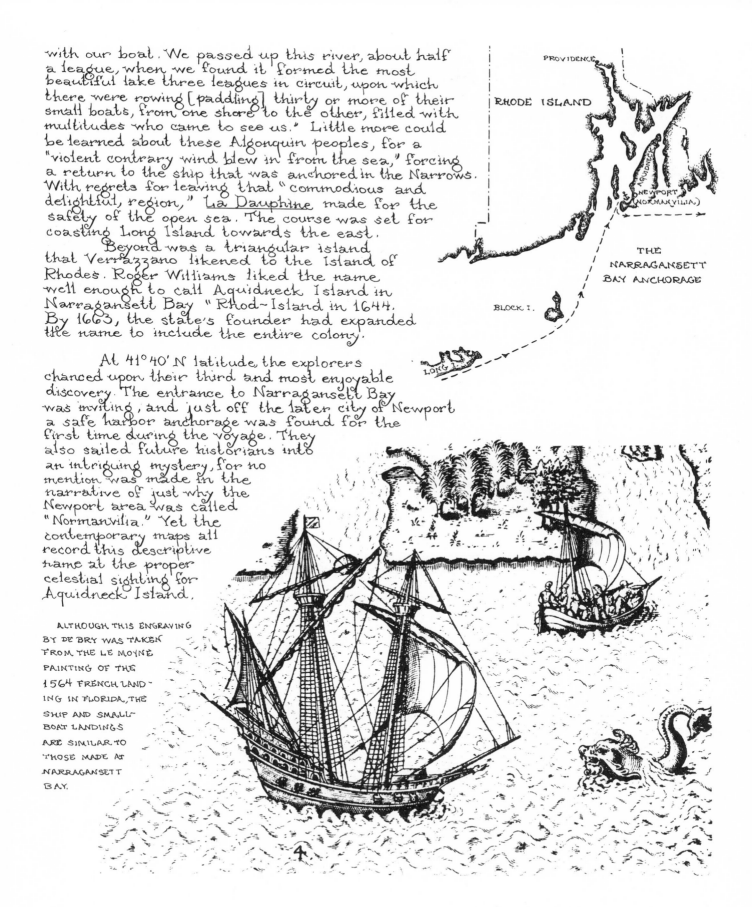

PROVIDENCE

RHODE ISLAND

AQUIDNECK

NEWPORT (NORMANVILIA)

THE NARRAGANSETT BAY ANCHORAGE

BLOCK I.

LONG I.

There remains the question of a Viking colony at Newport and its landmark of the Norman-style stone villa or tower. That ancient stone structure has weathered the centuries, silent and unperturbed by the controversy that still swirls around it.

There are, in addition, broad hints in the following narrative that other Europeans had preceded the La Dauphine to Narragansett Bay. Charles Willoughby, in his Antiquities Of The New England Indians, refers to the wrought copper plates mentioned by Verrazzano. "This copper must have been obtained from previous explorers of whom we have no definite account; for although an occasional implement and a few beads wrought from native copper have been found, nothing in the way of metal plates has been recovered in New England which was not made of European copper or brass. Many objects of those foreign metals have been taken from graves belonging to the sixteenth century…" One of the Wampanoag chiefs wore, according to Verrazzano, "a large chain ornamented with many stones of different colors," and there were other tribespeople who wore ear dangles of wrought copper.

The explorer for France also pointed out that "they are of very fair complexion, some of them inclined more to a white…" and later mentioned the Wampanoag precaution of keeping their women well out of the reach of the sailors. A 1578 letter from one Anthonie Parkhurst to historian Richard Hakluyt tells of some four hundred fishing vessels from various European nations working the vicinity of Newfoundland and Cape Breton. Willoughby goes on to say that "the New England coast was doubtless within this 600 mile area, and there seems to be no reasonable doubt that it was visited by many of these ships and that there was considerable intercourse between these vessels and the natives."

Keeping in mind such repeated contacts between the Old and the New World well before the 1524 visit by Verrazzano, we return to his detailed account of Narragansett Bay and its natives. There, "we found a very excellent harbour. Before entering it, we saw about twenty small boats full of people, who came about our ship, uttering many cries of astonishment, but they would not approach nearer than within fifty paces; stopping, they looked at the structure of our ship, our persons and dress, afterwards they all raised a loud shout together, signifying that they were pleased. By imitating their signs, we inspired them in some measure with confidence, so that they came near enough for us to toss to them some little bells and glasses, and

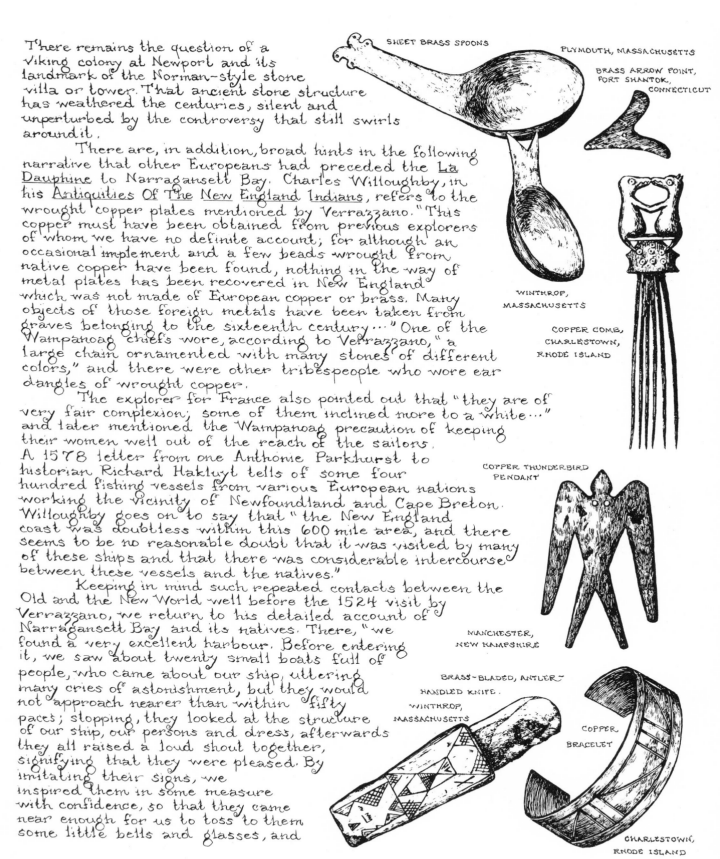

SHEET BRASS SPOONS
PLYMOUTH, MASSACHUSETTS

BRASS ARROW POINT, FORT SHANTOK, CONNECTICUT

WINTHROP, MASSACHUSETTS

COPPER COMB, CHARLESTOWN, RHODE ISLAND

COPPER THUNDERBIRD PENDANT

MANCHESTER, NEW HAMPSHIRE

BRASS-BLADED, ANTLER-HANDLED KNIFE.
WINTHROP, MASSACHUSETTS

COPPER BRACELET

CHARLESTOWN, RHODE ISLAND

TRADE METALS CRAFTED BY THE ALGONQUINS. (WILBUR, THE NEW ENGLAND INDIANS)

106

many toys [trinkets], which they took
and looked at, laughing, and then
came aboard without fear. Among them

were two kings more beautiful in form and stature than
can possibly be described; one was about forty years
old, the other about twenty~four, and they were dressed
in the following manner. The oldest had a deer's skin
around his body, artificially wrought in damask figures, his
head was without covering, his hair was tied back in various
knots; around his neck he wore a large chain ornamented
with many stones of different colours. The young man was similar
in his general appearance. This is the finest looking tribe, and the handsomest
in their costumes, that we have found in our voyage. They exceed us in size,
and they are of a very fair complexion; some of them incline more to a white, and
others to a tawny color; their faces are sharp, their hair long and black, upon the
adorning of which they bestow great pains; their eyes are black and sharp, their
expression mild and pleasant, greatly resembling the antique. I say nothing to your
Majesty of the other parts of the body, which are all in good proportion, and
such as belong to well~formed men. Their women are of the
same form and beauty, very graceful, of fine counte~
nances and pleasing appearances in manners and
modesty; they wear no clothing except a deer
skin, ornamented like those worn by the men; some
wear very rich lynx [bobcat] skins upon their
arms, and various ornaments upon their heads,
composed of braids of hair, which also hang down
upon their breasts on each side. Others wear
different ornaments such as the women of Egypt
and Syria use. The older and the married people,
both men and women, wear many ornaments in their
ears, hanging down in the oriental manner. We saw
upon them several pieces of wrought copper, which
is more esteemed by them than gold, as this is not
valued on account of its color, but is considered by
them as the most ordinary of the metals ~ yellow
being the colour especially disliked by them, azure
[sky blue] and red are those in highest estimation
with them. Of those things which we gave them,
they prized most highly the bells, azure crystals, and
other toys to hang in their ears and about their
necks; they do not value or care to have silk or gold
stuffs, or other kinds of cloth, nor implements of steel
or iron. When we showed them our arms, they
expressed no admiration, and only asked how
they were made; the same was the case with the
looking glasses, which they returned to us, smiling, as soon as
they had looked at them. They are very generous, giving away
whatever they have. We formed a great friendship with them, and one day we
entered into the port with our ship, having before rode at the distance of a league
from the shore, as the weather was adverse. They came off to the ship with a
number of their little boats, with their faces painted divers colours, showing us
real signs of joy, bringing us their provisions and signifying to us where we could
best ride in safety with our ship, and keeping with us until we had cast anchor.
We remained among them fifteen days, to provide ourselves with many things of
which we were in want, during which time they came every day to see our ship,

ALGONQUIN SLIT
SKIRT WITH SHORT
LEGGINGS.

WOMAN'S MANTLE.

bringing with them their wives, of whom they are very careful; for although they come on board themselves, and remained a long while, they made their wives stay in the boats, nor could we ever get them aboard by any en- treaties or any presents we could make them. One of the two kings often came with his queen and many attendants, to see us for his amusement, but he always stopped at the distance of about two hundred paces, and sent a boat to inform us of his intended visit saying they would come and see our ship~ this was done for safety, and as soon as they had an answer from us they came off, and remained awhile to look around; but on hearing the annoying cries of the sailors, the king sent the queen, with her attendants, in a very light boat, to wait, near an island a quarter of a league from us, while he remained a long time on board, talking with us by signs, and expressing his fanciful notions about every thing in the ship, and asking the use of all. After imitating our modes of salutation, and tasting our food, he courteously took leave of us. Sometimes, when our men stayed two or three days on a small island, near the ship, for their various necessities, as sailors are wont to do, he came with seven or eight of his attendants, to

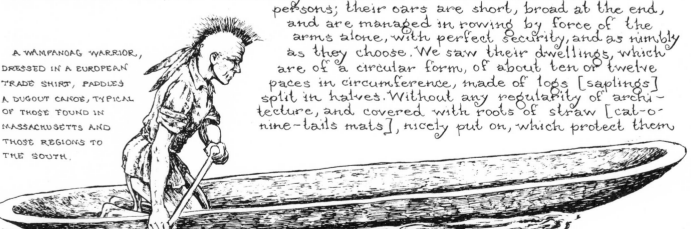

"THEIR ARROWS ARE WROUGHT WITH GREAT BEAUTY, AND FOR THE HEAD OF THEM, THEY USE EMERY, JASPER, HARD MARBLE, AND OTHER SHARP STONES, IN THE PLACE OF IRON."

inquire about our movements, often asking us if we intended to remain there long, and offering us every thing at his command, and then he would shoot with his bow, and run up and down with his people, making great sport for us. We often went five or six leagues into the interior, and found the country as pleasant as is possible to conceive, adapted to cultivation of any kind, whether of corn, wine or oil; there are open plains twenty~five or thirty leagues in extent, entirely free from trees or other hinderances, and of so great fertility, that whatever is sown there will yield an excellent crop. On entering the woods, we observed that they might all be traversed by an army ever so numerous [the Indians burned out the brush from their forests each spring and fall~ the towering trees were well above the flames and unharmed] ..."

They used "sharp stones in cutting down trees [with the aid of a controlled base fire], and with them they construct their boats of single logs, hollowed out with admirable skill, and sufficiently commodious to contain ten or twelve persons; their oars are short, broad at the end, and are managed in rowing by force of the arms alone, with perfect security, and as nimbly as they choose. We saw their dwellings, which are of a circular form, of about ten or twelve paces in circumference, made of logs [saplings] split in halves. Without any regularity of archi- tecture, and covered with roots of straw [cat-o- nine-tails mats], nicely put on, which protect them

A WAMPANOAG WARRIOR, DRESSED IN A EUROPEAN TRADE SHIRT, PADDLES A DUGOUT CANOE, TYPICAL OF THOSE FOUND IN MASSACHUSETTS AND THOSE REGIONS TO THE SOUTH.

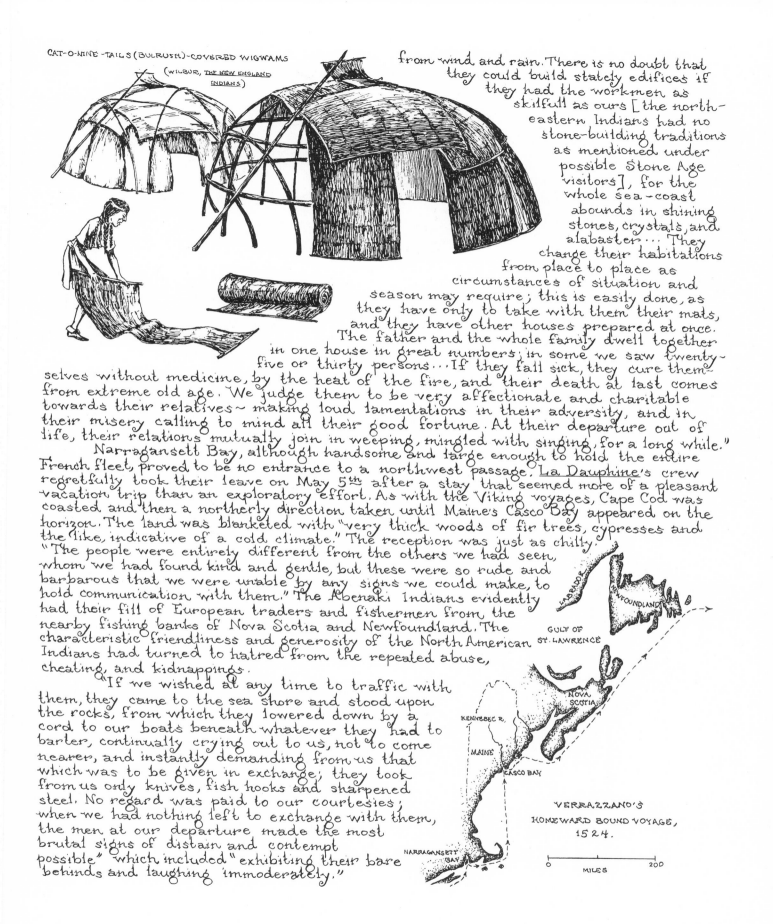

CAT-O-NINE-TAILS (BULRUSH)-COVERED WIGWAMS

(WILBUR, THE NEW ENGLAND INDIANS)

from wind and rain. There is no doubt that they could build stately edifices if they had the workmen as skilfull as ours [the north-eastern Indians had no stone-building traditions as mentioned under possible Stone Age visitors], for the whole sea-coast abounds in shining stones, crystals, and alabaster... They change their habitations from place to place as circumstances of situation and season may require; this is easily done, as they have only to take with them their mats, and they have other houses prepared at once. The father and the whole family dwell together in one house in great numbers; in some we saw twenty-five or thirty persons... If they fall sick, they cure themselves without medicine, by the heat of the fire, and their death at last comes from extreme old age. We judge them to be very affectionate and charitable towards their relatives~ making loud lamentations in their adversity, and in their misery calling to mind all their good fortune. At their departure out of life, their relations mutually join in weeping, mingled with singing, for a long while."

Narragansett Bay, although handsome and large enough to hold the entire French fleet, proved to be no entrance to a northwest passage. La Dauphine's crew regretfully took their leave on May 5th after a stay that seemed more of a pleasant vacation trip than an exploratory effort. As with the Viking voyages, Cape Cod was coasted and then a northerly direction taken until Maine's Casco Bay appeared on the horizon. The land was blanketed with "very thick woods of fir trees, cypresses and the like, indicative of a cold climate." The reception was just as chilly. "The people were entirely different from the others we had seen, whom we had found kind and gentle, but these were so rude and barbarous that we were unable by any signs we could make, to hold communication with them." The Abenaki Indians evidently had their fill of European traders and fishermen from the nearby fishing banks of Nova Scotia and Newfoundland. The characteristic friendliness and generosity of the North American Indians had turned to hatred from the repeated abuse, cheating, and kidnappings.

"If we wished at any time to traffic with them, they came to the sea shore and stood upon the rocks, from which they lowered down by a cord to our boats beneath whatever they had to barter, continually crying out to us, not to come nearer, and instantly demanding from us that which was to be given in exchange; they took from us only knives, fish hooks and sharpened steel. No regard was paid to our courtesies; when we had nothing left to exchange with them, the men at our departure made the most brutal signs of distain and contempt possible" which included "exhibiting their bare behinds and laughing immoderately."

VERRAZZANO'S HOMEWARD BOUND VOYAGE, 1524.

MILES

LABRADOR

NEWFOUNDLAND

GULF OF ST. LAWRENCE

NOVA SCOTIA

KENNEBEC R.

MAINE

CASCO BAY

NARRAGANSETT BAY

109

"Against their will we penetrated two or three leagues into the interior with twenty-five men; when we came to the shore, they shot at us with their arrows, raising the most horrible cries and afterwards fleeing to the woods. In this region we found nothing extraordinary except vast forests and some metalliferous hills, as we infer from seeing that many of the people wore copper ear-rings." Verrazzano was anxious to impress the Crown with the ore deposits and natural resources of North America that could be of tremendous value to France, even if a passage to Cathay remained undiscovered. (No doubt the copper dangles of the Abenakis, as with the Wampanoags, were of European trade metal and not of local origin.)

Departing that hostile country, they sailed to the northeast and were impressed by the "lofty mountains" and the "thirty-two islands, small and of pleasant appearance, but high and so disposed as to afford excellent harbors and channels." Continuing northward, the La Dauphine brushed the coast of Cabot's Nova Scotia and sighted Newfoundland. With his supplies dwindling, Verrazzano made a speedy crossing of the Atlantic and arrived at Dieppe on July 8, 1524. He had given France a belated claim to North America, a land that had great value in its own right.

Verrazzano never gave up his dream of a handy route to the Orient. In 1527, he probed the Brazilian coast, found no opening but did bring back a profitable cargo of Brazil wood for dyeing cloth. One year later he was in the Caribbean, and made the fatal mistake of wading ashore at one of the islands, probably Guadaloupe. While his horrified crew watched from the small boat beyond the breakers, Carib cannibals seized the explorer, diced his body and ate him on the spot. It was a sad end for a man who had given the world a sympathetic, idealistic picture of the North American natives and their vast shoreline that stretched from Florida to Nova Scotia.

CARTIER'S THREE VOYAGES FOR FRANCE

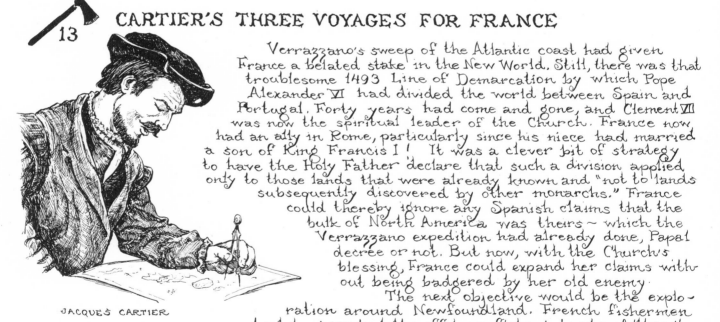

JACQUES CARTIER

Verrazzano's sweep of the Atlantic coast had given France a belated stake in the New World. Still, there was that troublesome 1493 Line of Demarcation by which Pope Alexander VI had divided the world between Spain and Portugal. Forty years had come and gone, and Clement VII was now the spiritual leader of the Church. France now had an ally in Rome, particularly since his niece had married a son of King Francis I! It was a clever bit of strategy to have the Holy Father declare that such a division applied only to those lands that were already known and "not to lands subsequently discovered by other monarchs." France could thereby ignore any Spanish claims that the bulk of North America was theirs ~ which the Verrazzano expedition had already done, Papal decree or not. But now, with the Church's blessing, France could expand her claims without being badgered by her old enemy.

The next objective would be the exploration around Newfoundland. French fishermen had long worked the offshore fishing banks. Although generally a closed-mouthed lot ~ just try discovering a favorite trout stream of an angler of this century! ~ there had been hints of an opening into the landmass beyond. With a passage to the riches of the Orient still very much in mind, Francis I commissioned French-born Jacques Cartier to make the voyage of discovery. Here was an admirable choice, for he was not only a master navigator, but it is probable that he had already sailed to Newfoundland and even Brazil. He was also "to discover certain islands and lands where it is said he should find great quantities of gold and other rich things" that might border an Asian passage. Verrazzano had implied such valuable ore deposits from his observations of the mountains and the many Indian ornaments he had seen.

110

FIRST VOYAGE TO THE GULF OF ST. LAWRENCE

On April 20, 1534, Cartier set sail from his home port of St. Malo with two sixty-ton ships, each with a complement of sixty crewmen. Aboard were provisions for fifteen months, enough for a trip to Asia and back. In just twenty days the Atlantic was crossed and a landfall made at Cape Bonavista at Newfoundland. The shore was ringed with ice, but safe harbor was found at the present port of Catalina. A brief outing to Funk Island, a lump of rock to the north, found a great feathery covering of squawking birds that included gannets and razor-billed and great auks. The latter were plump and as large as a goose with black and white feathers. The wings were "no bigger than halfe ones hand," and although they made efficient paddles in the sea, the birds were unable to fly. They made easy catches, and, in less than half an hour, two boatloads were filled, a fresh and welcome change from the salted meat diet. The Beothuk Indians of Newfoundland made frequent visits for these toothsome meals, and even a white bear, found swimming the thirty miles from the mainland, was on his way for a share. He, too, became part of the ships' menu.

The spring ice packs had effectively blocked the Strait of Belle Isle, and not until early June could the explorers chance a passage. Cruising the southern shore of Labrador, where Basque whalers would be harbored later in the century, the land was all "stones and wilde cragges, and a place fit for wild beastes. There was not a Cart-load of good earth," only "mosse and small thornes, scattered here and there, withered and dry. To be short, I beleeve that this was the land that God allotted to Caine." Ever since the Vikings called it Helluland, unfortunate Labrador has received bad press. Along that uninspired shore they set up a cross at today's Rocky Bay. Shortly after, they met their first humans— cod fishermen from La Rochelle who had lost their bearings! The lost countrymen were directed to nearby Cumberland Bay for anchorage ~ probably after recovering from such a surprise.

It wasn't long before they did have their first glimpse of the Native Americans. They were the Montagnais from the southwest (north of the undiscovered St. Lawrence River) and had come in their birchbark canoes to bring back fish and seal. They were "men of an indifferent good stature and bigness, but wild and unruly, they weare their haire tied on the top like a wreath of hay, and put a wooden pinne within it, or any other such thing instead of a naile and with them binde certaine birdes feathers." They were dressed in animal skins, "but that of the women, go straighter and closer in their garments than the men do, with their wastes girdled."*

On June 15th, they sailed southward and coasted the western shore of

THE RAZOR-BILLED AWK.
THE GREAT AWK WAS
EXTINCT BY 1844,
WITH GOOD REASON!

† = CROSS ERECTION

```
0        100        200
        MILES
```

* CARTIER'S NARRATIVE WAS TRANSLATED BY HAKLUYT, THE PRINCIPALL NAVIGATIONS, VOIAGES AND DISCOVERIES OF THE ENGLISH NATION, 1589.

Newfoundland. "Very steepe and wild hills" that "were all craggie, cleft and cut betwixt them and the Sea" could be seen as the explorers cruised the western shore. On July 1st, Prince Edward Island was spotted by the lookout. Thinking the sizable island was part of the mainland, they turned northward to follow the contour. The land was warm~a happy change from the chill of the Strait of Belle Isle. There was a blanket of such trees as cedars, pine, ash and willows on that low land and on the open fields grew a profusion of gooseberries, strawberries, blackberries and a "wild wheat like rye."

Running the mainland to the south, they rounded a projection of land that Cartier named the Cape of Hope, for it guarded a waterway that held promise of a northwest passage. This was the Bay of Chaleur, and a single longboat was launched to explore its reaches. There was cause for apprehension when forty or fifty birch canoes were seen crossing to a projection of land on the western bank," one part of which came to the said point, and a great number of men went on shore making a great noise, beckoning unto us that wee should come on land, shewing us certain skinnes upon pieces of wood, but because we had one onely boat, we would not goe to them, but went to the other side lying in the Sea: they seeing us flee, prepared two of their boats to follow us, with which came also five more of them that were comming from the Sea side, all which approached neere unto our boate, dancing, and making many signs of joy and mirth, as it were desiring our friendship saying in their tongue Napeu tondamen assurtah [we wish to have your friend- ship], with many other words that we under- stood not. But because (as we have said) we had but one boate, wee would not stand to their courtesie, but made signes unto them that they should turne back, which they would not do, but with great furie, came toward us: and suddenly with their boates compassed us about: and because they would not away from us. by any signes that we could make, we shot off two pieces among them, which did so terrifie them, that they put themselves to flight toward the sayde point, making a great noise: and having staid a while, they began anew, even as at the first to come to us againe, and being come neere our boat wee strucke at them with two lances, which thing was so great a terror unto them, that with great haste they beganne to flee, and would no more follow us."

It seemed clear that these Micmacs were up to no mischief and simply wished a friendly exchange of goods with the French. No doubt earlier swap sessions had taken place with European fishermen, and

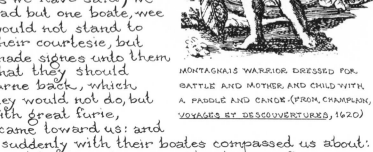

MONTAGNAIS WARRIOR DRESSED FOR BATTLE AND MOTHER AND CHILD WITH A PADDLE AND CANOE. (FROM CHAMPLAIN, VOYAGES ET DESCOUVERTURES, 1620)

The next day Cartier" made signes unto them, that we wished them no evill: and in signe thereof two of our men ventured to go on land to them, and carry them knives with other Iron wares, and a red hat to give unto their Captaine. Which when they saw, they also came on land, and brought some of their skinnes, and so, began to deale with us, seeming to be very glad to have our Iron ware and other things, stil dancing with many other ceremonies, as with their hands to cast Sea water on their heads. They gave us whatsoever they had, not keeping any thing, so that they were constrained to go back again naked, and made more signs that the next day they would come againe, and bring more skinnes with them."

For two days the explorers rowed and sailed their boats without finding any passage to the west, for a barrier of mountains rose beyond it. The disappointment was blunted when they found over three hundred Indians awaiting their return. Men, women, and children made welcoming signs and waved sealskins stretched on frames of saplings. Knives, hatchets, beads, and the like were brought ashore and another lively trading session began. "Some of the women which came not over, wee might see stand up to the knees in water, singing and dancing. The other that had passed the river where we were, came very friendly to us, rubbing our armes with their own handes, then would they lift them up toward heaven, shewing many

FRENCH TRADE KNIFE FROM BLOODY BROOK MASSACRE, 1675. MEMORIAL HALL, OLD DEERFIELD, MASSACHUSETTS

BONE-HANDLED TRADE KNIFE, UNEARTHED AT JAMESTOWN, EARLY 17th CENTURY. (NATIONAL PARKS)

TRADE KNIVES WERE HIGH ON THE WARRIOR WANT LIST, WHILE THE BELLS WERE POPULAR WITH THE WOMEN. BEHIND THE ENGLISH TRADERS ARE DUGOUT CANOES, INDICATING THAT THEY ARE NO FURTHER NORTH THAN MASSACHUSETTS. (DE BRY, AMERICA, 1634)

THE FRENCH
SMALL TRADE AXE, OTHERWISE
KNOWN AS THE TOMAHAWK OR HATCHET,
WAS FORGED BY BENDING A HOT STRAP OF IRON
AROUND AN IRON ROD TO FORM THE EYE, THEN WELDING
THE TWO ENDS TOGETHER TO COMPLETE THE BLADE. A
STRAIGHT WOODEN HANDLE WAS WEDGED INTO THE
EYE FOR AN EFFICIENT AND ECONOMICAL CAMP TOOL.

THE WARRIOR HOLDS HIS PRIZED
TRADE KNIFE.

figure des sauvages almouchicois

MICMAC INDIANS FROM A SECTION OF THE MAP OF
NEW FRANCE IN <u>VOYAGES BY CHAMPLAIN</u>, 1612

signes of gladnesse: and in such wise were wee assured one of another, that we very familiarly began to trafique for whatsoever they had, til they had nothing but their naked bodies; for they gave us all whatsoever they had, and that was but of small value." If nothing else, Cartier was a goodwill ambassador for those countrymen who would follow to New France.

After storms and contrary winds, the explorers reached the Gaspé Peninsula, where another delegation of two hundred native men, women, and children greeted them in forty canoes. These were Hurons from the Quebec area, and quite different from the Micmacs of Nova Scotia. They were thought "truely to be called Wilde," because "all they had together, besides their boates and nets, was not worth five sous. They goe altogether naked, saving their privities, which are covered with a little skin," and skins that acted as cloaks. They slept under their overturned canoes on the ground ~ but this was expedient for a fishing party who must travel lightly from a considerable distance, and not really a sign of poverty. "Their heads be altogether shaven, except one bush of hair which they suffer to grow upon the top of their crowne as long as a horse taile, and then with certaine leather strings bind it in a knot upon their heads."

When the French landed, the Indian men began to sing happily and dance about. "They had caused all their young women to flee into the wood,* two or three excepted, that stayed with them, to each of which we gave a combe, and a little bell made of Tinne, for which they were very glad, thanking our Captaine, rubbing his armes and breasts with their hands. When the men saw us give something unto those who stayed, it caused all the rest to come out of the wood to the end that they should have as much as the others. These women are about twenty, who altogether in a knot fell upon our Captaine, touching and rubbing him with their hands, according to their manner of cherishing and making much of one, who gave to each of them a little Tinne bell: then suddenly they began to dance, and sing many songs."

This is not to say that problems didn't surface between the two cultures. On the day of departure, July 25th, the French erected a thirty-foot cross at the tip of the Gaspé. At its center was secured a wooden shield, carved with three fleurs-de-lys and "Vivi le Roy de France." No sooner were the explorers back on board than the Huron chief, who had his brother and three boys with him in the canoe, paddled within shouting distance. Despite the language barrier, he made it clear that the countryside belonged to him, and he took a dim view of a cross being raised without his permission. Cartier chose to calm the troubled waters in a surprising way. Under pretense that an axe would be given in exchange for Chief Donnaconna's

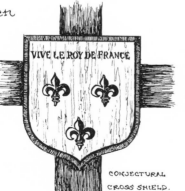

VIVE LE ROY DE FRANCE

CONJECTURAL
CROSS SHIELD.

* HERE WAS FURTHER EVIDENCE THAT SAILORS AND INDIANS HAD TRADED DURING THE EARLIER FISHING SEASONS.

114

bearskin mantle, they were enticed alongside. "One of our fellowes that was in our boate, took hold of theirs, and suddenly leapt into it, with two or three more, who enforced them to enter into our ships, whereat they were greatly astonished. But our Captain did straight-waies assure them, that they should have no harme, nor any injurie offred them at all, and entertained them very friendly, making them eate and drinke. Then did we shew them with signes, that the cross was but onely set up to be as a light and leader which wayes to enter into the port, and that wee would shortly come againe, and bring good store of iron-wares and other things, but that we would take two of his children with us, and afterward bring them to the sayd port againe: and so we clothed two of them in shirts, and coloured coates, with red cappes, and put about every ones necke a copper chaine, whereat they were greatly contented, then gave they their old clothes to their fellows that went backe againe, and we gave to each one of those three that went backe, a hatchet, and some knives, which made them very glad. After these were gone, and had told the newes unto their fellowes, in the afternoone there came to our ships sixe boates of them, with five or sixe men in every one, to take their farewels of those two we had detained to take with us, and brought some fish, uttering many words which we did not understand, making signes that they would not remove the crosse we had set up."

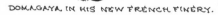

DOMAGAYA IN HIS NEW FRENCH FINERY.

One of the lads was the chief's son Domagaya, and his companion, Taignoagny. They would be sailing off on the adventure of their lives before returning to their Huron tribe. As for Cartier, it was his hope to have the boys learn French, and then give details of the lands that lay to the west.

The ships were off on a northeasterly course, arriving at the southern coast of Anticosti Island and thereby completely missing the entrance to the St. Lawrence River. After rounding that island, the tidal currents and the downstream winds made it impossible to make headway. With the late summer east winds beginning, it was time to head home before they became prisoners in the Bay of St. Lawrence. It was a wise decision, for even then the ships were tossed about by a vicious three-day easterly blow on their return. On September 5th, 1534, the explorers were back at St. Malo harbor with enough information and possibilities to plan for a deeper penetration beyond the Gulf of St. Lawrence.

SECOND EXPLORATION TO QUEBEC AND MONTREAL

LATER SHIPS' DETAIL FROM HUDSON'S MAP OF 1612. BECAUSE THERE WERE FEW ENGRAVINGS OF CARTIER'S DISCOVERIES ALONG THE ST. LAWRENCE RIVER, MANY OF THE FOLLOWING ILLUSTRATIONS ARE FROM CHAMPLAIN'S EXPLORATIONS BETWEEN 1604 AND 1611.

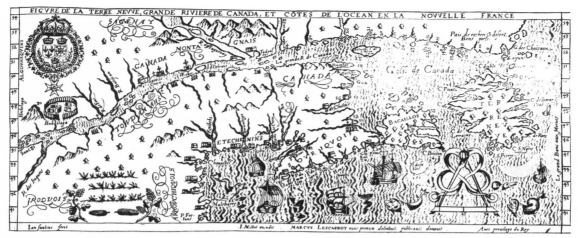

MAP OF NEW FRANCE, FROM LESCARBOT'S HISTOIRE DE LA NOUVELLE, 1611, AND BASED ON HIS EXPERIENCES WITH CHAMPLAIN IN 1606~1607. OF PARTICULAR INTEREST TO CARTIER WAS THE SAGUENAY RIVER, THE MYSTERIOUS LAND OF SAGUENAY TO THE NORTHWEST, THE HURON VILLAGES AT QUEBEC AND THE STOCKADE AT HOCHELAGA BY MOUNT ROYAL (MONTREAL), AND THE FIERCE IROQUOIS TO THEIR SOUTH.

Cartier's report of his first voyage dovetailed with Verrazzano's impressions. North America had natural resources in great plenty. True, no explorer had stumbled over golden nuggets or found an easy passage to the Orient, but the coast and rivers had cod, mackerel, and salmon in abundance, furs from the seal, walrus and inland animals, and the fertile soil grew mast trees, a variety of fruits and vegetables. Great ore deposits seemed likely, and the Indians around the Gulf of St. Lawrence had proved most friendly and helpful~willing traders and knowledgeable guides to whatever the interior might hold.

Domagaya and Taignoagny had learned to give the northwest passage dream a ring of truth. They told of a great waterway beyond the Gaspé that flowed from the setting sun. They called it Hochelaga, and it gradually narrowed as it passed by their tribal lands that they called Canada. Beyond, "there was fresh water [the Great Lakes] which went so farre upwards, that they never heard of any man who had gone to the head of it, and that there was no other passage but with small boats." Farther, they told of a well-to-do Huron town of Hochelaga upriver from their Canada. Still farther beyond lay the great and wealthy "kingdom of Saguenay." Could this river lead westward to Asia, with the town of Hochelaga along the way and Saguenay on its very outskirts? With these two boys as guides, Jacques Cartier expected to have those answers.

From the Gulf of Mexico to Labrador, the coastline had been mapped with some degree of certainty. The interior of North America, however, remained one vast unknown. The four Spanish survivors of the Narváez expedition would not reach civilization for two years, and Estévan would meet his maker in four years. As for Coronado's 1540~42 discoveries and De Soto's 1539~43 expedition, they had not yet reached the planning stage. And so the first real penetration was up to the French.

On May 19, 1535, Cartier's three vessels hoisted sail at St. Malo and were off to the great waterway into Canada. The flagship, the Grand Hermine, was about one hundred tons and bristled with twelve cannon. The Petite Hermine was sixty tons with four guns, while the Emerillon, a small bark capable of sailing shallower waters, was forty tons and with two guns.

Foul weather scattered the fleet during the westerly crossing. The Grand Hermine, with the two Indian boys aboard, was first to arrive off Newfoundland. During the eleven-day wait for the companion ships, it was worth another visit to Funk Island for the feathered feasts. Again, two boatloads of fresh provisions were carried off without making a dent in the auk population.

Once reunited at Blanc Sablon, Labrador, the fleet began its cruise of the coast. Cartier had no intention of missing a westerly passage on his way to the

116

boys' Canada. They passed north-ward of Anticosti Island, this time without bucking as many contrary winds and tides as the previous summer. Cartier was a thorough man and made several double-backs to the uninspiring Labrador coast. It being August 10th and the feast day of the Roman martyr, St. Laurence, he named the great gulf in his honor. Sailing westward, the ships entered the St. Laurence River. Island, reefs, rocks, shallows, currents, and tides made this obstacle course a navigational nightmare, but they continued on toward Canada without incident.

On September 1st, they came upon a spectacular river flowing from the north, deep and swift. Its entrance was guarded by three islands, and it "passeth and runneth along very high and steepe hils of bare stone, where very little earth is and not withstanding there is a great quantity of sundry sorts of trees that grow in the said stones," and yet large enough to make a mast of 30 tunne burden..." The boys said that this river "runneth into the country and kingdom of Saguenay"—hardly the westerly direction that Cartier had expected. But at least they were nearing Canada, for there they came upon four canoes filled with seal-hunting Hurons. The Indians were at first fearful of the unexpected fleet until the boys spoke to them in their native tongue. After the year in France, it was their first contact with their own tribesmen.

By September 7th, the ships had arrived at the well-populated Canada, and anchored between the Island of Orleans and the northerly mainland that one day would be called Quebec. The return of the two boys brought out great numbers of welcoming villagers in canoes, while on the beach a round of singing, dancing, and ceremonies were under way. Chief Donnaconna and his council were paddled to the Grand Hermine the following day. After his lengthy oration, Domagaya and Taigoagny told their countrymen of their visit to France and "what good enter-tainemen they had had." Donnaconna kissed Cartier's arm and placed it around his neck to emphasize the friendship they shared. After the visitors were wined and dined, the two boys left for their village of Stadacoma. The ships were then shifted to a more secure anchorage in the mouth of Ste. Croix River (St. Charles River) and close to the village. The shore continued to jump with happy tribespeople, with "the women still singing and dancing up to their knees in water."

The fleet briefly set sail for an exploration of the Isle of Orleans, which Cartier named Bacchus Island because of the profusion of grape vines growing there. Upon their return to the St. Charles River on September 14th, they found "Lord" Donnaconna, the two boys, and twenty-five canoe loads of greeters waiting. In spite of this show of affection, Cartier had his misgivings. Back at the Gaspé he had called them "Wilde men," and "no poorer people in the world" that "are very great theeves, for they will filch and steele whatsoever they can lay hold of." Briefly, then, they were not the cream of Indian society. Suspicions grew when the two boys said they would not guide the ships upriver to the rival town of Hochelaga as they had promised. Apparently the wily chief feared that these powerful allies would strike up a more lasting friendship with his more culturally advanced neighbors. Then those wondrous

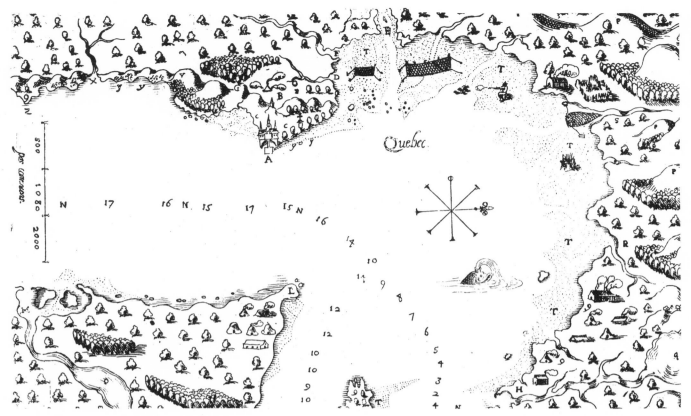

CHAMPLAIN'S MAP OF QUEBEC. A = SITE OF THE INDIAN VILLAGE OF STADACONE, NOW QUEBEC CITY; E = CARTIER'S ST. CHARLES ANCHORAGE WITH FISH WEIRS AT THE ENTRANCE; H = GREAT MONTMORENCY FALLS; L = POINT LEVIS ON THE EAST MAINLAND, AND SINCE ALTERED BY NATURE AND MAN; N = ST. LAWRENCE RIVER; S = MOULIN RIVER; T = FLATS COVERED AT HIGH TIDE.

trade beads, combs, knives, and hatchets would fall into other hands.

Realizing that Cartier was determined by any means, "as commanded by his king, to goe as far as possibly he could," with or without the boys as guides, Donnaconna reached deeply into his bag of tricks. First, he presented Cartier with his sister's ten or twelve-year-old daughter, as well as the son of his brother and another boy added for good measure. They were accepted without any altering of plans. Next, the chief asked for a cannon to be fired, since his people had never seen the likes of it. The French obliged by discharging not one but twelve guns. The broadside sent the cannon balls crashing into the woods, "at whose noyse they were greatly astonished and amazed, for they thought heaven had fallen upon them, and put themselves to flight, howling, crying, shrieking, so that it seemed hell was broken loose." Then Taignoagny, "a crafty knave," told Cartier that the smallest ship had killed two of their people. Such was not the case, for the cannon aboard that vessel had not been fired.

When Donnaconna found that he could not place the French in his debt, those god-fearing men might be persuaded to stay with the help of some supernatural hanky-panky. Three of his tribesmen were dressed as devils, "being wrapped in dogges skinnes white and black, their faces besmeered as black as any coales, with hornes on their heads more than a yard long." These counterfeit "Divels" paddled toward the ships, and made lengthy warning speeches before being chased away by Donnaconna and his good people. Domagaya and Taignoagny were in the next act, and they canoed to the ships, and with hands raised to heaven cried "Jesus Jesus Maria, James Cartier." They related that "there were very ill tydings befallen" and "that their God Cudruaigny had spoken in Hochelaga: and that he had sent those three men to shewe unto them that there was so much yce and snow in that countrey, that whosoever went thither should die, which words when we heard,

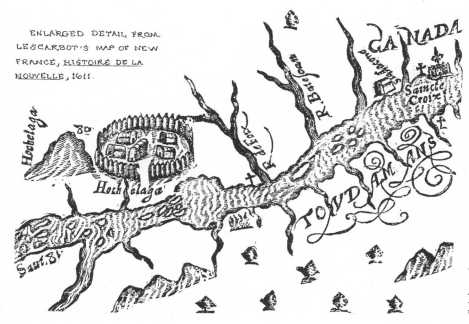

we laughed and mocked them saying, that their God Cudruaigny was but a foole and a noddie, for he knew not what he did or said..."

The unimpressed French sailed off the next day, September 19th, in the smaller Emerillon. The passage westward was pleasant, and although the two boys were not along, the Indians along the St. Lawrence were friendly and helpful. At St. Peter's Lake, the ship could make no farther way in the shallow waters. The longboats carried them beyond to Hochelaga. Well over a thousand of its people crowded the banks singing, dancing and bringing quantities of corn bread and fish for the visitors. They, in turn, were pleasured by gifts of such as tin beads and knives. Mothers pressed forward to have their youngsters touched.

The next day, Cartier led twenty-four of his men through oak groves and cornfields to the slope of a small mountain. This they called Mount Royal, and nestled at its southern slope was the large Indian town of Hochelaga that would one day become the city of Montreal. Surrounding it was an imposing stockade of some thirty feet in height. Crossed poles reinforced its wall and could be entered only by a single doorway. Two semicircular walls ringed the stockade, a first line of defense where the warriors could stand on an elevated walkway and hurl stones down upon any attackers.

Fifty large longhouses were within, each containing many rooms for communal living, and in the center of each was a large room that contained a common fireplace. Corn supplies were kept on atticlike platforms, ready to be ground with mortars and pestles, made into a paste, and cooked on hot flat stones. The explorers found all this quite a change from the more primitive living at Stadacona.

The explorers learned that nothing was more precious to the Hochelaga villagers than their beads of Asurguy ~ pure white wampum from the river clam made into perforated disks. After wrongdoers and enemy captives were put to death, multiple slashes were made into the buttocks, thighs, and shoulders, then weighted to the river bottom. The clams grew in these cuts, and the corpse could then be raised for harvesting. No doubt any luckless captive would consider

DETAIL OF AN ENGRAVING SHOWING A HURON LONGHOUSE, FRAMED WITH LOGS AND SAPLINGS AND SHEATHED IN BARK SHEETS. FROM CHAMPLAIN'S VOYAGES ET DESCOUVERTURES, 1620.

119

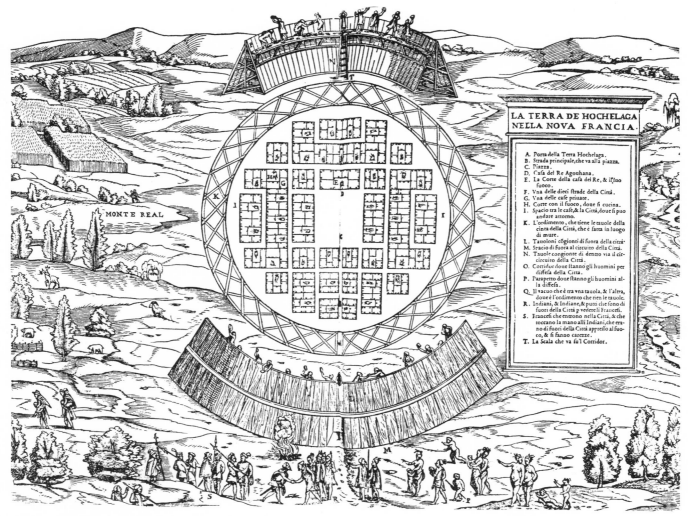

PLAN OF HOCHELAGA, FROM RAMUSIO, <u>NAVIGATION: ET VIAGGI</u>, VENICE, 1556. THE TWO SEMICIRCULAR OUTER DEFENSES WERE UNUSUAL WITH THEIR TRIANGULAR CONSTRUCTION. THEY WERE BUILT OF ROUND POLES, NOT THE EUROPEAN STYLE SAWN BOARDS AS ENVISIONED BY THE ENGRAVER. IT WAS BASED ON CARTIER'S DESCRIPTION.

this clam farm idea a high price to pay for a neck embellishment.

The explorers were led to a central plaza, where they were surrounded by womenfolk, anxious to "rubbe our faces, our armes, and whatever part of the bodie so ever they could touch, weeping for very joy that they saw us, shewing the best countenance that they possibly could, desiring us with their signes, that it would please us to touch their children." Then the great chieftain was carried through the crowds — a fifty-year-old ruler who was suffering from "palsie." He was obliged by Cartier when he indicated that he wished his trembling extremities to be rubbed. Then the sick, lame, and blind were brought forward for the healing touch. Cartier did so, but called upon a greater curative power by reading a lengthy passage from the Bible. The throng was "marvellously attentive, looking up to heaven, and imitating us in gestures." If the villagers lacked a full appreciation of the minisermon, they certainly had it for the hatchets and knives that were then given to the men, the beads and "other small trifles" given to the women, and rings and fancy tin brooches tossed out to a scramble of children.

Cartier concluded his version of winning friends and influencing people by ordering a grand finale of "Trumpets and other musical instruments." The natives must have been thrilled to their very bones!

Now the explorers were anxious to see the character of the countryside, and there could be no handier vantage point than atop Mount Royal, which rose a hundred feet above Hochelaga. The view was spectacular ~ the Green Mountains and the Adirondacks studded the horizon to the south, the Laurentians to the north, and the great St. Laurence River, like a silver ribbon, flowed from west to east. Just upriver from the longboats, they could make out a series of wild rapids, "the greatest and swiftest fall of water that any where hath been seene." Although their Indian guides indicated that once those three falls had been past, "a man might sayle the space of three monethes more alongst that River [the Great Lakes]," their hopes that this might be the northwest passage were dashed in the turbulence of the Lachine Rapids. (Much in the future, a modern canal would circumvent that fearful stretch of water.)

Beyond, to the northwest, the Hochelagas pointed out hills through which ran a sizable river ~ the Ottawa ~ through the Saguenay lands. With that, Cartier perked up his ears, for Domagaya and Taignoagny had said that vague kingdom was rich in silver and copper. Without prompting, their guides pointed to Cartier's silver whistle chain and then to the copper pommel of a crewman's dagger, and by signs indicated such metals came from there. Although "evill people" lived in Saguenay armed to the teeth and wearing armor "made of cordes and wood" ~ it was an objective for discovery, if only at a later date. But for now, the chill of October was upon them, and it was time to return to their anchorage by Donnaconna's village and weather the winter.

The return to Stadacone on October 11th touched off another round of celebrations. These powerful French with their wonderful gifts had formed no alliance with their upriver competitors. When Chief Donnaconna heard about the talk of Saguenay, he had no wish to be upstaged. He therefore embroidered a thread of truth to hearsay to give Cartier and his people a yarn that they wanted to hear. Yes, the people there were "clad with cloth as we are, very honest, and many inhabited townes and that they have a great store of Gold and red copper." There was much to mull over during the coming snowbound months.

Meanwhile, there was time to observe the villagers at Stadacone more closely. Cartier was amazed that in the coldest weather, they went about "starke naked upon snow and yce," and "are very much able to resist cold than savage beastes." As usual, the women were the real workers. Among their countless chores was digging the garden soil with pieces of wood "as big as a halfe a sword." Through their efforts were harvested corn (which must be stored, ground, and cooked), pumpkins, gourds, cucumbers, beans, and peas.

Generally, the men condescended to bend their backs over the tobacco crop, "and onely men use of it, and at first they cause it to be dried in the Sunne, then weare it about their neckes wrapped in a little beasts skinne made like a little bagge, with a hollow peece of stone or wood like a pipe: then when they please they make pouder of it, and then put it in one of the ends of the said Cornet or pipe, and laying a cole of fire upon it, at the other ende sucke so long, that they fill their bodies full of smoke, till that commeth out of their mouth and nostrils, even as out of the Tonnell of a chimney. They say that this doth keepe them warme and in health: they never go without some of it about them. We ourselves have tryed the same smoke, and having put it in our mouthes, it seemed almost as hot as pepper."
Males married two or three

GRINDING CORN WITH MORTAR AND PESTLE. (CHAMPLAIN, *VOYAGES*, 1620)

MAIDEN DRESSED FOR A DANCE, (FROM CHAMPLAIN, *VOYAGES*, 1620)

121

wives at Stadacone, but a widow never married again, and had to wear "a certaine blacke weede all the daies of their life, besmearing al their faces with cole dust and grease mingled togither as thicke as the backe of a knife."

Further, "they have a filthy and detestable [although possibly not to the crewmen] use in marrying their maidens, and that is, they put them all (after they are of lawfull age to marry) in a common place, as harlots free for every man that will have to doe with them, untill such time as they find a match. This I say, because I have seene by experience many houses full of those damosels, even as our schools are full of children in France to learne to reade. Moreover, the misrule and riot that they keepe in those houses is very great, for very wantonly they sport and dally togither, shewing whatsoever God hath sent them."

Sampling the simple pleasures of Indian life could be hazardous to one's health. Quite innocently the early explorers returned with more than trade goods ~ namely the tobacco habit and syphilis. But for the moment, Cartier had set about strengthening the fort on the shore of the St. Charles River, which had been built during his absence. Although "enclosed on all sides with large wooden logs, planted upright, with artillery pointing every way, and in a good state to defend us against the whole countryside," it was prudent to add a wide and deep trench about the stockade, with a drawbridge and gate to complete the defense. After all, Cartier was convinced that Donnaconna was a rascal and not to be trusted. Perhaps the chief's collection of five scalps, "spread upon boards" as trophies from "a people dwelling toward the South," also made him wary. The fierce Toudamans, probably the Iroquois, had burned their stockade on a Saguenay island two years before and killed nearly two hundred of the chief's people. There was no sense in being caught unprepared in the middle of an intertribal war.

These precautions were well advised, and particularly so when the garrison was dangerously weakened by scurvy. By the middle of February, many of the French were too ill to stand, their legs swollen and "sinnows shrunk as black as any cole." Skins were "spotted with spots

PIPE ~ SMOKING
IROQUOIS BRAVE,
SKETCHED BY CHARLES BÉCARD DE GRANVILLE, A FRENCH
OFFICIAL IN CANADA, ABOUT 1700

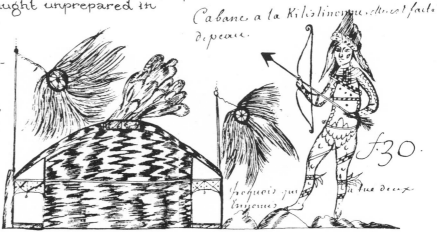

AN IROQUOIS WARRIOR BURNS AN ENEMY
LONGHOUSE. THE SCALPS, STITCHED ON CIRCULAR
FRAMES, ARE AMONG THE EARLIEST DRAWINGS
OF THIS PRACTICE. (GRANVILLE, c.1700)

of blood of a purple color, gums rotted and teeth falling out." Eight had expired and fifty more were rapidly approaching that end, Cartier made every effort to conceal the fact that but ten of the original complement could claim any sort of good health. Twenty-five deaths later, a cure came from unexpected quarters. Domagaya had also been wasting away from scurvy, but then cured himself by boiling a concoction of branch-lets and bark from the Northern White Cedar. The garrison was given the vitamin C drink until it seemed it would come out their ears, and the results were little short of miraculous.

NORTHERN WHITE CEDAR.

By April, the reduced but mended garrison broke up one of the ships for want of an adequate crew. A return to France was very much in mind, for Donnaconna seemed to be up to mischief. A considerable number of strange warriors were observed in Stadacona, and an attack on the fort might come at any time. It was then that Cartier decided "to play a prettie pranke" by enticing the chief, the two French-speaking boys, and a few important men into the stockade. They would then be taken to France as publicity agents for further exploration into that intriguing kingdom of Saguenay. When those people approached the fort in company with a mass of warriors, they were taken as unwilling guests for the voyage. The concerned villagers were assured that their leaders would be returned in ten or twelve months, and the two ships left the Saint Croix anchorage on May 6th, arriving at St. Malo by July 16, 1536.

CARTIER'S THIRD AND FINAL EFFORT

Donnaconna's audiences, including King Francis I himself, were held spellbound by his "kingdom of Saguenay" yarns. Wherever it was, there was "a large city called Sagana where there were many mines of gold and silver in great abundance, and men and women dress and weare shoes like we do; and there was an abundance of clove, nutmeg and pepper. Without much imagination, this could be a description of lands bordering the Orient! Other embellishments followed that included pigmies, fanciful one-legged men and even people there who drank and never ate." There was certainly enough enthusiasm for a third exploration, but yet another war with Spain proved to be a five-year distraction.

By 1541, the proposed expedition to Saguenay — and perhaps Asia itself — had grown to unexpected proportions. While the king was anxious to have Captain General Cartier continue his discoveries, he was determined to start the first colonizing effort at New France. The village would be protected by a well-garrisoned fort, and its growth and welfare would be the responsibility of the nobleman-soldier Jean François de la Rogue, seigneur de Roberval. As the first governor of the lands of Canada and Hochelaga, he would have the overall planning of the venture, while Cartier could prepare for his push into the deep interior. This was more easily said than done, for while the captain had his five ships ready for sailing, the governor was still rounding up cannon and provisions, convicts to build the homesteads and fort, and enough colonists to make the settlement a going concern. Now well into spring, the king ordered a restless Cartier to set sail with Roberval's blessing, and the governor would follow when all preparations were completed.

After leaving St. Malo on May 23, 1541, for a three-month voyage, Cartier's fleet once again anchored in their old St. Croix harbor. Unfortunately, none of the ten Huron children and adults were aboard to see their village of Stadacone again. All but one, the ten-year-old girl, had died in France during the interval. They were greeted by the acting Chief Agona, along with the usual merriment. "And after sayd Agona had inquired of the Captaine where Donnacona and the rest

MAP DETAIL BY CHAMPLAIN IN VOYAGES, 1612.

were, the Captaine answered him that Donnacona was dead in France [perhaps from all that high society living], and that his body rested in the earth and that the rest stayed there as great Lords and were married [indeed a fib], and would not returne backe to their countrey [indeed the truth]. "Agona did no unseemly handsprings or celebration dances, but "I think he took it so well because he remained Lord and Governor of the countrey by the death of said Donnacona."

The St. Croix anchorage in the St. Charles River could in no way accommodate the five vessels and those that would be arriving under Roberval's command. Cartier therefore moved his ships up-stream to the Cape Rouge River on the north bank of the St. Lawrence, named the place Charlesbourg Royal, and broke ground for the first French settlement. At the foot of Cape Rouge, a commanding bluff that overlooked the junction of the two rivers below, dwellings were built. Atop that prominence a stockaded fort gradually took shape to keep a watchful eye on the young colony. During those first days at Charlesbourg Royal, there was excitement aplenty when they found a "good store of stones, which we esteemed to be Diaments [quartz crystals]," a meadow a bit to the west with "gold and silver" (iron pyrites), and a "mine" or outcrop of iron ore as well. New France seemed to be off to a running start.

After a large garden field was cleared and planted, two of the ships left for France. Cartier could now begin his long-delayed exploration of the storied Saguenay. On September 11th, the small scouting party began rowing upstream in two boats. At an impassable first rapid, the explorers beached their boats and bypassed the tumble of water by a well-worn Indian trail above it. Friendly villagers offered four young guides to take them beyond the second run of rapids, the Lachine. That impressive rush of water dropped over forty feet within just two miles. The

CHAMPLAIN'S ASTROLABE (MARSHALL, <u>HISTORICAL WRITINGS</u>.)

CARTIER'S EXPEDITION 1541~1542

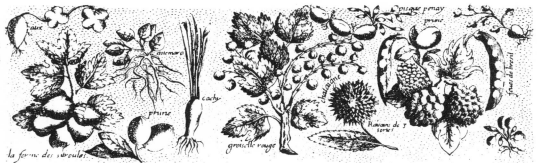

DETAILS FROM THE MAP BY CHAMPLAIN <u>VOYAGES</u>, 1612, SHOWS EDIBLE NORTH AMERICAN PLANTS SUCH AS VARIOUS GRAPES, PLUMS, PUMPKINS, ROOTS, RASP-BERRIES, CHESTNUTS, AND BEANS.

Indians made a diagram of sticks to show a third stretch of rapids ahead, and further still was the Ottawa River that pointed the way to Saguenay. Now that the topography of the land was in clearer focus, it was time to return to Charlesbourg Royal. Hopefully, Roberval's new infusion of colonists would be waiting for them, and a full-scale penetration of fabled Saguenay could get under way.

Returning downstream, Cartier's earlier misgivings of the Huron intentions began to surface. At Achelacy they were met by some four hundred villagers with "certain cries and ceremonies of joy. But a man must not trust them for all their faire ceremonies and signes of joy, for if they thought they had bene too strong forces, then they would have done their best to have killed us, as we understood afterward." When the French found the chief of that town absent, they learned "in truth he was gone to Canada to conclude with Agona what they should doe against us." Then, once back at the fort, they were told that the Hurons were "in a wonderful doubt and feare of us," and that many tribesmen were gathering near Charlesbourg Royal. To make matters worse, Governor Roberval had still not arrived to give a needed strength to the isolated colony.

HURON BRAVE IN BATTLE DRESS, FROM A CHAMPLAIN DRAWING BY JOHAN DE LAET, *L'HISTOIRE DU NOUVEAU MONDE*, LEYDEN, 1640.

Here, Hakluyt's narrative, the only known account of Cartier's third voyage, ends abruptly. This cliff-hanger has left our early American historians dangling in mid air. It may be that the Hurons were happy enough to swap for those much-wanted trade goods during the temporary French visits. But a fort that threatened with cannon, guarding an influx of foreign settlers on their tribal lands was not to their liking. Before matters got too far out of hand, the Hurons were ready to pit their Stone Age weapons and their guerrilla woodland warfare against the European arms and armor. A clash between these two vastly different cultures seemed inevitable—then and in the centuries to come. The highly individualistic style of Indian fighting and their inability to join forces with old tribal enemies for organized attacks on intruders would spell disaster for the Indian way of life.

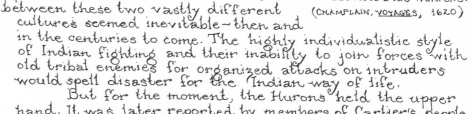

WARRIOR AND HIS WEAPONS.
(CHAMPLAIN, *VOYAGES*, 1620)

But for the moment, the Hurons held the upper hand. It was later reported by members of Cartier's people that several woodcutters were ambushed outside the fort. By the end of the scurvy-ridden 1541-42 winter, all of thirty-five lives had been lost to disease and Indian skirmishes. A push for Saguenay was out of the question. With their worthless (as it later proved) ore and crystal samples aboard, the remnants of the first serious North American colony sailed for home. When the ships put in at St. John's harbor at Newfoundland, they found Roberval's three ships riding at anchor! "Better late than never" was not good enough for the frustrated Cartier. When ordered to return to the abandoned Charlesbourg Royal, he flatly refused and sailed off to France.

The governor did continue on to occupy and enlarge his toehold in America. Apparently, no Indian attacks were needed, for another bitter Canadian winter accounted for fifty deaths from scurvy. The following June, the governor attempted to follow the Saguenay will-o-the-wisp, but with no better success than Cartier. Convinced that the lands of Canada and beyond had not been worth the effort and a sorry waste of the king's money, he returned to France September 11, 1543. But King Francis I had not been shortchanged. Early in the following century, Samuel de Champlain would build on Cartier's discoveries and establish the first permanent Canadian settlement.

THE PUSH TO COLONIZE

Just fifty years after Columbus had chanced upon the Caribbean Islands, explorations had largely defined the Atlantic coastline of North America. The Spanish had also penetrated much of the southern and southwestern interior, and the French knew something of the St. Lawrence watershed. Now, in the last half of the sixteenth century, the race was on to colonize and exploit those lands claimed by the right of discovery. Most, like Cartier's efforts, were doomed to failure. Out of the mother countries sailed soldiers, adventurers, and opportunists more intent on seeking their fortunes in gold, silver and pearls. And since America seemed an ideal dumping ground for convicts, the dregs of society, and the poor surplus population, they were but babes in the woods, ill-prepared for the realities of wilderness living. Conspicuous by their absence were families, farmers, builders, and craftsmen who would put down their roots in the isolation of the New World.

Two of the earliest settlements, although beyond our scope of exploration and discovery, did add considerable knowledge about the native Americans, their tribal lands, and the animals and vegetation that grew there. Both were accompanied by skilled artists prepared to picture the real America. Jacques Le Moyne de Morgues sailed with the French-Huguenot settlers to Spanish Florida in 1562. His illustrations, later engraved by de Bry, are to be found here and on the preceeding pages. John White accompanied the first English colonial effort to Virginia's Roanoke Island, and his drawings which follow, will speak for themselves. Both artists did much to spark the imagination and enthusiasm for further explorations and more permanent bases in America.

THE FRENCH INVASION OF SPANISH FLORIDA

By 1562, the French were ready for their second colonial venture, but with a different twist. An imaginative group of Huguenots were looking to America as a refuge for their Protestant faith. Well aware of Cartier's disastrous bouts with the harsh Canadian winters, they proposed a settlement in the very heart of unoccupied Spanish Florida. Once a well-garrisoned fort was established, the French would be within easy raiding distance of Spain's treasure galleon routes. Gaspard de Coligny, admiral of France and himself a Huguenot, and King Charles IX were enthusiastic backers of this intrusion into their old enemy's lands and the Huguenots were more than eager to seek out and destroy the religious fanatics.

Jean Ribaut was chosen to mastermind the operation. On February 8, 1562, the sea captain from Dieppe set sail with one hundred and fifty soldiers and sailors aboard his two

THE FRENCH IN FLORIDA, FROM LE MOYNE, ENGRAVED BY DE BRY, AMERICA, 1591

126

vessels. Landfall on May 1st was the St. Johns River, which he named the River of May and claimed the area for France. Reconnoitering northward, Ribaut's enthusiasm grew for this country that "lacketh nothing" with its "havens, rivers, and islandes of such frutefullness as cannot with tongue be expressed and where in shorte tyme great and precyous comodytes might be found." Near the present Port Royal Battery Creek, a small fort was built and thirty volunteers elected to remain to hold the land for France. When the Spanish learned of Charlesfort being erected, their protests were loud and vehement. "Florida," as far as they were concerned, extended all the way up to Newfoundland. However, their old enemies seemed to have developed a severe case of deafness.

With visions of a full-scale colony dancing in his head, Ribaut returned home, only to find a civil and religious war raging. Not to be denied, he sailed for England, knowing that Queen Elizabeth looked kindly on his country. It was agreed that supplies would be sent to Charlesfort, but the captain chosen turned rogue. The queen's ships were turned to Spanish privateering instead of crossing the Atlantic. Ribaut then found himself in jail because of a falling out between the two nations. Meanwhile, the thirty starving Charlesfort men, ill-equipped to cope with their surroundings, built a makeshift vessel and sailed for France. Soon out of their meager provisions, they turned to cannabalism. More dead than alive, they were finally rescued by an English privateersman.

While Ribaut was stewing behind English bars, René de Laudonière was paring for the colony's birth. As second in command of the Huguenot adventure, he got under way for St. Johns River with three ships, three hundred men, and four women. Artist Le Moyne was aboard, ready to begin his water color paintings. Fort Caroline, named in honor of the king, was built as more of a garrisoned fort than a town that could be self-sustaining. The Indians were friendly, but could only supply a limited amount from their food stores. Unrest and desertions followed, some making off with the barks to go privateering against the Spanish. Once again, the building of a ship was begun. They were unaware that Ribaut had been freed and was on his way with a fleet of seven ships, provisions and colonists. They also had no knowledge that the new Spanish governor of Florida, hard-as-nails Pedro Menéndez de Avilés, was on his way to rid his land of the heretics, once and for all. A collision course was in the making.

Menéndez, armed with full knowledge of the French fort from several deserters, anchored his five vessels thirty-five miles down the coast. Since it was August 28, 1565, and St. Augustine's feast day, he named the new settlement St. Augustine. As fate would have it, on that same day Ribaut arrived at Fort Caroline to inject new life into the flagging colony. Before long, the Spanish governor was on the move to test the French harbor defenses. Ribaut answered the challenge by sailing out to attack the enemy and destroy St. Augustine. He met with a far more formidable adversary ~ a vicious hurricane that scattered and sank the entire fleet.

Menéndez seized the opportunity and ran with it. Under cover of the same hurricane's lashing winds and rain, his army slogged through four days of swampy ooze and sawtoothed palmettos. It was worth the effort, for the fort was caught unawares. The garrison was

PORTION OF AN ENGRAVING SHOWING THE FRENCH LANDING IN FLORIDA. LE MOYNE/DE BRY.

overrun, and one hundred and thirty-two of the garrison met their death. Not all were put to the sword, for a number were saved for hanging. Under their swinging bodies, a happy Menéndez placed the inscription, "I do this, not as to Frenchmen but as to Lutherans."

There were no Spanish casualties. A handful of those at the French fort did escape on two small vessels that were anchored nearby. Artist Le Moyne and Laudonnière were among the fortunate, and the early water-color impressions arrived safely with them back in France.

Meanwhile, the bloody nightmare was far from over. Those who were able to reach shore from the sunken French fleet were soon facing starvation. Some two hundred struggled northward in an attempt to reach Fort Caroline. Menéndez learned of their plight and found them by the bank of an inlet too deep to ford. Accepting their surrender, he told them they would be brought to St. Augustine. After ferrying the prisoners over, ten at a time with their hands tied, each group was marched behind a sand dune and hacked to death with swords. Several days later, Ribaut and three hundred and fifty men were stopped by the same inlet. They surrendered and met the same Spanish version of honor. To this day, that watery barrier is called Matanzas Inlet — the Spanish word for slaughter.

Some two hundred others preferred to take their chances with the Indians by making their way south. They, too, were captured and eliminated near Cape Canaveral. The only survivors were a few who proved to be Catholic and had been weeded out before the carnage. Florida was again firmly in Spanish hands and Fort Caroline now flew the Spanish flag.

In France, disbelief turned to anger when the truth was out. Dominique de Gourgues, a French Catholic and at one time captured by the Spanish and chained in the galleys, swore his revenge on the bloody Menéndez. In August 1567, he sailed with three ships and one hundred and eighty men to attack the enemy garrison at Fort Caroline. All the defenders met their maker, including a number of Spaniards who were saved for hangings from the same trees that had served as gallows for their countrymen. De Gourgues had the satisfaction of burning into the tree trunks "I do this, not as to Spaniards or as Marranos [baptized Jews] but as to traitors, robbers, and murderers."

~ FORT CAROLINE ~

ON SEPTEMBER 20, 1565 ~ JUST AFTER THE DRENCHED AND EXHAUSTED SENTINELS HAD BEEN SENT TO THEIR QUARTERS ~ THE SPANISH LAUNCHED A 3-PRONGED ATTACK. ONLY 20 OF THE 150 FRENCH COULD BEAR ARMS, FOR RIBAULT HAD TAKEN ALL ABLE-BODIED SOLDIERS ABOARD HIS SHIPS. MEETING NO OPPOSITION, THE SPANISH SEARCHED THE BUILDINGS, KILLING EVERY MAN THEY FOUND.

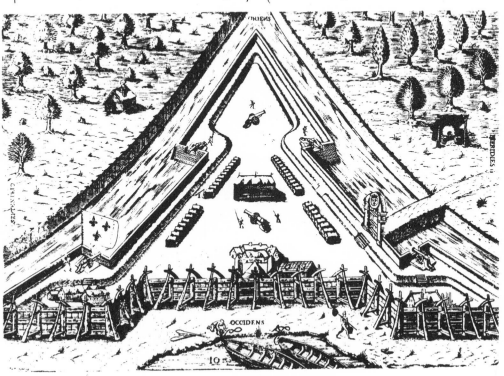

ENGLAND'S LOST COLONY

Nearly a century had passed since John Cabot had claimed Nova Scotia and the surrounding lands for England. Like a sleeping giant, that country had made no effort to exploit her American claims ~ and with good reason. There were more pressing problems, for a strong navy must be built to ward off a threatened invasion of their island by the French. When Mary Tudor married Prince Philip ~ soon to become King Philip II of Spain ~ England became something of a puppet to that all-powerful nation. Known as "Bloody Mary," she did her best to purge her country of the Protestant "heretics." And since Spain claimed the bulk of the American continent as her own, there could be no thought of any overseas expansion.

Not until Elizabeth came into power in 1558 did England awake to the possibilities that America might offer. Spain was guarding her colonial monopoly closely, had driven out the French garrison in Florida, and had forbidden all foreign trade with her possessions. It was past time for England to have a hand in the colonization of North America, and Walter Raleigh was given a patent by the queen to do just that. The first step was to find a suitable site somewhere on the lengthy coastline that Cabot, Verrazzano, Cartier, and others had defined. Raleigh chose two veterans, sea captain Philip Amadas and soldier Arthur Barlowe, to scout out the possibilities. With them would go the Portuguese pilot and master, Simon Fernandez, who had knowledge of the Florida lands. With him were artist John White and naturalist Thomas Hariot, ready to record what they saw and thereby interest English investors in the proposed settlement.

In April 1584, the two ships were sped westward by the trade winds and into the Florida Currents until the Carolina Outer Banks landfall was made. Coasting northward along the sandy barriers, they chanced upon a break in the shoals. Once through that entrance, the explorers anchored off the island of Hatorask. There they found the natives "very handsome and goodly people, and in their behaviour as mannerly and civill as any of Europe." These were Indians from nearby Roanoke Island, and, since their chief was not among them, his brother made the visitors welcome. The Roanoke lord seemed eager to trade. Barlowe continued that "when we shewed him all our packet of merchandize, of all things he sawe, a bright tinne dish most pleased him, which hee presently tooke up and clapt it before his breast, and after made a hole in the brimme thereof and hung it about his necke, making signes that it would defend him against his enemies arrowes: for these people maintaine a deadly and terrible warre, with the people and King adjoyning. We exchanged our tinne dish for twentie skinnes, woorth twentie Crownes, or twentie Nobles, and a copper kettle for fiftie skins woorth fiftie Crownes. They offered us good exchange for our hatchets, and axes, and for knives and would have given any thing for swordes: but wee would not depart with any."

Barlowe observed that "his wife was very well favoured, of meane [average] stature, and very bashfull: shee had on

QUEEN ELIZABETH

"A CHIEF LORD OF ROANOKE" BY JOHN WHITE, ENGRAVING BY DE BRY

T·B

129

her backe a long cloake of leather, with the furre side
next to her body, and before her a piece of the same:
about her forehead shee had a bande of white Corall,
and so had her husband many times: in her eares
shee had bracelets of pearles hanging downe to her
middle ... and those were of the bigness of good pease.
The rest of her women of the better sort had pendants
of copper hanging in either eare."

As for the country side, "the soile is the most
plentifull sweete, fruitful and wholesome of all the
world: there were above fourteene several sweete
smelling timber trees ... they have those Okes that
we have, but farre greater and better." The pines
were so large that a dugout canoe made from one
could carry twenty men. Divers kindes of fruites,
Melons, Walnuts, Cucumbers, Gourdes, Pease, and divers
rootes, and fruites very excellent good, and of their
Countrey corne, which is very white, faire and well
tasted ... " all grew there. "Our selves prooved the
soile, and put some of our Pease in the ground, and
in tenne dayes they were fourteene ynches high."

After visiting the tribes on the mainland
and their hosts at their stockaded village on Roanoke

"A NOBLE WOMAN OF POMEIOCK" BY WHITE / DE BRY

"THE ENGLISHMAN'S ARRIVAL IN VIRGINIA" SHOWS THE PINNACE UNDER SAIL, THE SHALLOW ENTRANCES THROUGH THE SAND
ISLANDS, INDIAN FISHING WEIRS, DUGOUT CANOES, AND STOCKADED VILLAGES. (FROM WHITE'S PAINTING, DE BRY'S 1590 ENGRAVING)

VIRGINIA

TITLE BANNER FROM
CAPTAIN JOHN SMITH'S
"A MAP OF VIRGINIA,"
ENGRAVED BY WILLIAM HOLE,
1612

ENGLISH SAILOR,
SOUNDING DEPTHS
WITH LEAD LINE.
SECTION FROM
THE MARINERS MIRROR
FRONTSPIECE, ASHLEY

Island, the explorers returned to England with the rave notices of their findings. With investors aplenty, Raleigh hastened preparations for a settlement and named it Virginia in honor of the Virgin Queen, Elizabeth. "Virginia" included those lands from Cape Fear to Cape Henry, and much of North Carolina and southern Virginia. When the queen refused Raleigh, her court favorite, permission to sail away, he passed the command to his cousin, Sir Richard Grenville. Grenville was a logical choice, for he had already made a name for himself raiding Spanish shipping in that undeclared war. Since the colony was to be more of a military garrison than a self-sustaining settlement, professional soldier Ralph Lane was chosen as governor.

Artist White and scientist Hariot were once again aboard. In April, 1585, seven ships and nearly six hundred men hoisted sail for North America.

After a close inspection of the Carolina Banks, Roanoke Island seemed to meet their needs. The Outer Banks offered protection from Spanish warships but could harbor English privateers within easy reach of the treasure galleon route. Being an island, it would be difficult for hostile Indians to take the fort by surprise. On July 29th, the expedition landed. When the fort was completed, Grenville left a force of one hundred and eight men and hoisted anchor on August 25th to search out more Spanish treasure. Unfortunately, the soldiers who remained were more interested in seeking their own fortunes in gold, silver, and pearls than planting and strengthening their Virginia holdings. The natives, tired of supplying the newcomers with their food reserves, became openly hostile. Skirmishes followed, and the Dasamonguepeuk chief and others were slain, endearing the English to no one. Isolated and wanting in provisions and morale, Raleigh's colonial dream was fast fading. These prisoners on their own island were overjoyed when the sails of Francis Drake appeared over the horizon. The sea rover was homeward bound, after relieving various Spanish convoys of their valuables, plundering Cartagen, San Domingo, completely destroying St. Augustine and in general "singeing King Philip's beard." Lane had his fill of the Virginia experiment, and the garrison sailed

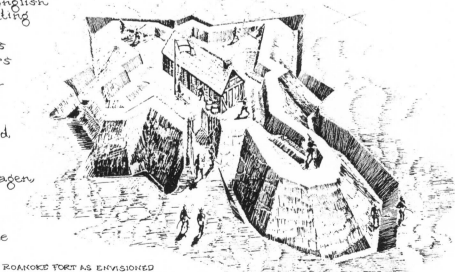

ROANOKE FORT AS ENVISIONED
BY A NATIONAL PARK SERVICE ARTIST

131

with Drake for the more hospitable shores of England.

Shortly after, Grenville arrived with the promised supplies and new settlers, only to find Roanoke's fort and dwellings forlorn and abandoned. Fifteen soldiers were left as a token force to hold the outpost, and Grenville was off again to worry the Spanish Main.

RALEIGH'S TWICE-LOST COLONY

Back home, the returned soldiers could only grumble about Roanoke. A more optimistic Raleigh was already planning a second colonial attempt, but this time to the more promising shores of the Chesapeake Bay. There, the deep harbors could accommodate shipping and those privateers ranging down to New Spain. White and Hariot had scouted the area, and the artist had made friends with the local tribesmen. He would make a level-headed, flexible governor. On May 8, 1587, three vessels steered westward with White and his small group of one hundred and ten colonists. According to plan, they would first stop by Roanoke and retrieve the fifteen soldiers before moving on to the Chesapeake Bay. But Simão Fernandes, the Portuguese master who guided the earlier voyages, had different ideas. More intent on collecting his share of Spanish prizes than a struggling settlement, he insisted that White and his people disembark at Roanoke when they arrived on July 22nd. And so the profitable business of privateering had shortchanged the colonization of North America. Nevertheless, the governor had every intention to make his way overland, as soon as possible, to the fresh Chesapeake beginning.

The fifteen Englishmen were nowhere to be found. It was learned from the friendly Indians on nearby Crotoan Island that eleven of their number had been approached, "with friendly signs," by thirty warriors from Scota, Aquascogoc, and Dasamonguepeuk. White related that "wherefore two of the chiefest of our Englishmen went gladly to them but while one of these Savages traiterously imbraced one of our men, the other with his sword of wood, which he had secretly hidden under his mantell [deerskin cloak], strooke him on the heade and slew him, and presently the other eight and twentie Savages shewed themselves…" In the following skirmish, another soldier was "shotte into the mouth" with an arrow. The outnumbered defenders managed to reach their boat and rowed for Hatorask Island. On their way, four of their fellows were picked up while oystering at a nearby creek. They landed on a small island near the "entrance into the harbor of Hatorask, where they remained a while, but afterwards departed, wither as yet we know not."

Meanwhile, on Roanoke Island, White's settlers made temporary repairs to the fort and outbuildings. The governor was prevailed upon by his people to return to England to hasten provisions, for their supplies were low and the planting season had passed them by. John White had an added incentive to plead the colony's case, for his daughter, Elinor Dare, had presented him with a granddaughter on August 24th. Christened Virginia, she was the first English

"GREAT LORD OF VIRGINIA" BY WHITE/DE BRY

WINTER DEERSKIN MANTLE, VIRGINIA

132

~HOW THEY EAT~

"THEY LAY A MAT OF TWIGS ON THE GROUND AND SET THEIR MEAT IN THE MIDDLE OF IT. THEN THEY ALL SIT AROUND IT ~ THE MEN ON ONE SIDE, THE WOMEN ON THE OTHER. THEIR MEAL CONSISTS OF BOILED MAIZE, WHICH HAS AN EXCELLENT FLAVOR, DEER FLESH OR SOME OTHER KIND OF MEAT, AND FISH. AS THEY ARE VERY TEMPERATE, BOTH IN EATING AND IN DRINKING, AND DO NOT OVERLOAD THEIR CONSTITUTIONS, THEY ARE VERY LONG ~ LIVED."

~HOW THEY BUILD BOATS~

"THE WAY THEY BUILD THEIR BOATS IN VIRGINIA IS VERY WONDERFUL. FOR ALTHOUGH THEY COMPLETELY LACK ANY IRON TOOLS SUCH AS WE USE, THEY CAN MAKE BOATS AS GOOD AS OURS, AND THESE BOATS ARE SEAWORTHY ENOUGH TO TAKE THEM SAILING OR FISHING WHEREVER THEY WANT TO GO.

"FIRST THEY CHOOSE A TALL, THICK TREE OF THE SIZE REQUIRED FOR THE BOAT'S FRAME. THEN THEY LIGHT A FIRE CLOSE TO ITS ROOTS, FEEDING IT BIT BY BIT WITH DRY MOSS AND SMALL CHIPS OF WOOD, KEEPING THE FLAMES FROM MOUNTING TOO HIGH. WHEN THE TREE IS ALMOST BURNT THROUGH, THEY MAKE A GOOD FIRE TO CAUSE IT TO FALL. THEN THEY BURN OFF THE TOP AND BOUGHS, TAKING CARE THAT THE TRUNK SHOULD NOT BE SHORTENED.

"THE TREE IS RAISED UPON A PLATFORM BUILT ON FORKED POSTS AT A HEIGHT CONVENIENT FOR WORKING. THE BARK IS STRIPPED OFF WITH SHARP SHELLS... A FIRE IS MADE ALL ALONG THE LENGTH OF THE TRUNK, AND WHEN IT HAS BURNED SUFFICIENTLY, IT IS QUENCHED AND THE CHARRED WOOD SCRAPED AWAY WITH SHELLS. THEN THEY BUILD A NEW FIRE, BURN OUT ANOTHER PIECE, AND SO ON···"

FROM DE BRY'S 1590 ENGRAVINGS OF JOHN WHITE'S VIRGINIA PAINTINGS AND DESCRIBED BY NATURALIST HAROIT.

133

subject to be born in America. Because the settlers would be moving on to their Chesapeake Bay destination, signs would be left to indicate their direction and if any problems had befallen them.

Stumbling blocks seemed to pave the way to an English America. There were the overriding incentives of privateering; cantankerous Fernandes leaving White's colonists on Roanoke, short of their goal; a lack of families to perpetuate the settlement; and badly scheduled shipments of supplies and knowledgeable farmers. Now came the greatest obstruction of all, for a formal war with Spain was near at hand. When Governor White arrived in England in November 1587, feverish preparations were being made to meet a threatened invasion by the Spanish Armada. King Philip was determined to revenge the lopping off of Catholic Mary Queen of Scot's head that year and to purge England of her Protestant rebels. Still, White was able to talk his way aboard a fleet under Grenville, preparing to sail against the colonies in New Spain that March. Before the raid-and-rescue ships could hoist anchors, all were requisitioned by the Royal Navy for the defense of the island.

That July, Spain's Invincible Armada, some one hundred great galleons bristling with heavy guns, sailed confidently into the English Channel. They were met and mauled by swarms of light, fast-sailing craft. The crippled Spanish ships attempted to escape around the northern tip of Scotland, only to be set upon by an unforeseen foe ~ a wild North Sea storm. Fewer than half of the ponderous galleons finally returned home, leaving England to rule the seas.

Now any seaworthy vessel with more than a shred of canvas was free for the easy pickings to be found off the Spanish West Indies. Such patriotic ~ and lucrative ~ adventuring gave little time or inclination for concern over the stranded Virginia colony. It was an anxious and frustrated Governor White who finally was granted a single passage aboard one such privateering fleet in 1590.

In his 1593 letter to his historian friend Richard Hakluyt, he recalled that "the leaders, captains, and sailors showed very small regard for the welfare of their countrymen in Virginia. There was nothing they wanted less than to touch those parts. Their whole desire was to plunder Spanish ships and take prizes, and they spent so much time doing this that summer was over before we arrived in Virginia."

It was August 15th when two of the ships finally anchored off Hatorask. The weather "was so foul and unseasonable" that one of the ship's captains and seven of his crewmen drowned when their boat capsized on the row to Roanoke. Not until the 18th could the crews be wheedled into another try. Darkness prevented a landing, but they sounded a trumpet call, and then played the tunes of many familiar English songs. We hailed the shore with friendly greetings, but got no answer. At daybreak we landed..." and the governor had touched the ground he had left over three years earlier.

"As we went inshore up the sandy banke upon a tree, in the very browe thereof were curiously carved these faire Romane letters C R O: which letters presently we knew to signifie the place [Croatoan], where I should find the planters seated, according to a secret token agreed upon betweene them and me at my last departure from them, which was, that in any wayes they should not faile to write or carve on the trees or posts of the dores the name of the place where they should be seated, for at my coming away they were prepared to remove from Roanoak 50 miles into the maine. Therefore at my departure from them in An. 1587 I willed them, that if they should happen to be distressed in any of those places, that then they should carve over the letters or name, a Crosse ✠ in this forme, but we found no such signe of distresse. And having well considered of this, we passed toward the place where they were left in sundry houses, but we found the houses taken downe, and the place very strongly enclosed with a high palisado of great trees, with cortynes [curtains] and flankers very Fortlike, and on one of the chiefe trees or postes at the right side of the entrance had the barke taken off, and 5 foote from the ground in fayre Capitall letters was graven CROATOAN without any crosse or signe of distresse; this done, we entered into the palisado, where we found many barres of iron, two

134

pigges [cast block] of Lead, four yron fowlers [myskets], Iron sacker-shotte [large cannon balls], and such like heavie thinges, throwen here and there, almost overgrowen with grasse and weedes."

Several chests were discovered that had been hidden by the colonists, including three that White had left behind, had their contents scattered about. "This could only be the deede of our enemies, the Savages at Dasamongpeuk, who had watched the departure of our men to Croatoan; and assoone as they were departed diged up every place they suspected any thing to be buried ... I greatly joyed that I had safely found a certaine token of their safe being at Croatoan."

Severe weather prevented a search of Croatoan the following morning, and the ships were eventually swept to England before the windstorms. So ended the search for the "Lost Colony," and the distressed governor had brought back more questions than answers. Only his drawings, later engraved by de Bry, would keep the mystery alive and give us his impressions of the Virginia he had hoped to colonize.

We do know that the settlers had every intention of going to Chesapeake Bay ~ about fifty miles by overland travel. But without food stores for the winter, they apparently left Roanoke for the hospitality of the friendly Croatoan Indians. They would return for their less necessary valuables, but did bring along the fort's small cannon for protection at the Chesapeake. In 1607, the more successful Jamestown colony learned of English people living on the mainland to the south of Albemarle Sound, but had no success rescuing them. Also, historian William Strachey recorded from a contemporary document, since partially destroyed, that they were massacred by order of Chief Powhatan just before the Jamestown group arrived in 1607.

If so, perhaps a mishap with their boats left them short of their land route. The powerful Powhatan may have considered the English as a danger to his authority and so eliminated that possibility.

THE POSSIBLE FATE OF ROANOKE'S "LOST COLONY."

ooo ? PLANNED ROUTE
--- ? SEA ROUTE

CONCLUSION

The Jamestown Colony, weak and tottery as a newborn babe, might have been snuffed out in a twinkling by the warriors of Powhatan. But a few minor skirmishes notwithstanding, the tidewater Virginian Indians and their new English neighbors realized that the advantages of peaceful coexistence and trade were to the benefit of all. Powhatan put it this way to Captain John Smith: "Why should you take by force from us that which you can obtain by love? Why should you destroy us who have provided you with food? ... I am not so simple as not to know that it is better to eat good meat, be well, and

135

sleep quietly with my women and children, to laugh and be merry with the English, and being their friend, to have copper and whatever else I want..."

Unfortunately, it was a peace-pipe dream that would one day dissolve in the smoke of battle. The Stone Age Indians knew only of their earlier contacts with these technologically advanced Europeans. Perhaps their ancestors had played willing hosts to the prehistoric stone builders and the Celtic and Irish holy men who followed. The rough-and-tumble Vikings were so outnumbered that they had little chance for a lengthy stay. Later explorers were content to poke along the North American shoreline and then disappear~perhaps with a few captives as souvenirs. Of course there were the Spanish conquistadors, those ruthless plunderers of anything that glittered. But after being swallowed up in the vastness of the southwest, pillaging South and Central America seemed more to their liking. The French to the north had established trading posts that were rewarding to both the red and white cultures.

Who in those early days of the seventeenth century could guess that the feeble Jamestown Colony was the beginning of the end for the native Americans? Farmers and artisans~no transients in the lot~the colonists were determined to plant their roots deeply and firmly on the New World soil. Possibilities were limited only by one's imagination and determination. Hard on their heels would follow countless shiploads of newcomers, all seeking their own piece of North American real estate. Their children would one day push westward clear to the Pacific coast. Many carried along an abiding prejudice and intolerance for any "pagan savage" who might object to being overrun. If Powhatan's medicine men could have forecast such history in the making, the chief would have no doubt ended the Jamestown experiment then and there.

Instead, new settlements would sprout along the old Indian trails throughout the eastern wilderness, and tribal lands would be boxed in by fences. At first bewildered by, and then vengeful of, these foreign intruders, the native Americans resisted as best they could~an act as futile as building a sand castle against the incoming tide. While the flintlock musket and the white man's diseases took a fearful toll of their numbers, Indian traditions and customs were being eroded in more subtle ways. Christian missionaries worked tirelessly to convert the "red heathen." Native crafts were running a poor second to trade goods. As more and more hunting grounds were sold off to the settlers, the tribespeople were losing their sense of identity and place. Too soon they would be sentenced to the confines of reservations by the sometimes bumbling governmental agencies. The clash of cultures had reduced a once proud race to second-class citizens in their own country.

The story has a happier ending. Due to changing times, there has been a gratifying rebirth of the Indian spirit. Tribal ceremonies and ancient crafts are well along on the comeback trail, adding to the color and richness of our multiracial society. A more sensitive schooling for the Indian youngsters is giving an appreciation of yesterday's heritage while helping them cope with the world of today. May they walk tall, as did their people before the coming of THE EARLY EXPLORERS OF NORTH AMERICA.

PLACES TO VISIT
Early Exploration Sites and Relics for You to Rediscover

ARIZONA
ARIZONA STATE MUSEUM, University of Arizona, Tucson.

CANYON DE CHELLY NATIONAL MONUMENT, Route 7, Chinle.

COLORADO RIVER TRIBES MUSEUM, Parker.

CORONADO NATIONAL MONUMENT, Hereford, Montezuma Canyon Road about 30 miles west of Bisbee. Exhibits along the path to Coronado Peak detail the 1540 march and wide-ranging views of the lands he explored.

HEARD MUSEUM OF ANTHROPOLOGY AND PRIMITIVE ARTS, 22 East Monte Vista Road, Phoenix.

MUSEUM OF NORTHERN ARIZONA, Flagstaff.

NAVAJO NATION MUSEUM, Window Rock.

PUEBLO GRANDE MUSEUM, 4619 East Washington, Phoenix.

CALIFORNIA
CABRILLO NATIONAL MONUMENT, Point Loma, 10 miles southwest of San Diego via U.S. 101. Juan Rodriguez Cabrillo, a Portuguese navigator sailing for Spain, landed here in 1542. Exploration was brief, for they were attacked by Indians. Fine view and visitor center featuring Spanish exploration.

FLORIDA
CASTILLO DE SAN MARCOS NATIONAL MONUMENT, St. Augustine. This well-preserved fortress was begun in 1672, two years after English privateersmen raided St. Augustine. The shellstone walls, 30 feet high and up to 12 feet thick, could absorb cannon balls with little damage.

DE SOTO NATIONAL MEMORIAL, 5 miles west of Bradenton on Tampa Bay, marks the general landing place of de Soto's army in 1539, of Ponce de Leon in 1513, and of Panfilo de Narvaez in 1528.

FORT CAROLINE NATIONAL MONUMENT, 10 miles east of Jacksonville, 5 miles north of Florida 10, has a reconstructed fort by the St. Johns River. In such a stronghold, the French defied the Spanish in 1564–65.

FORT MATANZAS NATIONAL MONUMENT, on Anastasia and Rattlesnake islands, 14 miles south of St. Augustine on Florida A1A. The 208 shipwrecked French soldiers were blocked by the inlet south of Anastasia Island in 1565. Upon surrendering, all but forty were slaughtered by the Spanish. A week later Ribault and 350 men met the same fate. "Matanzas" means slaughter. The present fort on Rattlesnake Island was built by the Spanish after an English siege of Castello de San Marcos in 1740. Across from it is the Anastasia Island visitor center.

MEL FISHER MARITIME HERITAGE SOCIETY, Green Street, Key West. Maritime artifacts from 17th and 18th centuries.

OLDEST HOUSE AND THE MUSEUM OF FLORIDA'S ARMY, Charlotte Street, St. Augustine.

THE SPANISH QUARTER, St. George Street, St. Augustine. Spanish-Colonial artifacts and restored or reconstructed Colonial buildings.

ST. AUGUSTINE. Here Don Pedro Menendez de Aviles established the first permanent settlement in the present United States. From this town Menendez marched to attack the French Fort Caroline to the north and to massacre the shipwrecked forces to the south. The narrow, winding streets thread by the public square, a 1703 house, the Old Spanish Treasury at the corner of St. George and Treasury streets, the Old Spanish Inn at 43 St. George Street, the Fatio House on Avites Street, and many others.

GEORGIA
ETOWAH INDIAN MOUNDS HISTORICAL SITE, Indian Mounds Road S.W., Cartersville. Prehistoric-Indian center.

KOLOMOKI MOUNDS STATE PARK MUSEUM, Route 1, Blakely.

OCMULGEE NATIONAL MONUMENT on U.S. 80 and 129, adjoining Macon. There are the remains of ancient Creek Indian towns, a site of a 1690 English trading post, a restored earth lodge and seven mounds used in religious ceremonies by the Indians, and the largest archaeological museum in the south at the visitor center.

MAINE
ABBE MUSEUM, Arcadia National Park, Bar Harbor. Archaic, Colonial, and contemporary artifacts.

COLONIAL PEMAQUID, Colonial Pemaquid State Park, New Harbor. Indian and Colonial artifacts, replica of Fort William Henry (1692).

POPHAM COLONY SITE at Sabino Head off Main 209 near Popham Beach. In 1607, 100 colonists attempted the first colony in New England, but it was abandoned the following year with the death of George Popham. A state museum holds discoveries and displays.

MARYLAND
HISTORIC ST. MARY'S CITY in St. Mary's City is an outdoor museum of history and visitor center, the 1634 village, and the replica ship *Maryland Dove*.

MASSACHUSETTS
APTUCXET TRADING POST, Aptucxet Road, Bourne. Reconstructed trading post on original 1627 site.

PLIMOUTH PLANTATION at Plymouth is a re-created Pilgrim village of the early 1600s—well staffed to give an authentic flavor. Fee. In town there is a replica of the *Mayflower* (fee) and The Pilgrim Century Museum.

NEWFOUNDLAND
L'ANSE-AUX-MEADOWS NATIONAL HISTORIC PARK of Canada with its remains of a Viking village, earthen huts, and discovered relics. Information 1-800-563-6353 (toll free).

NEW HAMPSHIRE
AMERICA'S STONEHENGE, Haverhill Road, North Salem. Possible origins of this controversial, prehistoric stone complex.

NEW MEXICO
ACOMA PUEBLO on New Mexico 23, about 13 miles south of U.S. 66, is the oldest continuously inhabited Indian settlement in the United States. Alvarado, one of Coronado's lieutenants, was the first to visit the pueblo in 1540.

BANDELIER NATIONAL MONUMENT, State Route 4, Los Alamos. Museum at archaeological site of prehistoric Pueblo Indians.

EL MORROW NATIONAL MONUMENT is 42 miles west of Grants. The 200-foot-high sandstone mesa has the most famous collection of inscribed names of early explorers. At the top are ancient Zuni Indian ruins that overlook the old Indian trail.

HAWIKUH, 12 miles southwest of Zuni Pueblo on the opposite side of the Zuni River, is northwest of Ojo Caliente village. Now in ruins, Hawikuh was the largest of the fabled "Cities of Cibola." There, on a low ridge of Zuni Reservation, Estevan was killed in 1539. Hawikuh was attacked by Coronado one year later.

INDIAN PUEBLO CULTURAL CENTER, 12th Street, N.W., Albuquerque. Archaeology-anthropology museum.

JEMEZ STATE MONUMENT, state highway, 1 mile north of Jemez Springs. Ruins of a pueblo and a 1620 Spanish mission.

MUSEUM OF CEREMONIAL ART, Camino Jejo off Pecos Road, Santa Fe.

PECOS PUEBLO on New Mexico 63, 4 miles north of U.S. 84–85. There Hernando de Alvarado first visited the pueblo and took the Plains Indian slave as a guide on the futile search for the riches of Quivira. This impressive ruin is near the Santa Fe Trail.

TAOS PUEBLO, 3 miles northeast of Taos, appears much the same as it did at the time of Coronado's march in 1540.

NORTH CAROLINA
FORT RALEIGH NATIONAL HISTORIC SITE on North Carolina 345, about 3 miles north of Manteo on Roanoke Island. A restored earthen fort is a reminder of the Lost Colony, first settled by the English in 1585.

MUSEUM OF THE CHEROKEE INDIANS, U.S. 441, Cherokee.

INDIAN MUSEUM OF THE CAROLINAS, Turnpike Road, Laurenburg.

PUERTO RICO

LA FORTALEZA, between Calle Recinto Oeste and San Juan Bay, was begun in 1533 as a defense against the Carib Indians and English and French privateersmen. In spite of alterations, the fort is basically unchanged and is one of the oldest structures in the New World.

SAN JUAN NATIONAL HISTORIC SITE of San Juan contains the forts of El Morro (1539), El Canuelo (1610), and San Cristobal (1633), reminders of the Spanish power in the Caribbean.

VIRGINIA

GLASSHOUSE POINT, just beyond the gates to Jamestown, has furnace ruins and a working furnace with daily demonstrations. Fee.

JAMESTOWN FESTIVAL PARK, Commonwealth of Virginia, has an off-site reconstruction of James Fort, replicas of the colonists' three ships, one Indian lodge, exhibit pavilions, and a cafeteria. Fee.

JAMESTOWN ISLAND NATIONAL PARK, 10 miles southwest of Williamsburg on the Colonial Parkway, was the site of the first permanent English colony in 1607. Originally a peninsula but now an island, it contains excavated foundations and the ruins of the 1639 brick church. Walking tour, markers, and visitor center displaying early relics.

Alexander, Michael, ed. *Discovery of the New World.* New York: Harper & Row, 1976. Based on the works of Theodore De Bry.

Anderson, Romola, and R. C. Anderson. *The Sailing Ship: Six Thousand Years of History.* New York: W. W. Norton, 1964.

Andrews, Ralph W. *Curtis' Western Indians.* New York: Bonanza Books, 1962.

Biddle, Richard. *A Memoir of Sebastian Cabot.* London: Hurst, Chance, 1831.

Biggar, H. P., ed. *Works of Samuel de Champlain, The.* Vols. I-IV. Translated by John Squair. Toronto: The Champlain Society, 1925.

Blow, Michael, ed. *The American Heritage History of the Thirteen Colonies.* New York: American Heritage, 1967.

Boland, Charles Michael. *They All Discovered America.* Garden City, N.Y.: Doubleday, 1961.

Bolton, H. E. *Spanish Exploration in the Southwest 1542-1706.* New York: Charles Scribner's Sons, 1916.

Brevoort, James Carson. *Verrazzano the Navigator.* Albany, New York: Argus Company, 1874. Extacted from the American Geographical Society of New York for 1873.

Brereton, John. *A brief and true relation of the discovery of the north part of Virginia.* London, 1602. Tracts appended from Massachusetts Historical Society Collections. Boston, 1843.

Burrage, Henry S., ed. *Early English and French Voyages: Original Narratives.* New York: Scribner's, 1906. Chiefly from Hakluyt 1534-1608.

Cumming, W. P., R. A. Skelton, and D. B. Quinn. *The Discovery of North America.* New York: American Heritage, 1971.

de Bry, Theodore. *Thomas Hariot's Virginia.* Ann Arbor, Mich.: University Microfilms, 1966.

de Champlain, Samuel. *Voyages of Samuel de Champlain.* Translated from the French by Charles Pomeroy Otis. Vols. 1-3. Boston: The Prince Society, 1880. Reprint. New York: Burt Franklin, 1966.

de Laudennière, René. *Notable historie containing four voyages made by certayne French captaynes unto Florida.* Translated by R[ichard] H[akluyt]. London, 1587.

Dillon, Myles, and Nora K. Chadwick. *The Celtic Realms.* New York: New American Library, 1967.

Fell, Barry. *America B.C.* A Domoter Press Book. New York: Quadrangle/Times Books, 1977.

———. *Saga America.* New York: Times Books, 1980.

Ferris, Robert G. *Explorers and Settlers.* Washington, D.C.: Department of the Interior, 1968. Historic places commemorating the early exploration and settlement of the United States.

Fischer, Joseph and Basil H. Soulsby. *The Discoveries of the Norsemen in America.* London: Henry, Stevens, Son & Stiles, 1903. Special relation to their early cartographical representation.

Forde-Johnston, J. *Prehistoric Britain and Ireland.* New York: W. W. Norton & Co., 1976.

Graham-Campbell, James, and Dafydd Kidd. *The Vikings.* New York: William Morrow & Co., 1980.

Gray, Howard F. *Leif Eriksson.* New York: Oxford University Press, 1930.

Hale, John R. *Age of Exploration.* New York: Time, 1966.

Haugen, Einar. *Voyage to Vinland.* New York: Knopf, 1942.

Haws, Duncan. *Ships and the Sea.* New York: Thomas Y. Crowell Co., 1975.

Herm, Gerhard. *The Celts.* New York: St. Martin's Press, 1975.

History of the Sailing Ship, The. New York: Arco Publishing Co., 1975.

Hodge, Frederick W., ed. *Spanish Explorers in the Southern United States.* The Narrative of Alvar Nuñez Cabeça de Vaca. The Narrative of the Expedition of Hernando de Soto. The Narrative of the Expedition of Coronado by Pedro de Castañeda. New York: Scribner's, 1907.

Howe, Henry F. *Prologue to New England.* New York: Farrar & Rinehart, 1943.

Holand, Hjalmar R. *Explorations in America before Columbus.* New York: Twayne Publishers, 1956.

Horsford, Eben Norton. *Discovery of America by Northmen.* Boston: Houghton, Mifflin and Company, 1888.

Journey of Coronado, The. Translated and edited by George Winship Parker. New York: Allerton Book Co., 1904.

Klindt-Jensen Ole. *The World of the Vikings.* Washington, D.C.: Robert B. Luce, 1970.

Landström, Björn. *The Ship.* Garden City, N.Y.: Doubleday, 1961.

Lorant, Stefan. *The New World: The First Pictures of America.* First rev. ed. New York: Duell, Sloan and Pearce, 1946, 1965.

Magnusson, Magnus. *Hammer of the North.* New York: G. P. Putnam's Sons, 1976.

Marx, Robert F. *The Treasure Fleets of the Spanish Main.* Cleveland, Oh.: The World Publishing Company, 1968.

Matthews, Washington. *Navaho Legends.* Boston: Houghton, Mifflin and Co., 1897.

Martinez-Hidalgo. *Columbus' Ships.* Edited by Howard I. Chapelle. Barre, Mass.: Barre Publishers, 1966.

Meigs, John Forsyth. *The Story of the Seaman.* Vol. 2. Philadelphia: J. B. Lippincott Co., 1924.

Miles, Charles. *Indian & Eskimo Artifacts of North America.* New York: Bonanza Books, 1963.

Morison, Samuel Eliot. *Samuel de Champlain.* An Atlantic Monthly Press Book. Boston: Little, Brown, 1972.

———. *The Great Explorers: The European Discovery of America.* New York: Oxford University Press, 1978.

Murphy, Henry C. *The Voyage of Verrazzano.* New York, 1875.

Newby, Eric. *The Rand McNally Atlas of Exploration.* New York: Rand McNally & Co., 1975.

Outhwaite, Leonard. *Unrolling the Map.* A John Day Book. New York: Reynal & Hitchcock, 1935.

Oxenstierna, Eric. *The Norsemen.* Greenwich, Conn.: New York Graphic Society Publishers, 1965.

Palmer, Rose A. *The North American Indians.* Vol. 4. Smithsonian Institution Series. New York, 1929, 1934, 1938, 1943.

Pohl, Frederick. *The Viking Explorers.* New York: Thomas Y. Crowell, 1966.

———. *The Viking Settlements of North America.* New York: Clarkson N. Potter, Jr., 1972.

Quinn, David B. *North America from the Earliest Discovery to First Settlements.* New York: Harper & Row, 1975. The Norse Voyages to 1612.

Quinnell, Marjorie, and Charles Henry Bourne. *Everyday Life in the New Stone, Bronze & Early Iron Ages.* New York: G. P. Putnam's Sons, 1923.

Rand, Rev. Silas Tertius. *Legends of the Micmacs*. New York: Longmans, Green, and Co., 1894.

Roberts, William. *An Account of the First Discovery and Natural History of Florida*. Bicentennial Florida Facsimile Series. Gainsville, Florida: The University Presses of Florida, 1976. A facsimile reproduction of the 1763 edition with introduction and index by Robert L. Gold.

Smith, Buckingham. *An Inquiry into the Authenticity of Documents Concerning a Discovery in North America Claimed to Have Been Made by Verrazzano*. New York: Printed by John F. Trow, 1864.

Smith, Joshua Toulmin. *The Northmen in New England*, or *America in the Tenth Century*. Boston: Hilliard, Gray, & Co., 1839.

Strachey, William. *The historie of travaile into Virginia Britania*. Edited by Louis B. Wright and Virginia Freunds. London, 1953.

Trento, Salvatore Michael. *The Search for Lost America*. Chicago: Contemporary Books, 1978.

Tryckare, Tre. *The Vikings*. Gothenburg, Sweden: Cagner & Co., 1966.

Weare, G. E. *Cabot's Discovery of North America*. Philadelphia: J. P. Lippincott Co., 1897.

Weeks, Stephen. "The Lost Colony of Roanoke; Its Fate and Survival." Papers of the American Historical Association V (1891): 107–46.

Weisberger, Bernard A. "American History Is Falling Down." *American Heritage*, February/March, 1987.

Wilbur, C. Keith. *The New England Indians*. Chester, Conn.: The Globe Pequot Press, 1978.

Willoughby, Charles C. *Antiquities of the New England Indians*. Cambridge, Mass.: Peabody Museum of American Archaeology and Ethnology, 1935.

Wissler, Clark. *Indians of the United States*. Revised edition. Garden City, N.Y.: Doubleday, 1966.

Wood, William. *New England's Prospect*. Edited by Alden T. Vaughan. London, 1634. Reprint. Amherst: University of Massachusetts Press, 1977.

INDEX